CHAWTON HOUSE LIBRARY SERIES

WOMEN'S TRAVEL WRITINGS IN IBERIA

T0326166

CONTENTS OF THE EDITION

Chawton House Library Series: Women's Travel Writings

Series Editors: Stephen Bending and Stephen Bygrave

Titles in this Series

Forthcoming Titles

WOMEN'S TRAVEL WRITINGS IN IBERIA

Volume 3
Lady Henrietta Chatterton,
The Pyrenees with Excursions into Spain (1843)
Volume I

EDITED BY

María Antonia López-Burgos del Barrio

Routledge
Taylor & Francis Group

LONDON AND NEW YORK

First published 2013 by Pickering & Chatto (Publishers) Limited

Published 2016 by Routledge
2 Park Square, Milton Park, Abingdon, Oxon OX14 4RN
711 Third Avenue, New York, NY 10017, USA

Routledge is an imprint of the Taylor & Francis Group, an informa business

BRITISH LIBRARY CATALOGUING IN PUBLICATION DATA

Women's travel writings in Iberia. – (Chawton House library series. Women's
travel writings)
1. Iberian Peninsula – Description and travel. 2. Travelers' writings, English –
Iberian Peninsula. 3. Women travelers – Iberian Peninsula – History – 19th
century – Sources.
I. Series II. Demetriou, Eroulla editor of compilation. III. Ruiz Mas, Jose
editor of compilation. IV. Lopez-Burgos, Ma. Antonia (Maria Antonia) editor
of compilation. V. Baillie, Marianne, *c.* 1795–1831. Lisbon. VI. Chatterton,
Georgiana, Lady, 1806–1876. Pyrenees. VII. Ellis, Sarah Stickney, 1799–1872.
Summer and winter in the Pyrenees.
914.6'0472'082-dc23

ISBN-13: 978-1-85196-647-9 (set)

Typeset by Pickering & Chatto (Publishers) Limited

CONTENTS

BIBLIOGRAPHY

Addison, J., Sir R. Steele and W. Bond (eds), *Spectator. A Weekly Journal of New, Politics, Literature and Science.* (London: Joseph Clayton, 1843).

Besas, P., *The Written Road to Spain. The Golden Decades of Travel 1820–1850* (Madrid: Limited edition published by the author, 1988).

Buckingham, J. S. and J. Sterling et al. (eds), *Athenaeum: A Journal of Literature, Science, the Fine Arts, Music, and Drama* (1843).

Dering, E. H., *Memoirs of Georgiana, Lady Chatterton from some Passages from her Diary* (London: Hurst and Blackett, 1878).

Inglis, H. D., *Spain In 1830* (London: Whittaker, Treacher, and Co., 1831).

—, [Derwent Conway], *A Tour through Switzerland and the South of France and the Pyrenees (1830–1831)* (Edinburgh: Constable and Co. and London: Hurst, Chance and Co., 1831).

Larousse, P., *Grand Dictionaire Universel du XIXeme Siècle* (Paris: Larousse, 1866).

Literary Heritage, 'Georgiana Chatterton' at http://www3.shropshire-cc.gov.uk/people/chattert.htm [accessed on 1 February 2013]

López-Burgos del Barrio, M. A., *Aportaciones Metodológicas al estudio de la Literatura de Viajes.* (Granada: Universidad de Granada, 1989).

—, *Siete Viajeras Inglesas en Granada* (Granada: Axares, 1996).

—, A *Portrait of Spanish Women in Travellers' Literature* (Melbourne: Australis Publishers, 2000).

—, *Viajeras en la Alhambra* (Sevilla: Consejería de Turismo, Comercio y Deporte. Junta de Andalucía, 2007).

—, 'Viajeras por España: Audaces, Intrépidas y Aventureras' in C. Medina Casado and J. Ruiz Mas (eds), *El Bisturí Inglés. Literatura de viajes e hispanismo en lengua inglesa* (Jaen: Universidad de Jaén y UNED, 2004), pp. 173–220.

—, 'Ventas, posadas y fondas en los relatos de viajeras inglesas de otros tiempos', in M. Carretero, E. Rodriguez and G. Rodriguez (eds), *De Habitaciones propias y otros espacios conquistados* (Granada: Universidad de Granada, 2006), pp. 23–33.

Shattock. J. (ed.), *Cambridge Bibliography of English Literature,* (Cambridge: Cambridge University Press, 1999).

CHRONOLOGY

1806   (11 November) Henrietta Georgiana Marcia Lascelles Iremonger is born at 24 Arlington Street, Picadilly, London.

1824   (3 August) Marries Sir William Abraham Chatterton of Castle Mahon, County of York.

1837   Lady Chatterton's first book *Aunt Dorothy's Tales or Geraldine Morton: A Novel* is published anonymously. Reviews in *Athenaeum*, 503 (1837) and *Spectator*, 10 (1837).

1839   Publication of *The Heiress of Drosberg and the Cathedral Chorister*, 3 vols (1839, 1840) and 1 vol. (1868, new edn). Reviews in *Athenaeum*, 633 (1839) and *Spectator*, 12 (1839).

1839   *Rambles in the South of Ireland during the Year 1838*, 2 vols, published with great success. Second edition published in 1839. Reviews in *Athenaeum*, 601 (1839) and *Spectator*, 12 (1839).

1841   Publication of *Home Sketches and Foreign Recollections,* 3 vols. Reviews in *Athenaeum*, 708 (1841), *Dublin University Magazine*, 18 (1841) and *Spectator*, 14 (1841).

1843   Publication of *Allanston or the Infidel* and *The Pyrenees with Excursions into Spain*. Reviews in *Athenaeum*, 810 (1843) and *Spectator*, 16 (1843).

1845–51   During the Irish Famine, the Chattertons move to a small residence at Bloxworth in Dorset where they live until 1852.

1848   Publication of *Reflections on the History of the Kings of Judah.*

1856   *Compensation: A Story of Real Life Thirty Years Ago*, 2 vols, published anonymously.

1857   Publication of *Life and its Realities,* 3 vols.

1858   Publication of *The Reigning Beauty,* 3 vols.

1859   Extracts from the works of J. P. F. Richter are selected and translated by Lady Chatterton.

1860   Lady Chatterton edits *Memorials Personal and Historical of Admiral Lord Gambier,* 2 vols, from *Family Papers.*

1862   Publication of *Selections from the Works of Plato Translated from the Greek.*

1863   Publication of *The Heiress and her Lovers,* 3 vols. Reviews in *Athenaeum*, 1879 (1863) and *Saturday Review*, 16 (1863).

1864   Publication of *Leonore, A Tale and other Poems* (1864, 1865, new illustrated edn) and *Quadmire Ahead*, privately printed.

1865   Publication of *Grey's Court*, 2 vols, ed. Lady Chatterton with E. H. Dering.

1867   Publication of *Oswald of Deira: A Drama* and *A Plea for Happiness and Hope*, a pamphlet printed privately.

1868   Publication of *Country Coteries*, 3 vols.

1869   Publication of *The Golden Bird: A Fairy Legend of the South of Ireland, The Oak, Original Tales and Sketches by Sir J. Bowring, Lady Chatterton, and others*, ed. C. Rogers, and *Lady May: A Pastoral Poem.*

1872   Publication of *The Lost Bride,* 3 vols (1872), 1 vol. (1875), 2nd edn. Review in *Athenaeum*, 2330 (1872).

1874   Publication of *Won At Last,* 3 vols. Review in *Athenaeum*, 2431 (1874).

1875   Private publications of *Extracts from Aristotle's Work selected and translated by Lady Chatterton, Misgiving* and *Convictions.*

1876   *The Consolation of the Devout Soul by Frassinetti* is translated by Lady Chatterton.

1876   (6 February) Lady Chatterton dies at Malvern Wells, Worcestershire, England.

LADY HENRIETTA CHATTERTON

In the year 1843 Lady Chatterton published in two volumes *The Pyrenees with Excursions into Spain*, a narrative of a long journey from Calais to the south of France and the Pyrenees including three short excursions into Spain. It constituted the second travel book of this prolific writer and was written after the great success of *Rambles in the South of Ireland*, published twice in 1839 within just a few months.

Although in *The Pyrenees with Excursions into Spain* Lady Chatterton does not reveal the exact year[1] of her journey even once, she is exhaustively precise in referring to days of the week and months. During the Chattertons's long journey from 1 May to the end of October, they visited (among many other places) Montreuil, Abbeville, Compiegne, Bernay, Amiens, Paris, Fontainebleau, Orleans, Blois, Tour, Poitiers, Angoulême, Bourdeaux, Bayonne, St Sebastian, Hernani, Passages, Bayonne, Cambo, Pau, Bagnères de Bigorre, Lourdes, Bagnères de Luchon, Venasque and Viella, which she describes in the first volume. In the second volume she includes descriptions of Bosost, St Bertrand de Comminges, Argeles, Cauterets, Lourdes, Pau, Oleron, Hospitalet, Tolouse, Carcassone, Narbone, Beziers and their return to Paris where they spent the winter of 1842. She gives a detailed account throughout of her travels in comfortable carriages, in Spanish diligences, riding donkeys or horses and on some occasions being carried in a sedan chair up the mountains by two men. Despite her delicate health and occasional low spirits, she made constant efforts to visit the interesting places in each village or town they went to, mainly describing churches and castles more than other buildings of interest. On the other hand, her detailed reports and description of the post houses, hotels, or even the private houses in which they were lodged, when hotels were full or non-existent, gave her the opportunity to depict their landlords, the food they were given and the society and standard of living of the places visited. Her continuous use of initials instead of full names to conceal the personality of the persons she meets or even the continuous use of the letter 'W.' to refer to her husband, Sir William Abraham Chatterton, dulls the book's reading. Furthermore, for the uninformed reader or in the case of readers not belonging to the society of the day, her attitude for preserving the privacy of friends seems quite absurd, although this was a tendency widely used in travel books at the time.

An indefatigable reader, in preparing for her journey she searched for information from previous books on Spain. We have proof of this in the various references she makes to Henry David Inglis and to his books, *A Tour through Switzerland and the South of France and the Pyrenees (1830–1831)* published under his pen name Dervent Conway, and his *Spain in 1830*.

Although most of Lady Chatterton's works were widely known, *The Pyrenees with Excursions into Spain* only went through one edition. Reviews of this book appeared in the *Athenaeum*[2] and the *Spectator*[3] in 1843.[4] In the *Athenaeum* review Chatterton's book is considered 'a pleasant reading and ought to satisfy many tastes', while that of the *Spectator* can be summarized in two main ideas:

> the main imperfections of Chatterton's book are its length, its slightness and its want of plan. The last want is in some sense inseparable from all travels; but when a person rambles from one place to another in a limited district, making this spot the starting point of lesser ramifications, this want is greatly aggravated. In short, a separation into parts might have facilitated casual reading and it could have been par example: Boulogne to Paris, Paris to Bayonne or Excursion into Spain, and so forth. These circumstances render the book better for occasional reading: a part is better than the whole.

In the *Spectator* we also read:

> the principal attraction in Lady Chatterton's narrative depends less upon her subject than her mode of treating it. She is of the class of the fine needlewomen – the materials may have little intrinsic worth but become valuable by the taste and delicate skill displayed in the workmanship. To the sentiment of the sex, the quickness of feminine perception and the refinement of a well-bred woman she adds a buoyancy and animation that fall short of being lively only from the restraint of habit or delicacy of temperament.

Notes

1.   See E. H. Dering, *Memoirs of Georgiana, Lady Chatterton from some Passages from her Diary* (London: Hurst and Blackett, 1878), where chapter 14 offers her account of their winter in Paris in 1842.
2.   Anon., [Review], *Athenaeum*, 810 (1843), p. 134.
3.   Anon., [Review], *Spectator*, 16 (1843), p. 447.
4.   J. Shattock, *Cambridge Bibliography of English Literature* (Cambridge: Cambridge University Press), p. 2073.

THE PYRENEES

WITH

EXCURSIONS INTO SPAIN.

VOL. I.

LADY CHATTERTON'S IRELAND.

Second Edition, in Two Volumes, post octavo,
With Illustrations,

RAMBLES IN THE SOUTH OF IRELAND.

BY LADY CHATTERTON.

" A charming book, full of picturesque descriptions, interesting observations on life and manners, amusing anecdotes, legendary lore, just feeling, and sound common sense."—*Literary Gazette.*

Sketched by Lady Chatterton and drawn on stone by Bichebois

Printed by Lemercier, Benard and Cᵉ

THE TOWNS OF FONTARABIA AND HENDAYE ON THE RIVER BIDASSOA.

THE PYRENEES

WITH

EXCURSIONS INTO SPAIN

BY

LADY CHATTERTON,

AUTHOR OF

" RAMBLES IN THE SOUTH OF IRELAND," " HOME SKETCHES,"

ETC. ETC.

IN TWO VOLUMES.

VOL. I.

LONDON

SAUNDERS AND OTLEY, CONDUIT STREET.

1843.

CONTENTS

OF

THE FIRST VOLUME.

iv　　　　　　　CONTENTS.

CHAPTER V.

CHAPTER VI.

CHAPTER VII.

CHAPTER VIII.

CHAPTER IX.

CHAPTER X.

CHAPTER XI.

CONTENTS.   V

vi   CONTENTS.

CHAPTER XIX.

CHAPTER XX.

LIST OF THE PLATES.

VOL. I.

VOL. II.

THE PYRENEES

ETC. ETC.

CHAPTER I.

Arrival at Montreuil—Historical Recollections of Abbeville
—The Battle of Crecy—Thoughts on the advantages of
experience and old age.

Friday, May 1.—*Montreuil, Hôtel de l'Europe.*—
We crossed over from Dover to Boulogne this
morning, and afterwards enjoyed the drive
here extremely. We were much amused at
the change of scene, the cheerful aspect of the
towns in this country ; and the contrast between
France and England seemed as striking as if
we had never been abroad before, yet this is the
ninth time I have crossed the Channel !

Then we had a lovely moonlight walk round
the ramparts, and were surprised at the deserted
look of the town. So few lights were twinkling

in the windows, and there was so little movement or noise in the streets, we could not
imagine what had become of the gay population
we had seen on our arrival.

The only thing that stirred seemed to be a
pension de jeunes demoiselles, who were walking
two and two, followed by some Black Nuns. We
saw them enter the gateway of a large gloomy
house, in which, like most of the others, there
were no lights visible through the open windows.

I delight in the cheerful aspect of French
inns, and their pretty light beds, which I always
think give pleasant dreams; and here, too, are
some venerable tapestry chairs, which look as
if they had been embroidered by Marie Antoinette's maids of honour.

Abbeville Hôtel de l'Europe, Saturday.—A hot
but pleasant drive of four hours and a half,
brought us here at three o'clock, and we have
got all our comforts out, and established ourselves, till Monday, in a very pretty apartment
looking on the garden.

To an invalid, almost the entire pleasure of
travelling depends upon the look of the rooms,
and the view from them, whether it be cheerful

or otherwise; and therefore I think a little tour in those countries which have good inns, must be of great use to the spirits, if not to the health of sufferers. In England the hotels are by no means so cheerful or amusing, nor in my opinion, half so comfortable, or the food half so good, as abroad.

The scenery is rather pretty about Nouvion— the last post before we reached Abbeville. It was a place often visited by Louis XI.; and there, the combination of light and shade along the avenue, a few peasants' carts, the steeple of a village church, and a group of rough, high-roofed cottages formed an interesting picture. Then, on our left, was the Forest of Crecy, whose fine beech trees are now in the full glory of their spring costume, and whose very name conjured up visions of valour and victory, and recalled pleasantly to mind the monument we saw only the day before yesterday at Canterbury Cathedral of the young hero of Crecy, whose touching epitaph in Norman-French (written by himself,) we tried to decipher; and about three leagues on our right was St. Valery, the place from which William the Norman embarked to conquer England.

4   LA TOUR D'HAROLD.

There is still a tower in the place called La
Tour d'Harold, into which Harold was thrown
by Gui, Count of Ponthieu, when that unfortunate prince was obliged, by a storm, to land at
St. Valery; and this scene is represented in the
famous Bayeux tapestry. Harold was, however, liberated by William of Normandy. He
returned to England, and, as we all know, on
the death of Edward the Confessor, caused himself to be proclaimed King. This exasperated
William of Normandy, who then collected his
troops, and embarked from St. Valery to invade
England, assisted by its Seigneur, and the
Count Gui de Ponthieu.

We could not see the spot, but its vicinity
made us imagine a race of still more bold and
hardy warriors than those of our third Edward,
traversing the old woods of Crecy: and I
thought of the ambitious dreams in which some
of those old Normans may have indulged—
dreams which, indeed, have not only been realized, but seem to survive in the minds of their
numerous descendants, who still bear, and
still do honour to their names. Eight hundred
years!—It is a glorious period—even in itself sublime; for, as Kant says, " eine lange

dauer ist erhaben ;" and when the same name, accompanied by the same noble spirit, is handed down through so long a period, there is something extremely interesting in its contemplation. But my scribbling will not become sublime, I fear, by being long, so I will merely add that, at Bernay, the post about half way between Montreuil and this place—there is a very good inn ; and this, to us degenerate travellers, is more to the purpose than all the conquests and glory of St. Valery and Crecy.

Evening.—We have been much surprised at the extreme beauty of the church here. The façade and two towers over the entrance are very highly ornamented—irregular, but magnificent. The exteriors of Gothic churches abroad always appear more rich than those of our own cathedrals, because the statues still remain in their niches : but the interior is seldom so highly ornamented, and the filthy pavement, and all the gilt gingerbread-looking ornaments of Roman-catholic shrines, have a tawdry appearance, which is always disappointing. Our cathedrals, too, are now restored, and so beautifully kept, that I fear we shall be more than ever disgusted with the interiors of the churches abroad.

6   HISTORICAL RECOLLECTIONS

We had afterwards a damp exploring walk through the town. We went round part of the ramparts, and saw a splendid sunset—lost our way, and made a great detour, which tired me extremely ; but I am now enjoying this pretty room (with its comfortable red velvet chairs and Louis XIV. furniture and decorations), and the moon is shining brightly through the two open windows which look on the garden, and the heavy thunder-shower has given a fresher smell to the lilacs and other sweet flowers which bloom there, and the soft summer lightning is gleaming in the horizon—now and then, bringing vividly to view the dark outlines of gable-ends and pinnacles ; at other moments, shining through the branches of the trees and illuminating the garden.

There are many interesting historical recollections connected with Abbeville, and I have been reading of several remarkable things which happened here in early times. Abbeville was the chief town of Ponthieu—at least, after the year 990—when it was surrounded with walls by Hugues Capet, for before that period Montreuil was the chief residence of the counts. Count Gui of Ponthieu fought at the battle of Hast-

ings, and afterwards, with Philip I. of France,
against Flanders,—as Louandre says, in his interesting History, — " Et reçu de ce prince
l'odieux mission de plonger dans un cachot la
Princesse Berthe, qu'il avait repudiée. pour
epouser Bertrade.   Renfermée à Montreuil-sur-
Mer, dans une tour qui subsiste encore dans la
citadelle, et qui parte son nom, la reine infor-
tunée y mourut de chagrin et de misère, vers
1095."   Count Gui died in 1101 : his daughter
and heiress, Agnes, married Robert (called Le
Diable) Count of Bellesme Alençon, who treated
her cruelly, kept her a prisoner in his Castle
of Bellesme, tried to poison her, and she at
last took refuge at Abbeville, where she died,
in 1120, at a house near the Porte Comtesse, and
which belonged since to the Knights Templars.

Adele, the beautiful daughter of Count Jean,
of Ponthieu, who lived in 1190, was married to
Thomas de St. Valery ; and having been mal-
treated by some brigands into whose power she
fell, her father caused her to be thrown into the
sea, thinking thus to efface " l'affront fait à son
sang." This subject has been chosen for several
tragedies and novels.   Her brother Guillaume
married, in 1196, Alix, sister to Philippe Au-

8 HISTORICAL RECOLLECTIONS.

guste, who had been affianced to our Richard Cœur de Lion, but the marriage was prevented by the infamous conduct of his father Henry II. The great-grand-daughter of the Count Guillaume, of Ponthieu,* was the celebrated Eleanor, wife of Edward I., who shewed his affection for her memory by the erection of those beautiful crosses at Northampton and other places. Edward did homage at Amiens to the French king for the Comté. He often came here; and fortified his castle near La Porte St. Gilles, on the Paris road, and embellished it with gardens, in 1282. He also obtained permission of Philippe le Hardi to coin money here.

Ponthieu then passed to England, and Edward II. came to do homage here, and married Isabella, daughter of Philippe le Bel. The vicissitudes of her life are well known. After various efforts she at last succeeded, with the assistance of Holland, in placing her son Edward III. on our throne. On her imprisonment in Castle Rising, for misconduct, the revenues

* His only daughter was Marie, whose eldest daughter, Jeanne, married Ferdinand III., of Castille and Leon, in 1237, and her daughter Eleanor afterwards married our Edward I.

of Ponthieu were assigned for her support. Our great Edward III., indignant at being obliged to do homage for Ponthieu, went to war with Philippe de Valois, and assumed a right to the crown of France for his mother.

Louandre gives a very interesting description of the battle of Crecy. Edward said, after having in vain attempted to enter Abbeville (which had been seized by Philip), " Je suis ici sur mes terres, et je veux les defendre." He chose an excellent position for the encampment of his army, and, on the evening before " the engagement, retired to his oratory, and prayed to God that, if he should combat his enemies on the morrow, he might come off with honour. The next day, he and the Prince of Wales heard mass, and communicated. The greater part of the army did the same, confessed, and made proper preparations."*

He (Louandre) attributes the defeat of the French, in some measure, to the impetuosity of the Duc d'Alençon, who commanded the men-at-arms. The king had given orders for the army to halt, in order to allow a little time for rest after a fatiguing march, before commencing

* Froissart.

10   THE BATTLE OF CRECY.

the attack. This order the Duke disregarded,
and advanced with his division ; others were induced to press forward, under the supposition,
when they saw the Duke's movement, that the
King's order had been countermanded, and thus
the army reached the ground in the greatest
disorder.

The Genoese archers, in the pay of France,
began the attack about three o'clock, in the
Valley of Troyelles. There had been a great
storm of rain, and, according to Froissart, " a
very terrible eclipse of the sun," which afterwards shone out brilliantly full in the faces of
the French, thus blinding the Genoese, while
the English archers had it in their backs. Besides this, the bowstrings of the Genoese were re-
laxed by the rain, whilst the bows of the English,
having been kept in their cases during the storm,
were in good condition. The Genoese were
thus unable to advance. The Duc d'Alençon,
exasperated by this check, led his troops forward through the broken ranks of his own
friends, exclaiming, " Tuez-moi cette canaille-
là !" Thus, numbers of them were trampled to
death, and the whole line thrown into inextric-
able confusion. When Philip rode up with

the reserve, in full expectation of victory, great was his horror to find the battle nearly lost. He made a gallant attempt to restore the fortune of the day, and had a horse killed under him; and it was only late in the evening, after his followers were reduced to not more than sixty men, that he suffered himself to be led off from the field. He at first took refuge in the Castle of La Broie, and from thence fled to Amiens.

The loss of the French was enormous,— almost incredible, when compared with the small force of the English army and its trifling loss. The brave but rash D'Alençon, the brother of the King of France, was among the slain; as was the King of Bohemia, whose heroic conduct was so conspicuous. He had lost his sight by means, it was said, of poison, in the Italian wars; yet, blind as he was, he requested that he might be led "so far into the engagement that he might strike one stroke with his sword." His wish was gratified, and the reins of his horse were attached to those of two of his knights. Their bodies were found together the morning after the battle, and it was his plume and motto, "Ich dien," which have furnished to our princes of Wales so interesting a memorial of this day's

12   THE BATTLE OF CRECY.

victory. The King of Bohemia was buried in the Abbaye des Valoires, with this inscription :—

> " L'an mil quarente six trois cents,
> Comme la chronique tesmoigne,
> Fut apporté et mis ceans,
> Jean Luxembourg, Roi de Bchaigue."

The conduct of the young Prince of Wales was admirable. The division which he commanded bore the brunt of the attack, and he was at one time in considerable danger from the impetuosity and numbers of his assailants. In this extremity, Sir Thomas Norwich was despatched by the Earl of Warwick to the King, to ask for reinforcements. " No," replied Edward, " let the boy win his spurs. I am determined, if it please God, that all the glory and honour of this day shall be given to him, and to those into whose care I have entrusted him."

There are some lines by an old poet, Jean Douchet, who in an epitaph on Philippe de Valois, wishes to shew that the defeat of the French is to be attributed to their dress:

> " Puis a Crécy perdis mes gindarmes
> Trente cinque mille nonobstant leurs grands armes,
> Par le moyen de leurs acoustremens,
> Et chaperons et autres vestemens,
> Lesquels flottoient de toutes parts en terre,
> Qui n'estoient bons pour gens de bien de guerre."

Philip's son, the unfortunate King Jean, was afterwards taken prisoner by our Black Prince, at the battle of Poitiers, and remained several years in London, till he at last signed the treaty of Bretigny, which restored Ponthieu to England, to the great despair of the inhabitants of Abbeville, who hated the English. Ringois, a rich citizen of this place, was taken to Dover Castle, and put to death by drowning, because he would not acknowledge the English dominion; and this event, too, has been made the subject of a tragedy. Soon afterwards, it came into the possession of the French, remained with them ever after, and the last Count of Ponthieu was poor Charles X., who retained that title after he lost his throne.

In old times the inhabitants of Abbeville seem to have had great taste for music and poetry, and there were " jeux floraux and combats of verse in the adjoining woods," at a place still called Fosse aux Ballades.

In 1463, Louis XI. arrived at Abbeville to repurchase the county of Ponthieu from Charles le Bon, Duke of Burgundy; but it fell again under the dominion of Burgundy, as Charles the Bold made his entry here in 1466. He, however, dying without issue, Ponthieu reverted to France,

14   HISTORICAL RECOLLECTIONS.

and Charles VIII. came to Abbeville on the 17th June, 1493.

Louis XII. was married here in 1514, to Mary of England, sister to Henry VIII., and the ceremony was solemnized with great splendour. The Princess entered the town on horseback, " moult triomphalement," by la Porte Merende, (the one through which we came yesterday from Montreuil.) She rode under a dais of white satin ; it was embroidered with roses and porcupines, (the device of King Louis,) and adorned with a fringe of red gold, and supported by silver batons, ornamented with leaves of pure gold. " Sa coiffure," says the old chronicle, " à la façon de son pays, etait enrichie de pierres precieuses à l'entour de ses templettes," and divers " beaux mystères et honnestes" were represented. Many cart-loads of filth were removed on the occasion from the streets, which were usually so dirty as to render boots or stilts indispensable. They were married at the Hotel Grutuze, an old house nearly opposite the church. It is now a magazin de sel; but we fancied, before we knew its name, that it must possess some historical interest, from its quaint and venerable appearance.

There existed some curious old customs in

Abbeville: a man condemned to be hung, might be saved if a woman offered, of her own accord, to marry him. This piece of good fortune happened to a robber at Hautvilliers in 1400; but the girl was lame, and he actually refused her, saying to the hangman, "Alle cloque, je n'en veux mie, attaqu' me;"—"She limps—I do not at all like her for a wife; tie me up."

It seems the echevins (sheriffs) and the mayor had all the authority in their own hands; but they were guided in their decisions by custom. Animals were sometimes executed: thus in 1413, a pig which had mutilated, or, as the old chronicle says, "murdry" a child, was dragged by the hind legs to the place of execution, and hung by the legs till he died. Sometimes animals thus condemned, were executed, dressed in men's clothes.

Plays taken from Scripture subjects were often represented. "The Passion" was played in 1451; and, in 1452, "Les jeux de la vie de *Monsieur* St. Quentin;" in 1493, those of *Monsieur* St. Roch.

Sunday Evening.—There was a tremendous storm of thunder and lightning last night—very awful: it lighted up my pretty Louis Quatorze bed-room in the most brilliant, but livid manner.

16   THUNDER STORM.

The outer Venetian blinds were closed, but the blue
flames seemed actually to dance about the room,
and were reflected in ghastly attitudes by the
numerous looking-glasses, highly polished floor,
and secretaire.   I drew round the blue silk
bed-curtains, and tried to go to sleep, by im-
pressing on my mind that silk is a non-con-
ductor of electricity, but it would not do.

We have had such a pleasant day ; I shall be
quite sorry to leave this delightful hotel, and
our pretty red sitting-room, and blue bed-room,
and the slippery stairs, and airy passage ; the
smiling waiter and good-humoured maid, and
the dear old landlady, who wears the same cap,
and looks exactly as she did sixteen years ago,
when I first came here—not a day older.

The nice dinners, too, with all the varieties
of petits plats, we both enjoy so much ; the
old tea-kettle, with its enormous handle, which
is sure to be hotter than the water it contains,
and the soft rich carpet, with its vivid flowered
pattern, which puts me pleasantly in mind of one
worked by Miss P——, two hundred years ago,
in my bedroom at poor dear old K——; so does
the elaborately carved pedestal to a marble-slab,
and the ornamented frame of a looking-glass in

my bedroom. It is strange that we have had a period of very ugly furniture since then, which France seems to have escaped. Why was this?

It is certainly delightful to travel for amusement; and I fear many of us who have the power of doing as we like, do not value this privilege as we ought. I mean that many people, instead of enjoying the independence they possess, long for some place or position in the world, which, however honourable it may be, must necessarily prevent them from going where they wish. Perhaps it is wisely ordained that such should be the case; ambition and vanity, though sad torments to those who possess them, have nevertheless their uses, and keep the world in a state of activity, which, in our degenerated condition, is necessary for its well being. They act like a high wind, and assist to blow away the pestilential influence of sloth and indifference.

·Well, be that as it may, I am right glad we have the entire disposal of ourselves, and have the whole world before us; and, what is better still, the whole summer—and even the spring. And this is a piece of good fortune that rarely occurs to those who, like us, have London, and all its pleasant world, for our dear home.

18   THOUGHTS ON THE ADVANTAGES OF AGE.

We have left it while the delicious long days are still lengthening, and are but too happy that we have neither parliament nor place to compel us to remain. We are happy, too, in possessing unprejudiced feelings and independent views, which are great sources of enjoyment. We look on the world as it is, and value all the various grades of our fellow-creatures according to their real merit, rather than by their supposed value in the world's eye.

Strange to say, I look forward with more bounding pleasure to this tour than I did when, at blooming fifteen, I set out on my first visit to France ; yet my health is not nearly so good as it was then, nor had I lost some of those dear friends whom I thought it impossible to survive. This wonderful improvement in cheerfulness as I have grown old should be a great encouragement to those who suffer from low spirits, and is chiefly to be attributed to the religious feelings I have attained. At fifteen I had no settled opinions on religion, and I trace my gradual improvement in happiness to the hope I have, by degrees, attained of enjoying eternal bliss in another world. The pleasure, too, that we derive from experience and the cultivation of our tastes,

increases as we grow old, and more than compensates for the buoyant animal spirits which
generally belong to youth. This is particularly
the case in the enjoyment of fine scenery, or
rather in the simple contemplation of nature. The
country between London and Andover always
appeared to me extremely ugly before I had
visited many beautiful scenes in other countries.

On returning home, I expected to be impressed more than ever by its want of beauty,
and was therefore much surprised on travelling
through it, to find myself admiring several parts
extremely; no spot appeared to me uninteresting. Here there was a new pleasure, a power
to find beauty in that which had before appeared
so plain; and this new faculty I attribute to the
intense enjoyment I had experienced in contemplating nature in its loveliest forms.

As a child, I used to long for beautiful scenery,
and felt convinced I should be happier if I lived
in a pretty country; and such I found to be the
case—not only when in the midst of beauty, but
afterwards also. The recollection of my enjoyment seemed to give me the power of finding
most unexpected charms in the plain aspect of
my native dells.

20   BEAUTIFUL SCENERY.

This longing to live amid fine scenery, which I cannot help thinking innate,—for, in my case, it was not caused by any outward impression,—proves to me that we are destined for a more perfect state, our aspirations being always after something more perfect than this world can afford. I have never yet beheld in reality scenes of such loveliness as I sometimes see in my dreams, nor heard music so exquisite as the strains which sometimes bless my slumbers.

21

CHAPTER II.

Journey to Compiegne—Comparison between the taste in furniture of Louis XIV. and Napoleon—Jeanne d'Arc—Arrival at Paris.

Paris, Wednesday.—We left Abbeville at seven on Monday morning,—passed through Picquigny, —where Louis XI. had an interview with Edward IV. on the bridge, and where the ruins of the old castle, celebrated by Madame Sevigné, above the town, is a fine object. We arrived at Amiens about half-past eleven, and were much pleased with the cathedral. It seems to have been finished in the manner intended when begun, which is not often the case with such a long and elaborate work as a highly decorated Gothic church.

It is in the form of a simple cross. The

entrance front, and indeed the whole exterior, is quite beautiful; over the centre entrance-door are colossal figures of the twelve apostles and other saints, very well carved; on the outside of the choir are some curious old coloured groups of carved figures. There was a dreadful massacre in the cathedral at the time of the Reformation, and the stones of the pavement are crossed in consequence. At the western end are fine recumbent figures, in brass, of the founders of the church, which narrowly escaped being used for cannon balls during the wars. " It was a pity they were not," said one of our party, " because they would have then been *canonized.*"

There is a spire over the centre of the transept, like those in some of our English cathedrals, which is very beautiful, but I thought it much too small for the size of the church; at least it appeared so to us, who have so lately seen and admired Salisbury's gigantic steeple. Much pleased with the town of Amiens. The houses in the older streets and in the place are very picturesque. We passed two pleasant, but fatiguing hours there, and reached Compiegne at half-past seven.

The view as we descended towards Compiegne

was very fine : the town, with its old towers and steeples, was below us, on the left the huge Palace, skirted by gardens and fine woods, its extensive park and forest covering the undulating heights around : the broad river Oise, passing through the town and then winding among green meadows to the right, reflected the brilliant colours of a sunset-sky, and gave animation to the whole scene.

We went, next morning, at eight, to see the palace. The original building was erected by the early kings. The palace was rebuilt by Louis XIV., and restored, after the sufferings of the Revolution, by Napoleon. The last time he was there was in 1811. It again suffered in the war of 1814, but is now in perfect order, and very magnificent. Many rooms are decorated with beautiful Beauvais and Goblin tapestry, and we admired it much more than the harsh, exaggerated paintings which cover the walls and ceilings of others. In the fine ball-room there are twenty-five long benches covered with tapestry, and each of them cost (according to our cicerone) £150!

I do not like Napoleon's taste in the furniture and decorations of his palaces. It has a tawdry

24   NAPOLEON'S TASTE IN FURNITURE.

and upstart appearance, shews an affected imita-
tion of the Roman, and has none of that genuine
grace and natural or hereditary royal splendour
of Louis XIV.'s style.   Napoleon's is too full of
the emblems of conquest, it speaks of newly-ac-
quired power, and is oppressed with massive
and tasteless gilding, which seems the out-
pouring of unexpected wealth.

It has perhaps more imposing magnificence,
but does not inspire half such pleasant feelings,
as the luxurious beauty of the old Bourbon style.
In fact, the character of an age, or of the person
who rules the taste of an age, is seen in nothing
more plainly than in its effect on the arts.

The painted ceilings &c. of Napoleon's time
are full of battle scenes ; in all the decorations
we see helmets and instruments of warfare,
or tokens of conquest, and even the silken
hangings of the walls are often supported by
bayonets.   The figures are harsh and stiff,
shewing, indeed, the youthful vigour of minds
just emerged from that temporary barbarism
which overspread France at the Revolution ;
whereas the decorations of the old Bourbons are
full of pleasant images of repose.   The graceful
shepherdesses, and exquisitely-carved Cupids and

Venuses, are the result of many centuries of internal repose and civilization; perhaps, indeed, their effeminacy and voluptuousness shew a state of over civilization, and consequent decadence.

Yet, though the apartments of Compiegne want the ease and grace of hereditary taste, one cannot but regard them with great interest, as the memorials of a man who exercised so extraordinary an influence over the age in which he lived.

It may seem strange, but so it is, that bad characters generally obtain more influence than the good. This is explained by the superior vigour with which bad actions are generally performed, and decision of action makes even vice attractive. Crimes are committed, ambition, envy, malice, &c. are indulged in, and their views carried out with the energy and vigorous impulse of the whole heart; whereas, lukewarmness and indecision too often characterize virtuous actions; besides, it requires an effort to subdue those bad feelings we all inherit with our fallen state, and this effort gives a restraint to the character by no means attractive.

It is seldom that persons not naturally good, however virtuous they may have become, obtain much influence by their goodness, though in reality they have more merit than those who are good without much effort. Our natural qualities alone give influence, because, as I have said above, all that springs from them is vigorous and attractive, and unfortunately they are more inclined to vice than to virtue.

In the evening, we walked round the town, and went to the bridge.

It was at the siege of Compiegne that Joan of Arc was taken prisoner, when heading a sally from its old walls, and the spot where the sad event occurred is still shewn.

After our own Mary Queen of Scots, there is no female character in history that has inspired so much interest, or received so many poetical tributes as Jeanne d'Arc. The last tribute contains more poetry than any written homage she has received, for though silent, it speaks more powerfully to beholders of all nations and languages, and though fixed and immovable, it seems to breathe the very living spirit of immortality. The immortality of thought, genius, and Christian devotion. All this is clearly stamped on that exquisite statue, moulded by Mary of Orleans, to the memory of France's

fairest heroine and to her own undying fame.
Mrs. Hemans could never have seen it, yet her
words seem to embody its loveliness :—

> " A still, clear face,
> Youthful, but brightly solemn !   Woman's cheek
> And brow were there, in deep devotion meek,
> Yet glorified with inspiration's trace
> On its pure paleness.
>   That slight form !
> Was that the leader through the battle-storm ?
> Had the soft light in that adoring eye,
> Guided the warrior when the swords flashed high ?
> 'Twas so, even so ! and thou, the shepherd's child,
> Joanne, the lowly dreamer of the wild !"

The statue expresses the heroine's feelings
even more eloquently than Schiller's words :—

> " So ist des Geistes Ruf an mich ergangen,
>   Mich treibt nicht eitles, irdisches Verlangen."

The drive out of Compiegne for several miles
was through the forest, and the smells delicious.
We admired the view of the town of Senlis, with
its beautiful church and airy spire, and other old
towers and buildings : also the fine prospect
we had looking back towards Compiegne, from
a high hill, up which we wound slowly after we
left Villeneuve.

We arrived here, (Paris,) about five o'clock,

28   ARRIVAL AT PARIS.

and had a great hunt for rooms—the place so
full, scarcely any to be had.   During the search,
my little dog, Frisk, and I, sat waiting in the
carriage, and the maid in the rumble behind,
whilst the post-boys stood leaning against the
railing of the Tuileries' gardens: thus we
passed two hours, much to the edification and
admiration of passers by. At last, we established
ourselves comfortably at Hôtel Wagram, au
troisième.   The situation very noisy, but the
view splendid, over the Tuileries' gardens—
smelling so sweet !

And now I am enjoying the moonlit view from
our windows, and the delicious smell of orange
and lime blossoms from the Tuileries, and the
pleasant repose of a comfortable sofa and dressing gown ; and this enjoyment is rendered still
more intense by feeling that I am not at Colonel
T——'s splendid party to which we were invited
to-night.   Had a delightful walk this evening in
the Tuileries, and sat down on the western terrace, overlooking the Place Louis XV., with its
obelisk and fountains, (which were in full play,)
and the Champs Elysées, as far as the splendid
Arc de Triomphe.   The prospect there on all
sides is very grand, and, animated by the gay

evening population of Paris, and the brilliant colouring of a fine sunset, was particularly beautiful and striking.

Friday.—The ball at Colonel T——'s was very splendid, and W. was much amused by the enormous bouquets and profusion of natural flowers worn by the ladies. The weather is so delicious one does not know how to enjoy it enough. This morning we went to the Louvre, and saw the new splendid collection of Spanish pictures. We thought some by Zurbaran very fine.

Lady I—— de C—— most kindly shewed me some casts of the Princess Marie's models. We admired particularly a figure of Jeanne d'Arc, on horseback; she is represented riding through a field of battle after an action, and contemplates the dead body of a warrior lying at her horse's feet; her countenance is finely expressive of grief.

The Princess Marie did not begin to model until two years before her death. Had she lived, what fame that wonderful genius would have acquired! It seems a great pity such a perfect creature should have been cut off, and yet perhaps the interesting Princess has attained a greater degree of happiness in heaven than if

30   SENSITIVENESS.

she had lived to receive more incense from an admiring world.

I often think that success is given by God not so much according to our deserts, as according to what we can bear, or may require for the good of our minds. Persons of genius who do not attain great celebrity during their lives, are perhaps those who would be too much elated by it. Scott had a mind which could not be spoiled by praise. I think, too, we are more depressed by ill success than we are by the consciousness of inability ; and characters differ from each other in nothing more than their requirement of encouragement, or the contrary. I am so dreadfully and fatally sensitive to the encouraging or discouraging opinion of others, that I often actually *become* what they think me. It is in the fatal power of the opinion of others to make me clever or stupid.

After the above sage observation, I found the following sentence in dear M——'s handwriting : —" A very good subject—do descant on it, and warn people against it, for I am afraid many persons are too apt to discourage, rather than encourage others, which is so dreadfully dangerous. Do say a great deal about it in your own wise way."

No, dear M——, I will not say any more; for, in the first place, I hope and trust there are not many people in the world so foolishly sensitive as I am to encouragement or the contrary; and, therefore, but very few would understand the feeling. In the next place, my "way" which you are pleased to call "wise," is not always so, or I should long since have got rid of the above uncomfortable quality.

Saturday, May 8.—Nôtre Dame, which we visited to-day, though very beautiful, struck us as being less fine and grand than the cathedral of Amiens. The exterior of the Madelaine is splendid, but I thought less beautiful than the last time I saw it, (four years ago,) from the joints in the columns being so much more apparent now than formerly. I was disappointed, too, in the size of the interior: it appears so much smaller than the magnificence of the exterior would lead one to expect. Admired some pictures at the Luxembourg more than I did during my last visit. It does not contain any of the best works of Delaroche; his death of Queen Elizabeth looks harsh; and I did not much admire his picture of Edward V. and Duke of York, nor that of Joash, saved by his

Aunt Athaliah—neither of them seemed in his best manner. I was very much pleased with a picture of H. Vernet's. It represents Michael Angelo in the Vatican, meeting Raphael surrounded by his scholars.—" You move about," said M. Angelo, " attended by a numerous suite, like a general." " And you," replied Raphael, " you go alone, like an executioner." The picture tells this anecdote well; but I think the expression with which the reply is given, is more contemptuous than Raphael's features could ever have assumed.   Among many good figures and groups in this picture, there is one of a Roman peasant with a child asleep on her knee, which is quite lovely, evidently from nature.   Vernet's Judith and Holophernes is fine, but she looks rather too like a Parisian beauty, with her hair dressed by the best coiffeur.

I admired Monvoisin's picture of the Death of Philip, Archduke of Austria.   The consequent madness of his wife, the unfortunate Jeanne of Castille, is well expressed, and contrasts strongly with the indifference which their son manifests on the occasion ;—that son was afterwards the celebrated Charles V.

To-day,(Tuesday,) passed some crowded hours

in the Louvre, trying to look at 2,280 modern pictures, and nearly a quarter of a mile of the ancient ones. Most of the best—indeed, the whole upper end of the long gallery—we found open, at least to strangers with a passport. So we lingered with great joy over our old friends, the Correggios—The Marriage of St. Catherine, and his Jupiter and Antiope, which came from Charles the First's collection at Richmond, with Titian's interesting picture of the Disciples at Emmaus.

Among the modern we liked some large French historical pictures by Alaux. The Duke of Orleans receiving hospitality under a tent of Laplanders in 1795, by Biard; and some rather exaggerated ones of Northern fishing among icebergs, by the same. The Interior of the Cathedral at Pisa, by Cibot, representing Galileo at eighteen, when he discovered the movement of a pendulum from observing the swinging of a lamp after it was lighted. He applied it to clocks many years afterwards; and this circumstance, like Newton's discovery of gravitation by the fall of an apple, is a proof of the advantage of not being absorbed in one thing—in fact, the use of inattention.

Peasants waiting for the arrival of a Ship, by
Delacroix, very good.   Portrait of La Duchesse
de D——, by Dubufe, we admired, and some
others by him ; also the Abdication of Charles V.
(a very large picture,) by Gallait.

These and many others we liked extremely :
I think the French are very superior to us in
their choice of interesting historical subjects,
and also in the power of painting large pictures.   But some particularly pink Eves and
naked goddesses are very bad, and their Holy
Families and Saints are not much better.   With
much of the power to execute, they seem to
want the sentiment of religion which produced the fine scriptural pictures of the old
masters.

Found le Comte de V—— when I went home :
he paid me a long visit—was very agreeable,
and more gentlemanlike than any Frenchman
I ever saw.   Handsome, too, and fair, and very
refined, without any affectation, but an amiable
wish to please ; in fact, I think he is very like
Cinq Mars, as described by himself, and that is
saying everything for him.

He spoke of the scenery of the Pyrenees in
very beautiful and glowing language, and

said the mountain outlines were plus doux, and there was more grace than in the Swiss landscapes. Of the Chateaux de Chambord, he said that it was unlike everything else : it was as if a number of people had tried to produce the most original building possible. He admired Richardson's novels more than any in any language. Said his best, Clarissa Harlow, I think, was composed after he was seventy ; M. de V——— was convinced the best novels were written by mature age. The result of thought and feeling, not the immediate action of either, being most conducive to excellence in writing.

36

CHAPTER III.

THREE DAYS AT VERSAILLES.

*Versailles, Friday, 2 May, Hôtel du Reservoir.—
Close to the palace and gardens.* The drive out
of Paris through the Place Louis XV., and
along the bank of the Seine, was to-day very
lovely. The sun shone brightly on the obelisk
and beautiful fountains, and lighted up the fine
views along the river, with a clear vividness
which our London climate, and our coal-smoke,
seldom allow. On coming direct from England,
or rather London, one of the greatest charms of
town scenery abroad is the clearness of city atmosphere. Yet the view from many of the London Bridges has perhaps more materials of beauty
than those obtained from the bridges in Paris.

The dome of St. Paul's is certainly finer than
the dome des Invalides; and the towers of

Westminster Abbey finer than those of Notre
Dame, but how seldom can we see them at a
distance very distinctly! At the same time, a
Frenchman may well ask where is to be found
such an arch as the Barrière de l'Etoile placed
in such a position, or such a building as La
Madelaine?

At Sevres we went to see the manufacture of
china. Some of the paintings are copies from
Raphael, and are beautiful; the vases, too, are
very fine; but the other things did not please me
near so much as the Dresden collection we saw
some years ago in Germany. There is nothing
in porcelain, I think, so graceful and pretty
as the embossed flowers of Dresden china.

Saturday.—Such a day! When I try to look
back on what we have seen, all seems like a
beautiful dream. First, we walked to the
Trianon, through beautiful sweet-smelling gardens, where birds of every variety of note were
singing in delightful harmony. We went over
all the rich apartments of the palace. After
the recollections of Marie Antoinette which
it excites, nothing interested me so much as the
apartments of the poor Princess Marie; they
adjoin those of her sister, Clementine, and the

chapel where she was married is not far off, under the same roof. Everything in her apartment looked so fresh and new—the yellow satin damask chairs and curtains — the bath, which forms a rich Turkish sofa, all—as if just newly furnished for her. In the chapel there is a fine picture, which looks like a Vandyke. It represents some · saint restoring a child· to life.

Many of the rooms have a very plain appearance from the carved walls being simply painted in white. They were all originally gilt, and in the gorgeous time of Louis XIV. shone no doubt in their full splendour; as the carving is extremely beautiful, the effect must have been very fine. Nothing can exceed the graceful minuteness of some of the wreaths and bouquets of flowers which ornament the doors and walls of even the smallest apartments. They are like our Gibbon's carvings in miniature. Another thing which gives, to our eyes, an unfinished and uncomfortable look, is the want of carpets, and to mine, above all things, the want of books, or even book stands, (except in the library,) or indeed, any sort of place where books, drawings, and comfortable litter could be put. Yet the royal family must read, and that they cultivate the arts with great success is shewn by the Princess Marie's beautiful models.*

But there was nothing in any of the rooms which gave token of ever having been inhabited; the chairs and sofas are in the most unvarying order; everything appears as if the palace was never used, though the family were in it last week, and, I believe, go there very often. Yet there is plenty of splendour. Malachite vases and pillars, given by the Emperor of Russia to Napoleon, and four onyx vases, given by the King of Spain, (in the great red gallery,) and an exquisite onyx intaglio, found at Pompeii, (over the chimney-piece in great drawing-room,) and many other fine gems set in clocks, &c.

The little Trianon is now used by the Duke of Orleans. It is very small, and has nothing particularly attractive, but the great interest given by the memory of Marie Antoinette. It was her favourite retreat, and near it is her bijou of a theatre, where she sometimes acted in the part of soubrettes; not far off is her dairy and her village, and here she enjoyed herself, and gave vent to the youthful buoyancy of a gay and good na-

* At Compiegne, indeed, there were some easels:

tured disposition. Here she played at shepherdess, at soubrette—at everything, perhaps, but formal etiquette; and thereby shocked the orthodox taste of the stately courtiers, without winning the love of the lower orders, whose manners she playfully imitated.

There was an air of melancholy in the Jardin Anglais, which surrounds the Petit Trianon and the dilapidated hameau and dairy, to which we walked—caused partly by the recollections of the miserable end of that young creature who formed them, and partly, indeed, by their neglected state.

The walls of a tower above the dairy, called " La Tour de Malbrouk," are fallen down, but a part of the staircase still remains, and these steps, which were ascended by the light feet of Marie Antoinette, that she might gaze from the height on the little paradise of her creation, now stand up against the blue sky like spectres, as if in mockery of what they had been. The tower was called " Malbrouk," from the air " Malbrouk est allé à la guerre," which was sung as a lullaby to the poor young Dauphin, (Louis XVII.) and was his favourite song.

The Swiss cottages are tumbling down; the

little lake is green, and overgrown with weeds ; and where children's mirth and joyous songs were once heard, the silence is now only broken by the croaking of large frogs, and the measured tread of a lonely sentinel, whose musket gleaming here and there among the trees, tells of past strife and present insecurity.

The play-ground of a beautiful Queen of France, a scene of rural life, where all was once peace and holiday enjoyment and farmyard festivity—how strange that its dilapidated remains, its crumbling, unroofed cottages, its stagnant ponds, and grass-grown walks, should now be guarded by military !

In these gardens it was that, when walking alone early one morning, she met a stranger, whose countenance filled her with such horror that she ran home and fainted.   This must have been a kind of presentiment of evil, for the man proved to be Santerre, who became her bitter enemy, and exercised so baneful an influence on her fate.

After lingering for some time in this strange scene we walked back to the great palace at Versailles, and, in spite of all fatigue, actually commenced the formidable task of seeing its

gigantic historical galleries, and launched our
tired selves into its hosts of recollections, associations, and splendour. Saw the north wing and
upper apartments of the centre. And so interesting was it all, that fatigue was forgotten; and
after several more miles of walking through the
splendid rooms, we were quite sorry when four
o'clock struck, and every one was turned out.

I was prepared to find the execution of many
of the modern pictures bad; but the subjects are
so interesting, and the explanation, names and
dates are so comfortably inscribed on everything,
that my only feeling was pleasure.   There is no
occasion to look in a catalogue, which to me is
as fatiguing as a dictionary.   And now it is
late, and we have walked out again since dinner on the terraces, and looked in at the windows, and thought again of all the kings and
queens who have lived, and rejoiced, and suffered, amid those splendid rooms.   But now that
I am sitting, in this comfortable room at the inn,
the whole thing, as I said before, seems like a
dream.   I see the statues in their old quaint
attires and kneeling attitudes.   That beautiful
young daughter of Francis I., with her pretty
jewelled head-dress; and the strange-looking

Isabeau de Bavière, wife of Charles VI., with her extraordinary attire and horrible countenance.

These, with Francis I.'s long nose, Louis XIV.'s large wig, Louis XVI.'s good-humoured, silly, fat face, and the last poor Dauphin's innocent stare, are all jumbled together before my eyes in strange confusion, but yet stand out more provokingly distinct than any of the other far more interesting objects we saw.

We were much amused by a picture of Louis XIV. and his family, in which he is drawn half naked, in his wig, without which, it is said; he was never seen, and Monsieur is in the same attire. The ladies, however, Madame (Henriette d'Angleterre), her mother, (the unfortunate wife of Charles I.), and the queen, are all very decently clad. Another picture, the Visit of Louis XIV. to the Invalides, is also very amusing. In it an angel is introduced completely naked and winged, among all the cocked hats, swords, substantial wigs, and the other ponderous realities of an armed court. Poor Louis XVI. is represented, in another picture, distributing charity to the poor. He looks like a great, bloated farmer, very foolish, and very hot, though snow covers the ground. But enough of this; his

44   SALLE DES CROISADES.

cruel fate has so hallowed this unfortunate monarch, that it is impossible to laugh at anything
connected with him.

Monday morning.—Before we again proceed
to the interesting but interminable labyrinth of
historical lore which the gigantic palace contains, I must say something of those parts we
saw yesterday. First, the private apartments
down stairs (seen by an order) are newly done
up, but not quite finished. The most beautiful
of these is the Salle des Croisades, which is
adorned in the Gothic and baronial style, the
ceiling and pillars emblazoned with the arms
of all the personages, both royal and knightly,
who went to the crusades.

Here, too, are some beautifully carved doors,
formerly belonging to a church at Rhodes, and
given by the Sultan to the Prince de Joinville.
After passing through several other rooms, we
went up stairs, and by means of our order were
admitted into the private apartments of Marie
Antoinette, which open from those of Louis XIV.,
and look upon an inner court of the right, or
south wing.

They are rather small and low, but adorned
with the beautiful gilt carving of, I believe, Louis

XIV.'s time, and furnished with green satin damask. Here is poor Louis XVI.'s oratory, separated from a small closet, which looks into the yard, by a thick, large pane of plate-glass. His guard stood on the outside, and could see the king, but not hear what he said.

We then returned to Louis XIV.'s bed-room, which is in the centre of the palace, and shewn to the public. It contains on each side of the state bed two beautiful pictures—a Holy Family, by, I believe, Vandyke; a Virgin and Child, by (the man said) Raphael, but we thought it appeared more like a good Andrea del Sarto.

It was on the balcony of this room that the unfortunate Louis XVI. and his family appeared when called for by the shouts and imprecations of a mad, infuriated mob. They then promised to return to Paris, which they did, guarded, or rather led as prisoners, by the refuse of the population, and insulted by the most turbulent spirits of that reign of disorder.

And this was the last time they beheld the palace of their ancestors. If Louis XIV. could, when reposing in that gorgeous bed, in the centre of the splendid pile he had reared, have

46   THE LIBRARY.

contemplated the remote effects of his lavish expenditure, would he have paused ?

We then went (still armed with our order, and therefore accompanied by another of the splendidly attired guardians who wait about in the public rooms,) to the private apartments of Louis XVI., first entering his bed-room, where Louis XV. died, in the left, or north wing. The next is called Salle des Pendules, ou du Meridien, and so on, through five splendid rooms (which, I believe, remain in the same state as when inhabited by the last unfortunate family,) to the old library.

Here there is a curious manuscript, framed— a plan for some improvements at Versailles, on which there are some marginal observations in Louis XIV.'s hand-writing. They are very characteristic of that gay and ever youthful monarch. He objects to the proposed plan, from the design of the figures being too serious, and that it wanted more youthfulness and " *gaiété;*" it must be more *plein de l'enfance.* This made us observe, that one of the great charms of most of Louis XIV.'s carvings and decorations are their being so full of youth, ease, and grace. All

the loves and graces which hover round the
ceilings, encircled with flowers and garlands in
gilt splendour, are teeming with youth and joy,
voluptuous but most refined. How different,
how clumsy, heavy, and tawdry do the gilt
carvings appear in some of the lately furnished
rooms.

From the Library we went to the Salon des
Porcelaines, which forms the corner of the second projection, and is very beautiful; and so
on through the billiard room to another, and
then back. Afterwards, we explored the south
wing, which contains the magnificent Gallerie
de Batailles. It has been lately renewed, is
lighted from the top, and shews to great advantage some fine pictures of Horace Vernet,
Sheffer, Schnetz, Gerard, Alaux, and other good
painters. A few are bad; but really, upon the
whole, there is much of excellence. I doubt
whether, if so many—and, above all, such *large*—
pictures had been done by English artists, they
would have been so good.

We thought the most interesting of these
gigantic pictures was the Battle of Fontenoy,
in which Marshal Saxe is the principal figure, by
H. Vernet, the little episodes in it are so well

48   BATTLE OF FONTENOY.

done.   On the right is a father embracing his son with intense joy for having won a cross of honour, his young comrades looking on—some envious, and others delighted at his success. The father's features seem quivering with emotion, yet only part of the profile is seen.   On the other side is a scene of sorrow—a mother leaning over her dying son; and a soldier, mortally wounded, gazing on his companion, who has just expired.

The lower part of that wing is occupied by the campaigns of 1796 to 1810; in short, it is devoted to Napoleon and all his glories.   There is a gallery on the second, or, as we should say, third floor, we saw to-day, which contains some very interesting old historical pictures—Blanche of Castille, Queen Elizabeth, Gabrielle, and Dianne de Poitiers Duchess of Valentinois, &c.

This morning, we saw the whole lower story of the centre part; containing a pleasant history of France,—portraits of its kings, its palaces, its celebrated warriors, from Pharamond down to the present time.

In the Gallerie de Louis XIII., in the middle of the front, are some good large pictures of the Marriage of Louis XIII. and Anne of Austria, and the interview between Louis XIV. and Philip IV. (father of his wife, Marie Therese, of Austria) on the Isle des Faisans.

We then went up to the second story of the north wing. It contains many curious old pictures. A very pretty one of Marie Stuart, that Queen—

" Dear to the Loves, and to the Graces vowed ;"

a curious one of the celebrated Agnes Sorel, half undressed ; one of Mary of Burgundy, daughter of Charles the Bold, and grandmother to Charles V.—her son was married to the pretty Jeanne la Folle of Arragon, daughter of Ferdinand and Isabella ; a good old portrait of Bayard. That of Du Gueslin disappointed me ; he is common-looking. There is a very curious old picture of a ball given by Henry III., in which his mother, Catherine de Medicis ; his wife, Louise de Lorraine ; and many others are dancing. There is also a portrait of Cinq Mars, and one of his love, Marie of Mantua, Queen of Poland, which I looked at with great interest, having just read again De Vigny's beautiful novel. A portrait of Rubens and one of Charles I. pleased me much ; another, Christina

50   CURIOUS PICTURES.

of Sweden, looks very much as if she could have
changed her religion, and be quite as capricious
as she was; she is represented with wild black
eyes, and hair which appears too self-willed ever
to submit to a coiffeur's dressing. The great
Prince of Condé disappointed me by his ugliness.
The portrait of Madame de Maintenon is very
good. She is in a black dress, and reminded
me strongly of Mrs. F——, such as I remember
her. There are three strange old pictures representing a fête given at Vienna, on the marriage
of Joseph II. to Josephine of Bavaria, in 1765;
they appear to be all children, and one of the
boys has wings.

On coming down, we passed again through
the upper statue gallery of that wing, and took
another look at the lovely statue of Joan of Arc.
What a face, and what a sublime expression!
None of the copies I have seen give one the idea
of its being half so beautiful and so inspired. That
dear Princess Marie!—she must have been almost
content to die, after leaving such a proof of her
beautiful mind and powerful genius to the world.

We came home when we were turned out, at
four; and now we have actually walked through
every part of the shewn apartments, and it

took us about twelve hours to do so, with scarcely any stopping. Yet, after all this hard work, I strolled each evening in the delightful gardens, where the nightingales sang, and the orange-flowers smelt so sweetly. We generally stayed in the gardens till we were turned out, soon after eight o'clock, when the harsh drums silenced the nightingales, but the screech-owls seemed to enjoy the noise, for, as we returned home through the dark alleys, they hooted over our heads in a very melancholy manner.

What a place is this for the Parisians to have so near to them ! It is far more magnificent in every way than I expected ; and, as merit of any kind is sure to do, it gains ground on acquaintance. The Terrace is peculiarly fine,— a gigantic undertaking well executed.

This evening we lingered out of doors for some time on the Parterre du Nord, and then crossed to the top of the steps which overlook the Tapis Verd of the great canal. How fine is the view from this point: here is seen to the best advantage the whole extent of Louis XIV.'s splendid addition, for it appears that out of respect for his father, he left that part of the palace standing which faces the entrance, and

52   PARTERRE DU MIDI.

surrounds the " Cour de Marbre." The garden-
front is thrown forward, and its noble wings,
from their great extent, and unity of design,
unbroken though ornamented by projecting
colonnades, have a grand effect.

We crossed to the Parterre du Midi, overlooking the curious Orangery, which is quite in
keeping with the Château. There are formal
parterres of flowers, and the broad walks are
bordered on each side by orange trees, which, to
the amount of some hundreds, are thus drawn
up, and look as stiff, and in the season must
smell as sweet as can well be imagined; noble
arched vaults constructed beneath the terrace,
serve as their winter residence.

Two splendid flights of marble steps, to the
number of 104, at each extremity of the parterre,
lead to the garden.

This evening I copied the following peaceful
effusion, which was scratched on the balustrade
of the Parterre du Midi :—

" L'ANTI-MARSEILLAISE.

Amour sacré de la Patrie,
La Patrie! c'est l'univers.
Révérons cette loi chérie,
C'est la loi des peuples divers,

PARTERRE DU MIDI.   **53**

C'est la loi de la Providence,
Qui nous créa pour le bonheur
De la grande et sainte alliance,
Des peuples à leur Créateur.
Plus d'armes et brisons,
Nos glaives destructeurs.
Jurons, jurons,
Qu'un saint amour unisse tous nos cœurs."

And below it, was written—

" Benit soit celui qui a écrit ces lignes,
   Puissent-elles être comprises."

54

CHAPTER IV.

Visit to Fontainebleau—Journey to Orleans—Blois—Its
old castle, and historical recollections.

Fontainebleau, Tuesday, May 18*th.*—We left our
pretty, comfortable rooms at Versailles this
morning, at seven o'clock, with much regret.

We found the scenery nearly all the way here
far prettier than we expected; and between
Versailles and Longjumeau there were some
beautiful spots.   Soon after leaving the horrible
pavé, we passed through the little village of
Bievres, and admired its old church and château,
with terraced gardens full of flowers, sloping
down a woody height to the river.   As we
wound down its little street, an extensive view
over a rich plain opened upon us, and here
we met an interesting procession.   Some

priests in their robes were chanting, accompanied
by one who played a huge trombone, and preceded by some girls, in white dresses, bearing
banners, embroidered in white.

After the descent of the hill, the road turns
to the left, and affords a picturesque view of
Bievres, and its old church; the road continued
through a rich and well-cultivated valley, bounded
by woods; some remarkably tall and very thin
poplars, looking like the ghosts of trees, gave a
peculiarity to the view.

Pear and cherry trees were abundant along
the road; narrow strips of various cultivation—
wheat, rye, peas, cabbages, vines. Some large villages, seen from the road—some country places,
—all had a pleasing and prosperous appearance.

Longjumeau occupies two hills, hence its
name; a translation of its Latin one, Mons
Gemellius. Before we reached it, passed Pa-
laiseau—a pretty little town, where is a well-
kept country residence. Beyond Longjumeau, we
remarked a curious old chateau; it consists of
a circular tower with smaller ones on one side,
and is surrounded by a moat; a modern building has been added. I think we heard, at Essone,
that its name was St. Geneviève; about twenty

minutes before reaching Essone, we came to
pavé and the Seine.

Chailly, our last relay, is famous for white
horses—we had a team, one of them cost 1000
francs—a good strong horse.   After leaving it,
we soon entered the Forest of Fontainebleau
(Fontaine belle eau), and inorder, I believe, to
shew it off, our postillion left the road, and
drove for a short way among the trees, a trying
undertaking for springs, and a shower-bath
occasionally for those behind; but it gave us
the sight of some of the finest oaks I ever saw,
—magnificent trees !   The country around very
singular ; masses of rock piled together.   How
splendid is this forest !—well worthy of having
days devoted to it for exploring.

On arriving here (at Fontainebleau), we first
drove to the Hôtel de France, where a very fat
landlady asked us eighteen francs for rooms.
Saussat thought it too much, so we decided on
going to another.   I own I regretted doing so ;
but from principle we yielded to our courier's
economy, and were rewarded.   We got very
comfortably lodged at the Hôtel de Lyons for
eleven francs, and five francs a-head for dinner.

Since then, we have visited the palace, which

PALACE AT FONTAINEBLEAU. **57**

has delighted me; it is very interesting, from its antiquity and the numerous historical events which have occurred here. The first rooms we were shewn were those occupied by the Emperor Charles V. during his visit to Francis I., and afterwards, in very different circumstances, by his descendant, Charles IV. of Spain. Pope Pius VI. was also, in Napoleon's time, a prisoner in these apartments; they now belong to the Duke of Orleans.

After seeing the large chapel of Henry IV., we passed through the long, quaint gallery of Francis I., which remains in its old decoration of blue and white, relieved by gilding and fresco painting. We then entered some gorgeous apartments lately restored, and Henry II.'s splendid hall; among its ornaments, the fair Dianne de Poitier's silver crescent is conspicuous. This is the most beautiful room I ever saw, and we lingered a few minutes to sketch it. We then proceeded to the old chapel consecrated by Thomas à Becket, and built, at the time of the original castle, by Louis VII., in 1169. It contains some beautiful painted glass windows, the designs for which were made by the late Princess Marie. The next room we visited was that of

poor Louis XVI. The walls are adorned with
fine tapestry, and satin embroidered in chenille,
presented by the town of Lyons to the king, on
his marriage. The walls of the bed-room are
also covered with the same costly material, in
graceful patterns of music and flowers. The
adjoining apartment was formerly called that of
Marie de Medicis, and in it Louis XIII. was
born. Napoleon occupied it as his bed-room;
and the small one beyond is the celebrated room
in which he signed his abdication. It has red
damask hangings, and contains two large looking-
glasses opposite each other. The important paper
was signed on a little, shabby-looking round table,
with a painted leg and unvarnished mahogany
top. It bears evident marks of being cut or
stabbed, as if in anger, with a penknife. In this
room there is a fac-simile of the celebrated do-
cument which gave peace to Europe; and we
remarked the blot after Napoleon's name. Did
this arise from accident or agitation ?

The Gallery of Diana is very fine. It was
built by Henry IV., the joyous king, who dated
some of his letters to the fair Gabrielle, " De
nos delicieux deserts de Fontainebleau." This
splendid gallery was afterwards restored by

Louis XVIII.; and under it is the Gallery of
Stags (des Cerfs) where Queen Christina of
Sweden caused Monaldeschi to be murdered.
How horrible are the details of that atrocious
action!

In the apartment of Madame de Maintenon
(which is near Henry II.'s Hall), the revocation
of the edict of Nantes is said to have been signed.
In Marie Antoinette's boudoir, the espagnolettes
of the windows were chiselled by her unfortunate
husband himself. They represent wreaths of
vine leaves, and are extremely beautiful.

St. Louis built a great part of the palace,
and, amongst other things, the Church of the
Trinity,—which, I think, was embellished by
Henry IV. It is much out of repair, but is soon
to be restored.

Philip le Bel was born here; so were Henry
III. and Louis XIII. Here, in 1636, the great
Condé died; and, in this palace, Louis XV.
married the Princess Marie, the daughter of
Stanislaus Lecksenski, the exiled King of Po-
land. Their son, the father of Louis XVI.,
Louis XVIII., and Charles X., died here, in
December, 1765, and within these walls, on the
30th of May, 1837, the marriage of the Duke

60   GARDENS OF THE PALACE.

of Orleans and the Princess Helene, of Meck-
lenbourg, took place—so there is no want of
historical interest.

Here, indeed, I seemed to be transported
several centuries back, and surrounded by the
spirits of celebrated characters.

> " They spoke unto me from the silent ground,
>   They look'd unto me from the pictured wall ;
>   The echo of my footstep was a sound
>   Like to the echo of their own footfall,
>   What time their living feet were in the hall."

In the evening we walked in the gardens, and
I took a view of the south-east front, containing
Henry II.'s room, the oldest chapel, and the little
oriel, or rather pavilion, where Louis XIII. was
baptized. I then drew one of the Cour des Fon-
taines, with the little lake and pavilion, or island,
where Napoleon is said to have often gone to
enjoy repose. This piece of water contains some
of the largest carp we ever saw, and in great
numbers. I thought of the various and different
feelings of Napoleon* in that venerable pile,

---

* There is a passage in Allison's History that describes so
well the desertion of Napoleon by his friends and servants,
that I will insert it :—

" And now commenced, at Fontainebleau, a scene of

where he enjoyed the height of prosperity, and experienced all the bitterness of adversity.

Orleans, Wednesday.—The dulness of this day's drive was quite a relief, as it gave one a little time to digest all the interesting sights of the last many days! I cannot bear to have too great a succession of interesting impressions—one has no time to chew the cud of them. But the cessation of interest did not last long, for the approach to Orleans is fine; the cathedral, with its two high towers and spire of Gothic lace-like tracery,

baseness never exceeded in any age of the world, and which forms an instructive commentary on the principles and practice of the Revolution. Let an eye-witness of these hideous tergiversations record them; they would pass for incredible if drawn from any less exceptionable source. 'Every hour,' says Caulaincourt, 'was, after this, marked by fresh voids in the emperor's household. The universal object was, how to get first to Paris. All the persons in office quitted their post without leave or asking permission; one after another they all slipped away, totally forgetting him to whom they owed everything, but who had no longer anything to give. The universal complaint was, that his formal abdication was so long of appearing. 'It was high time,' it was said by every one, 'for all this to come to an end; it is absolute childishness to remain any longer in the antechambers of Fontainebleau, when favours are showering down at Paris:' and with that they all set off for the capital. Such was their anxiety to hear of his abdication,

62　　　　　BEAUTIFUL SCENERY.

through which the sky is seen ; the domes of
smaller churches, and the first view of the majestic Loire—its vine gardens and its villaed
banks—then the fine bridge,—form a succession of pictures which called forth my little sketch
book from the bag in which it had peacefully
slumbered all day. But French pavé, with its dips,
and gutters, and French whip-cracking postillions
jolted too much to allow of even a scratch that
looks like anything, so my fingers were useless.
When we arrived at the Hôtel de la Boule d'Or,

that they pursued misfortune even into its last asylum ; and
every time the door of the emperor's cabinet opened, a
crowd of heads were seen peeping in to gain the first hint
of the much-longed-for news.' No sooner was the abdication and the treaty with the Allies signed, than the desertion was universal ; every person of note around the emperor,
with the single and honourable exceptions of Maret and
Caulaincourt, abandoned him :—the antechambers of the
palace were literally deserted. Berthier even left his bene-
factor without bidding him adieu ! ' He was born a courtier,' said Napoleon, when he learned his departure ; ' you
will see my vice-constable mendicating employment from the
Bourbons. I feel mortified that men whom I have raised so
high in the eyes of Europe should sink so low. What have
they made of that halo of glory through which they have
hitherto been seen by the stranger ? What must the sovereigns think of such a termination to all the illustrations of
my reign !' "

in a narrow street, it rained, and I hoped for a
quiet evening in our little, dark sitting-room,
looking on a small yard; but after dinner it
cleared up, and a bright gleam of setting sun-
shine attracted us to the old cathedral, which is
a fine building.

The exterior has been restored, and the buttresses are ornamented with large and handsome
pinnacles. It was too late to ascend the tower,
so we contented ourselves with an interesting
walk on the bridge.

Thursday, May 20th.—This morning, on our
way to the cathedral we saw the statue of Jeanne
d'Arc. The group which Inglis describes, stood
in the Rue Royale, and was erected, as he says,
by Charles VII.; but it was destroyed during
the Revolution. Inglis, then, could not have
seen it, and I cannot well imagine how he could
have been at Orleans without observing the
present statue.

It represents the heroine in female dress, with
flowing garments, wearing a cuirass, and in the
act of fighting; but I think that the statue of
the Princess Marie is much more accordant than
this, with the enthusiasm of Jeanne's character
and her strong devotion. The costume, too, is

64   THE CATHEDRAL.

infinitely better.   On the pedestal are bas-reliefs
in bronze, representing the four principal inci-
dents of Jeanne's career: the statue itself is in
bronze.

We found some one in the sacristy of the cathedral, and ascended one of the towers—a good
appetite-giving operation, for the twin towers
over the western entrance are 240 feet high;
they are richly ornamented; the figures of four
angels stand at the angles of the balustrade,
these are 15 feet high; so the entire height is
255 feet.

There is a lofty, but not a handsome spire,
which rises directly from the roof in the centre
of the church, its cross is 260 feet high. This
spire inclines very perceptibly; it has been
propped up, and no danger is apprehended.
According to our informant, this cathedral is
400 feet long, and 100 feet high.

The original structure was of very ancient
date, so far back as the time of Constantine, for
Orleans was the ancient Gebanum : Henry IV.
commenced its restoration, which was continued
by subsequent kings, until Louis XV. built the
towers. The exterior is very rich. Its buttresses,

which are numerous, perhaps eleven or twelve, have upon each, three rows of tall and ornamented pinnacles; these have all been recently restored. The interior is very plain—the simplicity of the early English—no screens. A handsome modern grille separates the choir from the nave.

The view from the top of the tower is extensive; but over a flat country. The course of the Loire is traced for some distance, and on a clear day, with a glass, the castles of Chambord and Blois are visible. The town is tolerably large; its population 40,000. The new street (Jeanne d'Arc) is a great improvement; we saw the tracings of the railroad to Paris, now in progress.

Thursday, 20th. — In the carriage. Rather disappointed in the views on leaving Orleans. Country flat, and too many poplars—but the broad river looks well, and the scene is enlivened by the square, white sails of boats sailing up and down; and they continue to be seen through the trees, though we have lost sight of the river. The garden-like vineyards are very neat, bordered with walnut-trees, and some surrounded by great wooden railings, or trellices.

Then, here and there, in the midst of them,

VOL. I.   F

appear little farm-houses, to each of which a
long avenue of quaintly-cut lime-trees leads from
the road; and these buildings, with their old
high roofs, green blinds, and formal little flower
gardens, have a rural and homely air, far preferable to that of the spruce villas of retired
merchants, usually seen in the neighbourhood
of large towns, and look as if they contained a
far happier class of people.

Just changed horses at the little village of
St. Ay, and passed two campagnes surrounded by
beautiful gardens; where a profusion of roses and
stocks smelt very sweet; and peonies of various
colours and great size gave a most brilliant air
to the formal, but well-kept flower-beds.   I
rather like formality, particularly in gardens.

The country has now become more flat; and
we have lost the river, but the quaintly-shaped
church of Nôtre Dame de Clery has come in
sight on the opposite bank.   It was built by
Louis XI., for his favourite Madonna, his " chere
petite maitresse;" to whom he was overheard
asking pardon for having caused his brother to
be poisoned.   Under its roof he was buried;
and the heart of his son, Charles VIII., is pre-
served there.

I have heard a curious legend of that old church, which states that, when any one in danger at sea vowed a ·pilgrimage to Nôtre Dame de Clery, the bell used to toll of its own accord.   And now we have left it behind us ; and the pretty village of Meung is just seen at the end of a turn in the road, with its church and a fine old red-brick château, embosomed in woods, and surmounted by high pinnacles.

It is gone; but the ancient town of Beaugency has appeared, and its fine ruined castle, close to the river, which winds along to our left.

We got out, and while horses were changing, walked down through the little winding narrow streets of Beaugency, to see the old castle.

The outer walls of one large square tower remain.   It is of great height, and is said to have been built in the time of Julius Cæsar. The windows are still ornamented with beautiful carving, and the floors only fell in about three years ago.

In many of the little streets are old houses and half ruined towers, some beautifully ornamented; and not far from the old castle, there is a curious high tower, surmounted by small

pinnacles, and the remains of some arches at the
bottom, ornamented inside, which appear to be
Roman.

Another irregular street, with carved doorways opening into little garden-courts, led us
down to the river, and its long bridge of thirty-
nine arches, (we could only count twenty-nine.)
The opposite bank appears flat and uninteresting, but we liked Beaugency much. It is a
clean and pleasant-looking little town, in which
there seemed to be few indications of either
poverty or riches; no large modern mansions,
and the old dilapidated houses are only half
inhabited — sometimes only a few of the windows, or a single story, had glass in them,
shewing that those rooms alone were occupied;
but they were full of flowers, and luxuriant
vines trailed along the old carving of the
ruined and glassless windows, and over the little
Gothic doorways—giving a cheerful air, and
making the half-deserted abodes of former
splendour appear venerable, but not gloomy.
One of them reminded us of the finely-carved
house at Stirling, (of the Regent Morton, I believe,) near the old palace, which was never
finished.

VILLA OF MADAME DE POMPADOUR. 69

Soon after leaving Beaugency, the country became very bare, and we saw no beauty of any kind. At Mer, where we next changed horses, there was nothing remarkable but the highly-decorated tower of its Gothic church.

At the next post, Ménars, we went to see the villa of Madame de Pompadour, and were much disappointed with it; though the house is well built, and comfortable-looking. The garden terraces, which slope down to the river, are ornamented with statues and sculptured vases; but the view they command is by no means pretty; the only interest about it is derived from its former celebrated possessor, and from the dark Forest of Chambord, which covers the flat plain beyond the villages and poplar-bordered vine grounds on the opposite bank.*

The whole place has a deserted and neglected look; the terraced parterres are turned into corn fields, and the borders (in which, however, some beautiful roses were blooming) are overgrown with weeds. The redeeming feature in this, as in many ill-kept French châteaux, is the profusion of orange trees, in large green boxes, which

---

* Inglis has made a mistake about this villa, which he places at Beaugency.

70   MADAME DE POMPADOUR.

adorn the walks. We could not see the interior, where some of Madame de Pompadour's furniture still remains, because it was jour de fête, and the servants were all amusing themselves.

The same sort of flat country till we approached near Blois. The town extends on both sides of the river, and, with its fine old castle and church, which stand on the height to our right, and the sloping gardens and noble bridge to the left, forms an interesting and beautiful picture.

Six o'clock. — In the Hôtel d'Angleterre at Blois, close to the bridge, where our sitting-room at the corner commands a view up and down the river, and is approachable only by an open balcony, full of flowers. Very pleasant such a mild evening as this, but in rain or cold would make us grumble. W—— met a gentleman on this romantic-looking balcony, who told him some good traits of the first possessor of Menars, and one very creditable to the present owner also.

The road formerly went on the outside of Madame de Pompadour's grounds ; and to save the public this detour, she offered to allow it to pass, as it now does, close to her château. Its present possessor, the Prince de C——, has erected a large school and gymnase, entirely at his own expense. It was the fine building near the château, which we saw.

We are delighted with Blois, and the air seems so light and gentle here, that, compared with the depressing heaviness of some other places, it feels like eating soufflé after a tough bit of beef.

The people are very civil and talkative. A nice old woman shewed us the castle. We met, too, a pleasant old French gentleman, and afterwards a farmer, who, with his little son, accompanied us in our walk home. He was full of information, and shewed us the church of St. Nicholas : a fine old building—which has lately been restored—it suffered much during the revolution, and was used as a stable.

The old castle here, and indeed the whole place, puts me in mind of Stirling—not in form, but it has the same character—a deserted royal residence, full of interesting recollections, the remains of ancient splendour mingled with present decay and misery. The part of it, too, where Guise was assassinated by the order of Henry III., corresponds in position (overhanging a high precipice) with that part of Stirling Castle where Douglas was murdered.

The exterior of this castle, and the interior of

the court, with its curious open staircases, are
most picturesque. The part built by Louis XII.,
is of red brick, with stone friezes and quaint
carvings : the bricks look so fresh, that it
appears of a much later date than the buildings
of his son-in-law and successor, Francis I. Louis
XII. was born there ; his young wife, Anne of
Brittany, occupied the upper apartments erected
by him. These were afterwards inhabited by the
Duchess de Nemours and Duchess of Guise,
during the fatal catastrophe which occurred in
the reign of Henry III, the too-confiding Duke
of Guise occupying those below. At the time
of the murder, Henry III. occupied the upper
part of Francis I.'s building, over the apartment
of his mother, Catherine de Medicis.

The Salle des Etats, a fine old room, with a row
of Gothic pillars and arches, was erected by St.
Louis (IX.) The only apartments which retain
any of their old carved wainscots, are those of
Catherine de Medicis ; the ceilings of these are
beautiful, particularly her oratory, a sort of
large oriel window projecting over the dizzy
height on which the castle is built; and the
room beyond it from whence poor Marie de Medicis, (wife to Henry IV.,)made her escape by
a ladder of ropes, when imprisoned here by

Richelieu. Near this spot are the dungeons called Les Oubliettes—a name which awfully proclaims their destination—they are at the bottom of an old round tower; and here the Cardinal de Guise was murdered the day after his brother.

The oldest part of the castle is a massive tower at the western corner, erected by the early Counts of Blois. And on this spot, where our King Stephen once lived, Catherine de Medicis built her observatory, and the stone table where her horoscope stood is still there. We ascended the same old wooden staircase, so often trodden by that imperious queen; it is now very crazy, but I thought this the most interesting part of the whole castle. It commands, too, a good view of the other portions of the building, with that of the whole town and river below. What a mixture of religious observance, superstition, and cruelty, was Catherine! Close to her oratory was the gloomy dungeon where she confined her enemies, and to it was an entrance even from her room.*

---

* On considering over the numerous old places I have seen possessing interesting historical associations, I find none gave me so much pleasure, or transported me so vividly into the past, as Linlithgow. Queen Margaret's bower, the room where Mary was born, and the chapel, where the ghost is said

74   GLOOMY PREDICTIONS.

She died here in 1588, soon after the murder of Guise by her son. The castle is now a barrack ; the part where Guise was murdered being devoted to soldiers' bed-rooms, so that the smell, the noise, and bustle of its present occupants destroy all romance. I could think of nothing. The disagreeable present put all thoughts of past interest to flight, and proved too much even for the graphic description of the scene in James's Henry of Guise, or for the recollection of that lovely Margaret de Valois who was here married to Henry IV.

It is strange how often we find that some apparently absurd prophecies have been fulfilled, and rhymed sayings, which have foretold terrible events, have come to pass.

In allusion to the murder of Guise, l'Almanac de Billy gravely said that, Pasquier prognosticated nothing good for all the year 1588, and less still for the month of December. Indeed, all the predictions were threatening. The people expected to see realized the prophecy of Nostradamus :—

to have appeared to James, warning him of danger—all these have an undisturbed look, as if desolation had reigned there ever since, and carry the imagination back, without ption, to the scenes of past centuries.

" Paris conjure un grand meurdre commettre,
 Blois lui fera sortir son plein effet."

The friends of Guise commented on—as the fatal announcement of some dreadful event which should strike the House of Lorraine—these four verses des Centuries, which the credulity of the epoch made terrible :—

" En l'an qu'un œil en France regnera,
 La cour sera en un bien facheux trouble,
 Le grand de Bloys, son amy tuera ;
 Le regne mis en mal et doute double."*

A strange circumstance is connected with the murder of Guise, and is an instance of the retributive justice which we often see, in history, pur-

---

* Another of these remarkable sayings was fulfilled in the reign of Louis XIII. It was said that sometime before the tragic end of the interesting Cinque Mars and his friend De Thou, Nostradamus composed the following enigma :—

" Quand *bonnet rouge* passera par la fenêtre,
 A *quarante onces* on coupera la tête et *tout* perira."

Bonnet rouge proved to be the Cardinal Richelieu, who at his great fête, was carried through a window to go to the theatre. A mark was eight ounces ; therefore, forty ounces made five marks (Cinque Mars). At the same time that his implacable enemy was triumphant at Paris, poor Cinque Mars, (forty ounces,) was beheaded, and De Thou (Tout) perished with him on the scaffold.

suing criminals. It is said that, in the very room where Guise was murdered, he himself plotted, sixteen years before, the massacre of the Huguenots. The man who destroyed him, too, Henry III., seems never to have enjoyed any peace or happiness after he had committed the horrible crime, and was himself murdered not long afterwards.

Friday, 21.—Rainy and cold. The romantic balcony where I lingered last night on my way to the bedroom, gazing at the stars, was this morning so wet as to oblige me to put on goloshes, and hold up an umbrella in going from one room to the other. In the evening, the weather cleared up, and we had a pleasant walk to the Cathedral, and in the gardens of the "Eveché." The Cathedral is not so fine or so large as the church of St. Nicholas, which we saw last night. A violent thunderstorm drove us home, but after dinner we were again attracted out by a fine sunset, and went up to the old castle. I tried to sketch the interior of the court, but such numbers of soldiers surrounded me, that I could not do it satisfactorily. We got a recollection, however, of Louis XII. and Francis I. buildings, with the three curious open stair-cases; and imagined what it must have been when first built by Louis XII., "tout de neuf, et

tant somptueux qui bien sembloit œuvre de
Roi," so said an old chronicler, Jean of Auton.

Besides the number of celebrated historical
events which happened at Blois, there are many
less known, but almost as interesting.

Here the young Queen Isabella of Valois,
widow of King Richard II., and called the
Little Queen, found peace and joy with her
second husband, the Duke of Orleans.   Our
unfortunate Richard was murdered when his
young Queen was only thirteen years old ; and
she was so shocked at his tragic end, that even
after many years had elasped, she steadily refused the hand of the gallant Henry of Mon-
mouth, though, as Froissart said, " Richard of
Bourdeaux, (II.) had been far too old for her ;
but the person now offered was suitable in every
respect, being no other than the Prince of
Wales."   She continued, however, to refuse this
accomplished prince (afterwards Henry V.) " in
a manner," says Monstrelet, "exceedingly touching, as all who approached her, French or English, bore testimony."   She was after some
delay and difficulty restored to her father, the
King of France, and as we read in Shakspeare's
tragedy :—

78   VIOLANTE OF MILAN.

> " My Queen to France from whence set forth in pomp,
>   She came adorned hither, like sweet May,
>   Sent back like hallowmas, or shortest day."

Some time afterwards she accepted the offer
of her cousin, Charles of Orleans ; and it is delightful to think that after all her vicissitudes
and misfortunes, she enjoyed great happiness
in this venerable castle of Blois.

She was idolized by her husband, and he was
not only amiable and valiant, but one of the
most accomplished Princes in Europe, and composed many beautiful poems.*

His mother, Violante of Milan, was a very interesting person, and during the first year of her
son's marriage, she came to Blois, almost broken-
hearted for the loss of her husband, who had
been basely assassinated by his kinsman, the
Duke of Burgundy. Here she took for her
" embleme," une chante-pleure (un arrosoir),
between two SS, initials of soupir and souci,
and the melancholy device—

> " Rien ne m'est plus,
>   Plus ne m'est rien."

---

* There is a richly illuminated copy of poems in the British Museum, which is supposed to have been transcribed
for Henry VII.

was embroidered on the walls of her apartments, which were hung with black. This unfortunate widow found great pleasure in the
society of Isabella, and her last hours were
soothed by the presence of her beloved daughter-
in-law.

But our poor Queen Isabella's happiness did
not last long; at the early age of twenty-one,
she died, after giving birth to a daughter. The
Duke of Orleans was almost frantic at the loss
of his beautiful wife, and eloquently deplored
her untimely end in some lines, which begin—

" J'ai fait l'obseque de madame."

I will quote a translation that Miss Strickland
has given of them in her interesting history
of this Queen's life.

" J'AI FAIT L'OBSEQUE DE MADAME.

" To make my lady's obsequies
    My love a minster wrought,
And, in the chantry service there,
    Was sung by doleful thought.
The tapers were of burning sighs
    That light and odour gave,
And grief illuminèd by tears
    Irradiated her grave ;
And, round about, in quaintest guise,
    Was carved—' Within this tomb there lies
The fairest thing to mortal eyes.'

" Above her, lieth spread a tomb
  Of gold and sapphires blue :
  The gold doth shew her blessedness—
  The sapphires mark her true ;
  For blessedness and truth in her
  Were livelily portrayed ;
  When gracious God, *with both his hands*,
  Her wondrous beauty made ;
  She was, to speak without disguise,
  The fairest thing to mortal eyes.

" No more, no more ; my heart doth faint,
  When I the life recal
  Of her who lived so free from taint,
  So virtuous deem'd by all ;
  Who in herself was so complete,
  I think that she was ta'en,
  By God to deck his Paradise,
  And with his saints to reign ;
  For well she doth become the skies,
  Whom, while on earth, each one did prize—
  The fairest thing to mortal eyes !"

This accomplished prince was afterwards
taken prisoner, when fighting valiantly at the
battle of Agincourt, and sent by Henry V. to
England. Some of his most beautiful poems
were composed during a weary captivity of
twenty-three years in the Tower of London.

" It was at the Château de Blois," says Saussaye, " that Charles d'Orleans, one of the first

days of the first spring which smiled on him since his return to France, when beholding the magnificent country which he saw from the height of his royal residence, and enjoying the beauties of nature with the feeling of a captive before whose eyes the prison doors have just opened, composed this charming rondel :"—

> " Le temps a laissié son manteau
> De vent, de froidure, et de pluye,
> Et c'est vestu de broderye,
> De soleil raiant* cler et beau.
>
> " Il n'y a beste, ne oiseau
> Qui en son jargon ne chante ou crye :
> Le temps a laissió son manteau
> De vent, de froidure, et de pluye.
>
> " Rivière, fontaine, et ruisseau
> Portent, en livrée jolie,
> Gouttes d'argent, d'orfevrerie ;
> Chacun s'habille de nouveau,
> Le temps a laissié son manteau
> De vent, de froidure, et de pluye."

The following ballad was also written at the Château de Blois :—

> " En tirant d'Orleans à Blois,
> L'autre jour par eau venoye
> Si rencontrai, par plusieurs fois,
> Vaisseaux, ainsy que je passoye,

---

* Rayonnant.

82   CHARLES THE FIFTH.

Qui cingloient leur droite voye
Et aloient legièrement,
Pour ce qu'eurent, comme veoye*
A plaisir et à gré le vent.

" Mon cueur, penser et moi, nous trois,
Les regardasmes à grant joye ;
Et dit mon cueur, à basse voix,
Volontiers en ce point seroye ;
De confort† la voile tendroye,
Si je cuidoye‡ seurement
Avoir, ainsy que je vouldroye,
A plaisir et à gré le vent.

" Mais je trouve, le plus des mois,
Le eaue de fortune si quoye:||
Quant ou bateau§ du monde vois
Que jamais d'espoir je n'auroye ;
Souvent en chemin demouroye,¶
En trop grant ennuy longuement ;
Pour néant en vain attendroye
A plaisir et à gré le vent.

" Les nefs dont ci devant parloye
Montoient et je descendoye ;
Contre les vaques du tourment,
Quant il lui plaira, Dieu m'envoye
A plaisir et à gré le vent."

The Emperor Charles V. passed through Blois
and stopped at the castle. His visit was de-

---

* Comme je vis.   † Consolation.   ‡ Si je pensais.
|| L'eau de fortune si calm.
§ Au bateau.   ¶ Demeurerais.

scribed in a short poem, little known, composed on the occasion of this fête, by Claudius Chappuis, valet to the king:—

> " Blois, noble ville, à sa joyeuse entrée
> Triomphalement a esté accoustrée ;
> Ne délaissant aucun poinct en arrière,
> Pour luy monstrer affection entière," &c.

Mademoiselle de Montpensier thus speaks of a visit she made to her father, the Duke d'Orleans, at Blois, in 1655:—" L'air de Blois me donna un rhume épouvantable qui dura trois semaines, je ne sortais, ne dormais, ni ne mangeois; je m'amusai à jouer, parceque cela m'ennuyoit moins que d'entretenir les gens que je voyois."

Her description of the visit of Louis XIV. there, three years afterwards, when on his road to St. Jeanne de Luz, to marry the Infanta of Spain, is rather amusing:—" On alla diner à Blois, où mon père donna à manger au roi dans le château. Mes sœurs vinrent au bas des degrez (le grand escalier à jour) reçevoir sa Majesté. Par malheur, de certaines mouches que l'on nomme cousins, avoient mordu ma sœur; comme ce qu'elle à de plus de beau est le teint, elles le lui avaient si gâté et la gorge qu'elle avoit maigre, comme l'ont ordinairement les

84   CHARLES THE SECOND AT BLOIS.

filles de quatorze ans, qu'elle faisoit pitié à voir. Ajoutez à cela le chagrin ou elle étoit d'avoir cru épouser le roi. On lui avait toujours tenu ce discours, et on l'appeloit toujours la petite reine."

It was during this short sojourn of Louis XIV., at Blois, that he saw, for the first time, Madlle. de la Vallière, whose mother had for her second husband M. de Saint Remy, first master of the household to the Duke of Orleans.

In the following January, Charles II., then an exile, visited the Castle of Blois, on his return from the Pyrenees, where he had vainly endeavoured to enter into negotiations with Mazarin. Gaston, the Duke of Orleans, made, in favour of his youngest daughter, another attempt at marriage with the English prince, which his eldest daughter had equally thought of, in her innumerable projects of an establishment. " L'on ajusta fort ma sœur," said Mademoiselle de Montpensier, who does not seem to have been very fond of her sister, " parceque l'on là vouloit marier à quelque prix que ce fût."

In later times, also, this old town of Blois was the scene of interesting events. The Empress Marie-Louise took refuge here after Paris was

taken; and, when the news arrived of Napoleon's abdication, she was shamefully deserted
by nearly all her attendants.*

* Allison says, in his most interesting History of Europe,—" Meanwhile, the Imperial Court at Blois, where the
Empress Marie Louise and the King of Rome had been
since the taking of Paris, was the scene of selfishness more
marked, desertions more shameless, than even the saloons of
Fontainebleau. Unrestrained by the awful presence of the
emperor, the egotism and cupidity of the courtiers there
appeared in hideous nakedness, and the fumes of the Revolution expired amidst the universal baseness of its followers.
No sooner was the abdication of the Emperor known, than all
her court deserted the Empress: it was a general race who
should get first to Paris to share in the favours of the new
dynasty. Such was the desertion, that in getting into her
carriage on the 9th April, at Blois, to take the road to
Orleans, no one remained to hand the Empress in but her
chamberlain. The Empress, the King of Rome, were forgotten; the grand object of all was to get away, and to carry
with them as much as possible of the public treasure which
had been brought from Paris with the government. In a
few days it had all disappeared. At Orleans, the remaining
members of Napoleon's family also departed:—Madame
Mere and her brother, Cardinal Fesch, set out for Rome;
Prince Louis, the ex-king of Holland, for Switzerland; Joseph and Jerome soon after followed in the same direction.
The Empress at first declared her resolution to join Napoleon; maintaining that there was her post, and that she
would share his fortunes in adversity as she had done in
prosperity. The wretched sycophants, however, who were
still about her person, spared no pains to alienate her from
the emperor: they represented that he had espoused her

86   MARIE-LOUISE.

only from policy; that she had never possessed his affections;
that during the short period they had been married he had had
a dozen mistresses, and that she could now expect nothing
but reproaches and bad usage from him.   Overcome partly
by these insinuations, and partly by her own facility of character and habits of submission, she, too, followed the general
example: her French guards were dismissed, and replaced
by Cossacks; she took the road from Orleans to Ram-
bouillet, where she was visited successively by the emperor
her father, and the Emperor Alexander; and at length she
yielded to their united entreaties, and agreed to abandon
Napoleon."

87

CHAPTER V.

EXCURSION TO THE CHATEAU DE CHAMBORD.

Saturday.—Passed at Chambord. We were delighted with the old palace, which belongs to the
poor Duc de Bordeaux, and is the only possession he retains in all France. The road there,
and indeed, the country about it, is very ugly. I
do not see the " gloom" which the descriptions
I have read generally talk of—the avenues of
little stunted poplars, the ditches, and fields are
too trivial and common-place to be gloomy.

We passed just opposite to Madame de Pompadour's villa, and congratulated ourselves on
not having followed the advice of the postmaster at Menars, who wanted us to be ferried
across the river, and go direct from thence to
Chambord. The road is so very bad, that had
we done so, our carriage would probably have
been broken or upset.

The last league was the worst, particularly within the wall — that nice old wall which encircles the demesne, as is the case so frequently in Ireland; our postillion, however, differed from his Irish brother in driving slowly, thus affording us, as we approached, full leisure to contemplate the beauties of the château. In Ireland we should have rattled along, as Pat infallibly reserves " the trot for the avenue."

And magnificent indeed is the château. Striking is the view of the mighty pile, with its vast assemblage of towers, lofty roofs, points, highly-ornamented chimneys, and cupolas, with the graceful pinnacle, surmounting the great staircase du Lys in the centre. It struck me as perhaps the finest specimen of a French château, I had ever seen. The effect was dignified, yet mournful, when one thought that after all the immense sums expended there, it was impossible that the palace could ever again be turned to account, for were it to be repaired, it would not be suited to modern wants, or to the present state of things ; but there it stands, a lone monument of by-gone splendours, a sad possession of one now exiled, perchance for ever, from his native land, and the throne of his ancestors.

I am not quite certain whether the upper part is not overwrought in comparison with the severe simplicity of the basement story. I am aware that it is the usual march of buildings, (as in the coliseum and a hundred others,) to rise from the substantial and solid to the light and ornamented ; but still the eye should not be hurt by the least want of congruity in the parts. And very beautiful as the exterior of the main building is, with its exquisitely wrought details, the effect is, I think, much injured by the low buildings added in the time of Louis XIV.

The interior, in general, presents an immense number of rooms, of no great size, and almost totally devoid of anything accordant with the date of the building ; but the external staircases at the two corners are extremely elegant, and richly worked ; and the cruciform Salles des Gardes, despite the injury done them by being lopped of their height by an intervening floor, are very beautiful. They surround the famous escalier Du Lys ; and this floor, which so nearly spoils one of the grandest designs in architecture I ever saw, is said to have been introduced by Louis XIV. That a Prince so celebrated for his taste and grandeur, should have done this bar-

90   CHATEAU DE CHAMBORD.

barous act, seems most wonderful. In one place,
too, the beautiful balustrades of the staircase
have been sacrificed to make room for the King's
box ,when plays were represented in one of the
four rooms.   Molière's comedy of the Bourgeois
Gentilhomme, was performed for the first time
here.

I much admired Francis the First's decoration
of the vaulted ceilings : his initial (F) and his device (the Salamander) occur in alternate com-
partments ; they strongly reminded a friend of
mine who had lately travelled in Egypt, of the
beautiful arched apartments at Abydos, (Arabat
el Matfoon,) which are similarly ornamented,
with the name and the prefix of Osirei I., father
of Remeses the Great.   I much liked, too, the
little cabinet, where the same ornament is repeated in miniature.

It was in this room that Francis I., in a fit of
jealousy or disappointment, caused by the fickle
conduct of the fair Diane de Poitiers, wrote
with the point of a diamond these well known
words on a window-pane :—

> " Souvent femme varie,
>   Mal habile qui s'y fie."

Saussaye says, that Louis XIV., " in quite

a different disposition, because he was young and happy, sacrificed these lines of his ancestor to Madame de la Vallière, and broke the pane to shew his high opinion of woman's constancy." In this room, too, Madlle. de Montpensier is said to have breathed on the window, and written with her finger the name of Lauzun—a first confession of her affection for that celebrated Duke.

I was rather disappointed at the effect of the chapel at the other side of the palace, into the decorations of which, the crescent of Diane de Poitiers has so strangely crept—the device of a goddess, anything but chaste. But I was specially charmed with the grand staircase du Lys—the gem of the whole—the conception beautiful, and charmingly executed; and its double spiral lines rising conjointly, now spreading, now crossing, suggested to me the idea of arms gently extended, the most graceful contours, and a multitude of wild, but delightful fancies. Catherine de Medicis used the pavilion at the summit of this staircase as her observatory. It was a pleasing occupation to try to re-clothe those deserted halls and galleries with their rich hangings and gorgeous tapestries, and to re-people them with the

92   STAIRCASE OF THE PALACE.

gay and lovely dames, and the gallant bearded
cavaliers, rustling in their gold and jewels,
their velvets and satins, who formed the brilliant courts of the luxurious monarchs who
there pursued their mad revels and mysterious
intrigues.

The best description I ever read of this celebrated staircase, is given by Madlle. de Montpensier, when speaking of her first visit to
Chambord when quite young : " Une des plus
curieuses et plus remarquables choses de la
maison, c'est le degré, fait d'une manière qu'une
personne peut monter et l'autre descendre sans
qu'elles se rencontrent bien qu'elles se voient, à
quoi Monsieur, (her father,) prit plaisir à se
jouer d'abord avec moi. Il étoit au haut de
l'escalier lorsque j'arrivai ; il descendait quand
je montai, et rioit bien fort de me voir courir
dans la pensée que j'avois de l'attraper : J'étois
bien aise du plaisir qu'il prenoit, et je le fus
encore d'avantage quand je l'eus joint."

After we had passed several hours wandering
about the palace, I went to make some sketches,
one of which is here introduced, as it gives a
general idea of the pile, though it is not nearly so
picturesque as some I took in the interior of the

Sketched by Lady Chatterton and drawn on stone by Bichebois.

Printed by Lemercier Benard and Cⁱᵉ

THE CASTLE OF CHAMBORD.

courts. We were so delighted with the place, that we could easily imagine the Emperor Charles V.'s admiration of it must have been sincere, when he said the palace was " Un abrégé de ce que peut effectuer l'industrie humaine." He was there in 1539 ; and, as an old account of Chambord says, " Il y passa quelques jours pour la délactation de la chasse aux daims qui estoient là dans un des plus beaux parcs de France, et à très grand foison."

There are various superstitions connected with the first origin of this castle, in early ages, that have amused me by their extreme contradiction : some ascribing it to the powers of evil, others to the actions of good spirits. The most popular, perhaps, is the legend of the Chasseur Noir. " When," says an old chronicle, " the timid countryman, after having walked on the ' herbe qui égure,' finds himself, about midnight, near the pavilion of Montfrault, he is likely to meet the terrific figure of the nightly horseman, clad in black, and followed by his coal-black hounds. This was no other than Theobald of Champagne, called ' The Old,' and ' The Cheat,' the first hereditary Count of Blois, and the most complete type of those barons—hard as iron—

94   SAUSSAIE'S ACCOUNT OF BLOIS.

who lived in the first period of the feudal system.
This same baron, during the fine nights of autumn, may be heard starting from Montfrault,
with a great troop of men, horses, dogs, and
horns, to hunt in the air. After having rested
a little at the ruins of Bury, they return to
Montfrault. The same noise which was heard
at their departure continues during this aerial
hunt, though neither horses, dogs, nor hunts-
men were visible."

We purchased, yesterday, a very interesting
account of Blois, written by M. de Saussaie. Its
historical details are excellent, and well told. It
contains much valuable information in a small
compass. I discovered by it that the swan
pierced by the dart—an ornament which I observed on the ceiling of one of the rooms at
Chambord, of Catherine de Medicis' apartment,
—was the device of Claude, the eldest daughter
of Louis XII. and Anne of Brittany, who married Francis I., and must have been the first
occupant of these apartments. Her device was
the swan, with three C's—Clauda Candida Can-
didas, Blanche parmi les blanches.

95

CHAPTER VI.

Carriage notes between Blois and Tours—Expedition to
Chenonçeaux—Legend of the Ambitious Jewess.

Notes scribbled in the Carriage.—Soon after we left
Blois, on looking back,we caught a fine view of
the town; and now the country improves, and we
begin to see the truth of de Vigny's description
of Loire scenery.   Four boats are generally fastened together, to present, I suppose, with their
large square sails, a greater resistance to the current than they could do singly.   They have a
very good effect.   Just passed a pretty, comfortable-looking château, on the other side, belonging to Baron Sygomen.   The road keeps
close to the river, which is very pleasant ; the
smells of vegetation are so sweet, after the rain
of yesterday—quite delicious !   I cannot spoil
my enjoyment by writing ; and yet the object of

96   CASTLE OF CHAUMONT.

doing so is to prolong the enjoyment, by trying
thus to impress it on our minds.

At the first post, Chousy.—The river and its
banks look pretty and calm—rather tame, but
the sort of scenery, " qui," as Balsac says, " repose l'ame." The river winds through meadows
and vine-banks, and then appears to lose itself
in a forest, which closes the picture, not very
far off.

Marshy ground and uninteresting country for
a little more than a mile, and then the Castle of
Chaumont comes in sight. It was given to
Diane de Poitiers, by Henry II. ; she afterwards
resigned it to Catherine de Medicis, who gave
her Chenonçeaux, in exchange.

It was built in the fifteenth century, by the
family of Amboise, and the cardinal of that
name (Louis XII.'s minister) was born there.
Besides all this, it is to me very interesting from
being the residence of Cinq Mars.   The situation beautiful—much the prettiest bit we have
yet seen on the Loire.   Chaumont is, indeed, a
noble building, with numerous towers, pinnacles,
and picturesque irregularities, and stands on a
high perpendicular bank embosomed in fine
woods, with the chapel described by De Vigny,

half way down, and the pretty village below, close by the river's side.

Changed horses at Veuvex, the second post, and we can still see Chaumont in the distance behind us. It is quite a redeeming feature in the far-famed, but, to us, rather disappointing, Loire scenery.

Afterwards, there was nothing very particular till we came in sight of Amboise. The ancient palace there is a noble pile, situated on a precipitous rock, overlooking the old town and the Loire, with its little island and two long picturesque bridges.

It rained heavily on our arrival at the inn, but we got into a nice little carriage there, and drove to the castle, crossing the river by the two bridges. We dismounted at the bottom of a curious large round tower, which flanks the high rock on which the old palace is built, and forms a covered and well-defended road up to it. We entered the large tower, and walked up the winding road inside. The ascent is very gradual, and was used even for carriages in ancient times. Its arched roof is beautifully carved, and ornamented with grotesque figures ; and Gothic windows, pierced through the thick walls, give good light.

The interior of the pillar, round which this road-staircase winds, was formerly used as a prison, and is lighted by smaller windows, which give a borrowed light, or rather gloom, from the staircase outside. How tantalizing it must have been to the prisoners in these dungeons to hear the tramp of steeds and men ascending and descending around them, telling of liberty and joy no longer theirs !

We came out at the top of this strange place into pretty gardens and terraces, bordered with orange-trees, which led us to the old castle. The furniture of this royal residence is plain, but the rooms looked comfortable, and the views from their windows are very fine. There is some beautiful carving on the corbels in the lower galleries; we admired particularly a sentimental bat, with its claw on its heart, and its eyes full of languishing melancholy; the feathers are beautifully carved, and the expression of the face most pitiful. Bats and owls occur in great numbers : they seem to have been here a favourite device.

But the gem of the place is the little chapel,

CHAPEL OF THE PALACE.   **99**

built by Charles VII.; to which we went, through
the gardens, after we had seen the palace.   It
stands, like the castle, on the very edge of a
perpendicular rock, overlooking the town.   It is
very small—a cross of only twenty-eight feet by
thirty-six; but the form, the carving, and the
windows are exquisitely graceful.   Over the entrance, on the outside, is carved the chase of
St. Hubert.

This is not only one of the most beautiful bits
of ornamented Gothic architecture I ever saw,
but it derives an additional beauty from the
situation.   It is in a garden—graceful acacias
wave over it, orange trees bloom around, and
roses beneath, rendering the spot quite en-
chanting.

Church decoration is so often accompanied
with bad smells in the narrow streets of a
crowded town, that the lovely, peaceful, and
sweet-smelling chapel of Charles VII., at Amboise,
really gains by the contrast.   The whole place
has been well restored, and belongs to the present king.   Louis XI. lived often in this castle;
and his son, Charles VIII., was born and died
here.   A Protestant conspiracy was carried on
within these venerable walls, in 1560, during the

100   DRIVE TO TOURS.

reign of Francis II., who was married to Mary
Queen of Scots.

The scenery, during the remainder of the
drive to Tours, was pretty, but not very striking.
The first glimpse of the town, in the distance,
very beautiful: the two towers of its fine
cathedral; the long bridge, then near us on the
right; the curious arches and mysterious-looking
remains of Marmoutier Abbey; and, a little further on, the ruins of the old bridge, whose grey
spectral arches span a branch of the river on
our left, and are lost among the tall willows on
a pale-green island.   The colouring is certainly
pale in this part of France, more so than in England, and in England more so than Ireland.   I
have, indeed, never seen in any country the
colouring so vivid as that of the Green Isle.

Tours, Monday evening.—Hôtel du Faisan.—
Just been to the cathedral, and admired its
painted glass windows and the pretty monument
of two children of Charles VIII.   The arms of
Blanche of Castille, mother of St. Louis (the
Ninth) are still visible in the windows of the
choir; and here that good and beautiful queen
may have offered up prayers for the success of

her son's arms in Palestine. It was of this queen Shakspeare said,—

> " If lusty Love should go in quest of beauty,
>   Where should he find it fairer than in Blanch ?
>   If zealous Love should go in search of virtue,
>   Where should he find it purer than in Blanch ?
>   If love ambitious sought a match of birth,
>   Whose veins bound richer blood than Lady Blanch ?"

Part of the original church was burnt in 561.

> " Le temple Saint Gatien sentit aussi le feu,
>   Mais estant secouru, n'en brusla que bien peu,"

says Olivier Cherreau, in his poetical history of the Archbishops of Tours. He says nothing, however, of what struck me as being so odd, that the church is crooked, the left wall and pillars of the nave not being in a line with the choir.

Tuesday 25th.—Expedition to Chenonçeaux.— We were nearly four hours going. The country pretty, but very tame, and the day hazy and lazy ; everything looked and felt quiet. The wind too indolent to blow, the sun to shine, or the clouds to rain. It was indeed repose, or rather stagnation ; for the green pools we constantly passed looked as if they had not moved since the creation. Before the end of our long drive, our whole party felt the influence of this stagnation, and fell fast asleep. The road was very good, and runs, for about half of the way, along the left bank of the Loire. We had a good view of the ruins of Marmoutier Abbey, and also of the curious high tower, on the opposite bank, called " Lanterne de Roche-corbon," which leans considerably. There are stalactite grottoes under it, and curious ancient staircases cut in the rock.

After leaving the river, we had a very gentle ascent through vine-gardens bordered with fine walnut trees. Passed several pretty villages, and the town of Bleré. In one of the villages, a marriage fête was celebrating. The bride did not appear to be very young; but I believe that the women in this country soon look old, for I remarked that we seldom see anything but young girls and old women. It was a very pictu-resque spectacle; the whole party were dancing " rondes" in great glee, and the bright-red pet-ticoats of the women, with the white cap and blue boddice, looked very vivid and pretty. The young men danced without coat or hat, and wore at their waistcoat buttons large bouquets of flowers; forming a good contrast to the

cocked hat and loose blue frock, which was the
graver costume of the older gentlemen. The
whole scene was very animated; and it had certainly escaped the contagion of laziness, which
this hot day had brought on us.

When we arrived at Chenonçeaux, we were
so delighted with the venerable appearance of
the old castle, that all sleepiness was dispelled
in a moment. It quite justifies the description
given by the old poet, Loret, in his " *Voyage de
la Cour a Chambord.*"

> " Basti si magnifiquement,
>   Il est debout comme un géant
>   Dedans le lit de la rivière,
>   C'est à dire dessus un pont
>   Qui porte cent toises de long,
>   La reine y faisoit sa prière,
>   Et le baillif de Chenonceaulx
>   Estoit monsieur de Villarceaux."

Chenonçeaux is full of interesting recollections. The rooms of Catherine de Medicis, her
bed, &c., are in the same state in which she occupied them. There are reliques, also, of Diane
de Poitiers, and the chambre de deuil of poor
Louise, the widow of Henry III., remains un-
touched. In it is a looking-glass which belonged
to Mary, Queen of Scots. She paid a visit to

104 .   PICTURES IN THE PALACE.

Chenonçeaux in the happy days of her youth;
and there was something very touching in being
thus reminded of these two fair widows of brother kings.   Both began their career with every
prospect of happiness.   Poor Louise, ill treated
by a husband she loved, perhaps found peace at
last in the quiet retirement of Chenonçeaux.
Mary began life more happily, but found peace
only in the grave.

Many of the old pictures are very curious.
There is a good one of Ninon de l'Enclos, and
one of Diane de Poitiers, as Diana; also origi-
nals of Rabelais, Louis XI., and Gabrielle
d'Estrées.   There is, too, a good bust of Agnes
Sorell, whose quaint device was $\left| \frac{A}{L} \right|$ A sur L—
Agnes Surelle.

 It is on record that a fête was given here, in
1577, by Catherine de Medicis to her son, Henry
III.   The place itself brought the scene strongly
before one.   What a strange mixture of pro-
fligacy and grandeur !   " Le service," says the
chronicler, " était fait par les plus honnétes
belles de la cour, à moitié nues," and this in the
presence of the meek and guileless Louise and
the imperious and haughty Catherine !   Many
years afterwards, Chenonçeaux ceased to be a

royal residence, and came into the possession of Madame du Pin. During this time, Rousseau was often here, and took a part in its private theatricals—then so celebrated—and has immortalized its groves in his verses.

Chenonçeaux is built *on* the river Cher; the body of the castle on a little island, or rock, which it completely covers, or rather overhangs; and the long wing extending from it (containing Catherine de Medicis' fine picture gallery) is built on six massive arches, over the main branch of the Cher. Over it, at the further end, is the theatre where Rousseau played.

Francis I. often lived there, as his numerous salamanders and initial (F) shew. But the great embellisher and heroine of it was Diane de Poitiers, who after her royal lover's (Henry II.) death, was obliged to give it up to his widow, Catherine de Medicis. It is singular, that in the chapel and other places, the two devices of these rival dames should be united— Diana's crescent and Catherine's initial, forming the following monogram.

In other places, Diana's two D's make Henry the second's H.

106   CASTLE OF CHENONCEAUX.

The sofas, toilette tables, cups, glass, china—everything, remains the same as in their time; and what is most rare, the walls are covered with the very same hangings which then adorned them. Some are of stamped leather, others of canvas, painted in large and vivid, yet dark patterns, as if to imitate tapestry. The doors are hung with tapestry, or rather worsted-work, (cross-stitch,) in flowered patterns, whose colours remain quite vivid.

Whilst I was sketching the view, which is here given, I saw a boat carried down the river—it upset just under the walls of the chapel, and totally disappeared. This shews how deep the water must be, and the current is so strong, that it seems wonderful the castle, massive as it is, has not been carried away during the many centuries that have past since it was built. It now belongs to Le Comte de Villeneuve, great-nephew of Madame Du Pin. He is proprietor also of the Castle of La Carte.

Though Chenonçeaux is so interesting from being a perfect and unaltered specimen of the manners &c. of olden time, and indeed, also from the beauty of its architecture, yet I think Diane de Poitiers made a very good exchange

Sketched by Lady Chatterton and drawn on stone by Bichebois.

THE CASTLE OF CHENONCEAUX.

Printed by Lemercier, Benard and C

to Chaumont. The situation of that castle on the Loire, is so much finer and more cheerful.

After our visit to the castle of Chenonçeaux, we passed some hours strolling in the gardens, and under the thick shade of the old groves in which Rousseau loved to wander. His favourite walk was " *l'Allée de Silvie*,' of which he says—

> " Qu'à m'égarer dans ces bocages
> Mon cœur goûte de volupté !
> Que je me plais sous ces ombrages !
> Que j'aime ces flots argentés."

There is a legend of an enchanter called Orfon, who is said to have exercised so much influence over the early inhabitants of Chenonçeaux, that I will relate the story. In the forest of Loches, is a barrow called the Monument of St. Nicolas—a work, no doubt, of the ancient Gauls, but the tradition of the country gives it a supernatural origin. It is said that a formidable magician, named Orfon—a prince, who owed his power to the hidden authority he exercised over nature—lived for a long time in a palace in this neighbourhood, surrounded by thick forests, and invisible to the eyes of men : he was the inheritor not only of the immense riches of the Druids, but of their super-natural knowledge also.

108   ORFON, THE ENCHANTER.

As avaricious as any king who was not a magician, Orfon buried in the caverns of the neighbourhood his heaps of gold, always choosing to count his wealth on the night of our Lord's nativity.

Every year there arose a terrible tempest on Christmas-eve. Furious winds swept along the immense forest of Loches, and the trees, bending to the earth under their influence, prevented all approach to the abode of the magician, and deprived the inquisitive of any desire to interrupt him in his absorbing calculations. However, as if in mockery of the misery of his poor neighbours, he who paid attention, might hear, even in the midst of the furious tempest, the sound of pieces of gold pouring down one after the other.

Even in the very churches during the solemnity of that service which celebrates the anniversary of the coming of the Divine legislator, whilst all hearts were raised to heaven, by those Christmas hymns, which bore testimony to the joy of our ancestors, the sound of gold would suddenly penetrate into the midst of the kneeling multitude, and call back their thoughts to the joys of a terrestrial and perishable world.

DEATH OF THE ENCHANTER. 109

Jingling of money, and the fury of tempests, were the objects of Orfon's enjoyment. If any wretched man committed a theft, Orfon was sure to have been the instigator; if a young girl committed a fault, Orfon's music was the excitement. Thus he was the universal execration, and the entire neighbourhood re-echoed with exorcisms against so wicked a king.

At last, whether that his time was come, or, as has happened since to so many other princes, that he was conquered, and forced to yield to an insurrection of his people,—one night in the month of December, when the earth was covered with snow, and the cold almost insupportable, during the celebration of Christmas, instead of the usual noise of gold, suddenly a great cry was heard, and all the lights of the chapel of St. Nicholas were at once extinguished. Orfon had just expired! Orfon, buried in the vast vaults of his former residence, continued, indeed, in possession of his treasures, but had lost his accursed power, and his empire over the elements.

It is true, indeed, that every year during the solemnities of Christmas, when the hour of the nativity approaches, Orfon may still be heard groaning in the depths where the exorcisms have

110   SUPERSTITION.

bound him, and counting his innumerable piles
of gold ; but it is not easy to hear him,—perhaps
it is that his treasure has diminished since he is
no longer permitted to employ it, or that he
has some misgivings as to the corruptions of the
age—certain it is, that he is much more tranquil,
and that it now requires to be one of the initiated to hear him, or a man must possess a
delicacy of ear, such as does not fall to the lot of
every citizen of the department.

In the middle ages, however, the enchantments
of Orfon reigned in full force ; and the simple
peasantry of this country imagine it was the fatal
sound of Orfon's treasure that destroyed, in this
very province, the happiness of three of its fair
and once innocent beauties—Agnes Sorel, Gabrielle d'Estrées, and Louise de la Vallière. Agnes
Sorel, (whose name has become celebrated as
the mistress of Charles VII.) was in the fourteenth century so enchanted with the distant
sounds of Orfon's fatal coin, that she accepted a
situation in the queen's household, and yet
Schiller says of her :—

> " Zieren würde sie,
> Den ersten Thron der Welt—doch sie verschmäht ihn."

The old historian Monstrelet admired her

character so much, that he scarcely allows one
to suppose there was anything wrong in the
King's partiality for her.   " For," says he,
" people are more inclined to speak well than ill
of their superiors.   The affection the King
shewed her, was as much for her gaiety of temper, pleasing manners, and agreeable conversation, as for her beauty.   She was called the
fairest of the fair, and most liberal in her alms,
which she distributed among such churches as
were out of repair, and to beggars."   King
Francis the First, wrote under a portrait of La
" Gentille Agnes"—

> " Plus de louange et d'honneur tu merites,
>   La cause étant de France recouvrer,
>   Que ce que peut dedans un cloitre ouvrer,
>   Close nonain, ou bien devot hermite."

And it seems certain that, she always insti-
gated the King to act bravely in his defence
against the English.

The influence that women have often exercised over the destinies of nations, induces some
persons to imagine that their mental powers are
naturally not inferior to those of men.   I think,
however, this influence arises, not from the
superiority, but on the contrary, from the in-

feriority of their intellect. To be influenced is rather a sign of a superior intellect that can afford to bow down, and give way to the weaker sex. Obstinate, and narrow, or weak-minded men, are rarely influenced—they are, indeed, often compelled and driven—by a clever wife or mistress, but this is quite different from being influenced.

To return to Agnes Sorel : in order to escape the too-fascinating attractions of gold, and all the dangers of a court life, she is said to have retired to the castle of La Guerche, not far from this place. With all her faults, that beautiful Agnes had many redeeming qualities, and it is very possible, that she often intended to repent, and saw plainly that the court of her royal lover, with even all its honours and pleasures, was not equivalent to the peace of mind she had lost.

Tours.—Wednesday.—This old town seems full of traditions—almost every street has some name for the origin of which a wonderful story is told.

The oldest street in Tours is that of la Porte Hugon, and from this name the celebrated term of Huguenot is said to have sprung.

LEGEND OF A JEWESS.   113

It would be endless to relate them all; but one of the most remarkable is that of the Rue des Trois Pucelles, a well-authenticated local tradition, and which illustrates a great moral truth.   It shews that

> " Ambition is a vulture vile,
>> That feedeth on the heart of pride,
>> And finds no rest when all is tried;
>> For worlds cannot confine the one,
>> The other lists and bounds hath none;
>> And both subvert the mind, the state,
>> Procure destruction, envy, hate."—DANIELL.

Many centuries ago, a rich and honest Jew lived in the Rue des Trois Pucelles.   He had, as most rich Jews seem always to have, an only daughter, who was surpassingly beautiful, and of a pleasant and sprightly temper; and this daughter, of course, had a lover who adored her, but who, as usual, was handsome and poor.   But here the common version of such stories ends : for instead of a cruel and worldly-minded parent, who wished to sacrifice his daughter's happiness to ambition, this honest son of Israel desired nothing more than to see his darling child married to the poor young Tobias.   The girl, too, loved the youth well, but she wished to see a little more of the

114   LEGEND OF A JEWESS.

world, and when her father, in the kindly simplicity of his heart, proposed she should accept the
offer of humble young Tobias, great was his
surprise to find that she refused it.

The old Jew, however, was a sensible man :
he made no remark, but simply gave her answer
to Tobias, who in consequence quitted Tours in
despair. Now this was more than the young
Jewess intended, and he was no sooner gone
than she suddenly discovered that she could not
live without him, and fell into such a fit of
melancholy, that her mother and most of her
friends began to fear she would die. Not so the
old man, he only smiled and rubbed his hands with
glee. " Well," said his wife one day, bursting
into tears, " I see you will never be satisfied till
our poor child lies in her grave. Why will you
not send a messenger for Tobias ? You know
she loves him, only the darling child is too
proud to confess it. I was just the same at her
age."

" She *is* proud," said the father, looking
grave, " and ambitious too, which thank God
you never were, or we should not have lived so
many years happily together ! She fancies all
sorts of foolish things about the happiness to be

found in the splendour of courts and earthly greatness; and she would not believe a plain old-fashioned sort of man like me, or our good Rabbi either, if we preached to her by the hour, so she shall see, and judge for herself. And as she has thoughtlessly and unfeelingly rejected that good young man, who is so worthy of her love, I swear that nothing shall induce me to consent to her marriage with him, until she has received the proposals of a prince, an abbé, and a knight. If then she reject their offers, — after having seen that world which appears to her so delightful,—if she still love poor Tobias, and wish to marry him, I will gladly consent. Go and inform her of my positive conditions."

The fair Miriam heard her father's proposal with extreme surprise—it roused her, indeed, from the state of despair her own wilfulness had caused; but she had already discovered how deeply her heart was engrossed by Tobias, and her happiness wound up in his, so that she shrank with terror from the ordeal. A splendid court without the man she loved, seemed to have now no attraction; however, her father was inexorable. He swore by the God of his fathers that Tobias should never again visit the house till the

116　　　LEGEND OF A JEWESS.

conditions were fulfilled.　On the other hand, he promised to furnish her with a brilliant escort, splendid jewels, and everything requisite to shine in the luxurious courts of Paris or Bretagne, in order to facilitate the fulfilment of the conditions he had imposed.

So Miriam rose from her bed of sorrow, and attired in splendid robes, started for the court of Brittany.　She was attended by twelve young damsels, brilliantly adorned with costly jewels, as many pages, and a large retinue of serving men and women.

The arrival of a strange beauty at the King of Brittany's court, caused a great sensation, and as Miriam concealed her real name, she was called " La Pucelle Inconnue."

Few weeks passed before she had a numerous host of valiant knights at her feet.　Some were handsome and accomplished, and swore to adore her for ever ; but none pleased her so much as the poor Tobias.　The pleasures, indeed, of the court were great : a constant succession of fêtes and tournaments ; but Miriam sighed for one half hour's conversation with Tobias under the trees in her father's garden, and began to think the song of birds which then accompanied their happy talk, and which she had once almost despised as common and homely, now sounded more beautiful in memory's ear than all the martial music, or even the gay minstrel's song. But as yet only one of her father's conditions had been fulfilled, therefore, she dared not return home : many brave knights had sought her, but no prince or abbé had yet sued for her hand.

So the Jewess continued to array herself in the most splendid manner, and sought to win the applause of the young Princes of Bretagne. She was very lovely, and excelled too in many of the accomplishments of those days ; therefore, before long, the King's eldest son, Prince Adelbert, swore he would marry no one but the fair stranger, and threw himself at her feet. Miriam did not at once refuse either the prince or knight, but according to her father's orders, told each separately she had made a vow not to decide for six months, but if they chose to be in a certain street in the City of Tours, on the succeeding Good-Friday, she would give her answer. They both murmured at the delay ; but, seeing her resolution was unchangeable, promised to be there at the appointed time. There now only remained an abbé's heart to win,

118   LEGEND OF A JEWESS.

which did not take long. So Miriam, who had
become quite tired of her life of pageantry
and heartless career of gaiety, returned home,
wiser, perhaps, by a few months' experience of
the hollow realities of that world's glitter which
she had once sighed for, than, as her father
remarked, if she had received endless sermons
from the wisest heads. All her fear now was,
that Tobias might be changed, for he had never
been undeceived, and still believed her indifferent
to his love. But her dear father, who was
enchanted to see her again, promised to write
immediately to explain everything, yet he still
insisted the ceremony must not take place till
her three admirers appeared at their rendezvous.

Good-Friday was fast approaching ; but now
began the difficulty of the three lovers, for they
had been only informed of the town, but were
ignorant of the fair stranger's name.

" The Prince," says an old chronicle, " sent
immediately some of his attendants to inquire
in every street for the handsome noble young
lady called, ' La Pucelle Inconnue.' The Abbé
made the quête for his convent, from door to
door, in the hope of meeting ' son amie ;' but
as he took care not to beg from the Jews, he of
course failed in his object. As to the Chevalier,

who, like his brotherhood, possessed more courage than wit, he contented himself with sending formal challenges to the knighthood of Touraine, who took no notice, but left him in quiet repose. Great indeed was the disappointment of these three personages.

" At length, one fine morning, each of them received a note, informing them of the street in which their researches should be made, directing also that they should go from door to door, and make whatever inquiries they thought proper, until they received the answer, ' Here I am, at your service.'

" Thereupon, the lovers were immediately on the alert. The Jewess attended them, dressed as a page, and, as it was dark, without running any risk of being recognised. At first, the Prince and Monk got on tolerably well, but at last they became fatigued. Besides, the good citizens of Tours were not always inclined to answer their foolish questions, so that all parties got angry — invectives followed, and ' La Pucelle Inconnue,' was sent to the devil five hundred thousand times. The Chevalier, indeed, as from his warlike habits might be expected, began . where the others left off.

" At last, they all reached the place of rendez-

vous, though not together. The Abbé arrived
first: on receiving the wished-for answer, he
rushed into a large and dark apartment; and he
was just beginning the recital of his disappoint-
ments, when the Prince, in his turn, arrived.
He was received in the same manner, and with
still greater impetuosity rushed into the house,
without, however, finding what he sought for.

" He at first had some hope; but you may
judge of his anger, when, instead of a graceful
and delicate head, his hand lighted on a thick
beard and bloated countenance. Cries of " treason! treason!" resounded through the house.
The Chevalier entered at that moment, with his
dagger drawn, and their cries, struggles, and
explanations lasted until daylight, when all
three—wounded, furious, and breathing death
and vengeance—recommenced their researches in
Tours.

" They continued in the same embarrassment
until Easter-week, when they received a note in
the same hand-writing, signed by the daughter
of Israel. This letter announced to them that
the maiden they sought for, was at that moment
the wife of young Tobias, having preferred Metz
to Tours, and a simple child of Moses to those

great ones of the earth, who, under soft words, concealed a deadly poison, and the envenomed dart, which drove mankind from the sanctuary of Eden."

Wednesday evening.—Still at Tours, and more and more pleased with the place. The girls who wait in all these inns are very nice and pretty. They are full of good humour and civility; yet they have a very hard life. One of them sits up every night; and as there are generally only three in an establishment, they have not much sleep. We are tolerably comfortable here in this hotel, but the court-yard and staircase are very dirty, and I think the Hôtel de Londres looks to be a better house.

To-day is very hot, so we did not drive out until after dinner, when we visited Plessis les Tours. But little of Louis XI.'s celebrated castle remains; it has been all destroyed except one wing of brick with stone carvings, and a winding staircase in a tower at the corner. In the garden are some remains of walls, and we descended some steps to reach the dungeon where Louis XI. confined Cardinal de la Ballue for nine years. We also saw, in a field adjoining, but at a little distance, the oratory, or little chapel, where Louis XI. used to pray, which exactly resembles the one described in Quentin Durward. It is now used as a stable.

As we lingered among the ruins of Plessis les Tours, I thought of Monstrelet's description of its strange inhabitant. During Louis XI.'s last illness, and not long before his death, the old historian says, — " At this time the king sent for a number of musicians, who played on low-toned instruments, whom he lodged at St. Come; near to Tours. They were about six score in number, and with some shepherds from Poitou, that played on their pipes, assembled before the king's apartments, but never saw him, and there played for his amusement, and to prevent him from falling asleep. On the other hand, he collected a great many devout people of both sexes, such as hermits and others of holy lives, to pray incessantly to God that his days might be prolonged."

But prayers and musicians were alike unavailing, and on the 11th of August the king died, and having previously given orders that he should be buried at his favourite Nôtre Dame de Clery, the old church which we saw, and that forms such a fine feature in the landscape on the

ABBEY OF MARMOUTIER.   123

opposite bank of the Loire, on the road from Orleans.

We afterwards crossed the bridge, and drove to the Abbey of Marmoutier. It was from it that Jean Sans peur, Duke of Burgundy, carried off Isabella, Queen of Bavaria. We saw the place this beautiful evening to great advantage. Its lonely and romantic position seemed to point it out as just the scene for such an enterprise. We have arranged to quit Tours to-morrow. I find that this interesting old town belonged to Mary Queen of Scots, in her own right.

124

CHAPTER VII.

Carriage notes from Tours to Poitiers—Antiquities of
Poitiers.

Thursday, 27.—In the Carriage.—A fine view
back on Tours, as we ascended the hill after
crossing the Cher.   Country very riante and
luxurious, but pale and quiet-looking.   The
number of poplars, alders, and willows, add
much here to the usual paleness of French colouring; and the walnuts, which grow in
great profusion, seem also paler than in England, though very large and fine trees.   Just
come in sight of the pretty valley of the Indre,
with the little town of Montbazon in the centre,
and its old castle perched on an abrupt rock
above.

Fine avenue of walnut trees nearly all the
way from Montbazon to the next post, Soligny;

they smelt sweet, and gave us pleasant shade. Fields beyond, but no distant view — very flat.

Afterwards, a woody height, before we came to St. Maure (post); near which place, on the left, is Fierbois, where Jeanne d'Arc came for her sword to the tomb of a knight. And now we have got into that sort of plain and featureless country, where the most interesting and conspicuous object is the broad high road, which extends, in a white undeviating line, straight before our faces for many a dusty mile. We are fortunate, however; for the heavy rains which swelled the Loire and Cher have spared us from much dust,—that great enemy to travelling enjoyment,—and the only sensation they have left us, is the freshened smell of earth and tree; indeed, the day is quite perfect.

At Les Ormes (post.)—We have passed a nice-looking *terre*, belonging to M. d'Argentin; and afterwards, on a fine woody height to the left, the fine old chateau of Madame Cassin; opposite to it a pretty village, and several smaller chateaux,—a comfortable English-looking valley.

Chatelherault.—A very nice town, with a fine bridge over the Vienne—one end of which is

guarded by two ancient towers, with little quaint
projecting turrets, and surmounted by pinnacles.
There are pretty walks, gardens, and country-
houses along the banks of the river, and a
little island, covered with large trees, in the
middle of it,

Chatelherault is famous for its cutlery, and,
on stopping at the *poste*, we were besieged by
women, who placed themselves on chairs at the
sides of the carriage, and, armed with knives
and scissors, held them up with pathetic entreaties to buy. We bought some, which looked, at
least, very good.

I like all this country much better than the
banks of the Loire. It is more clean, lively,
and healthy-looking, and has none of those stagnant ditches and green ponds which rendered
the scenery there so dull and uncomfortable.
Here are bright fields, red and white clover,
and all the varieties of green corns and grass,
dotted over with very large walnut and cherry
trees; then the surface of the country is
much more undulating. We have now and
then a good distant prospect; and old château
and country-houses, nestled in woods, crown
most of the heights.

Poitiers.—Hôtel de France.—We passed near some woods as we approached this place, where the fine walnut and other trees put me in mind of Ariosto's description, in his " Orlando Furioso." They are, indeed, most probably the remains of that forest in whose umbrageous depths the tomb of the prophet Merlin was situated, and where Bradamante came to inquire of the fate of her lover, Ruggiero.

> " Pensò al fin di tornare alla spelonca,
> Dove eran l'ossa di Merlin profeta.
> *　　*　　*　　*　　*　　*
> Con questo intenzione prese il cammino,
> Verso le selve prossime a Pontiero,
> Dove la vocal tomba di Merlino
> Era nascosa in loco alpestro e fiero."

On approaching this ancient town, the country-houses and people assumed a much more southern look. Low, broad roofs of ribbed tiles overshadow the wide open windows of the cottages ; the road runs at the bottom of a winding range of grey rocks, overhung in many places with terraced gardens, and villas at the top ;—on the other side, the finest wall of poplars I ever saw—river and gardens beyond. We ascended a steep hill into the town, through

narrow winding streets, containing many gate-
ways and blind houses. By blind, I mean gable-
ended, looking into gardens or courts, but having
no windows towards the street. Others had iron
gratings on their lower windows, with vines
trailing among them, or trees peeping over the
windowless walls, which gave to the ensemble a
cheerful look.

After dinner, we went to the cathedral. It is
a fine and peculiar building; the side aisles,
nave, and transepts are all of the same height.
The whole of the interior is rather low, but,
owing to its continuity of breadth, has a very
grand effect. We then proceeded to the church
of Sainte Radegonde, which is a very ancient
structure. We gratified an old woman by buy-
ing candles to burn at the shrine of the saint,
which lies beneath the raised choir. Over the
steps which lead down to the shrine, is a curious inscription of Anne of Austria, who made
an offering to the saint on the recovery of her son.
This church has no side aisles, and the east end
is rounded like a Roman temple. Out nexr visit
was to the church of St. Jean, the oldest in
France. It is now secularized, as were numerous
other churches, and has been very fitly appro-

priated to a museum for antiquities. It was built of Roman bricks, and has some Cipolino pillars near the altar, but they are now painted over. The collection is young, and does not as yet contain many things of great interest, but, with industry, it will soon become valuable. It has now some interesting remains from Château Bonnivet, of the time of Francis I. The arabesques resemble those of the staircases at Blois and Chambord, and are of fine execution ; and we remarked, also, a large Roman monumental stone, which was purchased by the society, and thus fortunately saved from destruction. The letters are in a handsome, bold style ; the inscription has suffered much, but it has been deciphered. · It is interesting, as it shews how much refinement of feeling existed in this remote place, at the period. The inscription was as follows :—

" Claudiæ Verenillæ Claudii Vareni Consulis Filiæ Civitas Pictonum Funus Locum Statuam Monumentum Publicum Marcus Censor Pavius Legatus Augusti Pro Præces Provinciæ Aquitanicæ Consul Designatus Maritus Honore Contentus Sua Pecunia Ponendum Curavit."

The French translation is this :—

" A Claude Venerille, fille du Claudius Consul Varenus. La Cité des Pictons a voté des Funerailles, un lieu de Sepul-

ture, une Statue, un monument publique. Marcus Censor
Pavius, Lieutenant de l'Empereur, Gouverneur de la Province de l'Aquitaine, Consul designé, Son mari, touché de
tant d'honneur, a fait elever le monument à ses frais."

I doubt whether the translation " touché de
tant d'honneur" gives the full force of the original " honore contentus."

There is here also an old Roman altar, found,
I think, at Boares.

We returned by the promenade formed on the
old ramparts. Much has lately been done—fine
walks made, with a good jet d'eau in the centre.
It forms a very good promenade—here a valuable thing, for the pavement in the streets is
detestable. In the cool of the evening we and
our homely guide, who, luckily for himself,
has a most exalted opinion of the productive
powers of his " beau pays," started for the
" Pierre levée."

It lies about a mile from the hotel. We
crossed the " Clan," and on the heights beyond,
came to the stone. It resembles in every respect
the Druid monuments which we saw in Ireland—
the same form and the same inclination. It is
supported by two rude stones at one end, and
unites at the other with a stone, which at first I

thought formed part of it.   We measured it in
a rough way: it is twelve-and-a-half feet long,
twelve wide, and three thick.   Reichart gives it
far greater dimensions : he makes it thirty feet
long, and seventeen feet wide.   Rabelais, whose
curious portrait we saw at Chenonçeaux, to give
an idea of the strength of his hero, asserts that
as Pantagruel returned from his walk, he took
up the stone, and walked off with it under his
arm.   This is a shameful interference with the
exploits of Sainte Radegonde, who is said, on
undoubted authority, but for what purpose does
not quite appear, to have carried the large stone
on her head, and the small ones in her apron.

I find that the opinion of the country people
is, that the battle called that of Poitiers took
place at Maupertuis, on the Rochelle road, about
three leagues from Poitiers.   This was confirmed
by the postmaster of Croutelle, the first stage
from Poitiers, who said he had sent some English-
men there to see the field of battle.   There is
nothing but tradition to indicate the exact position.

On our return to the town, we again took
a walk on the promenades, which are extremely
beautiful : they command fine views over all the

surrounding country, and we had the enjoyment
of one of the finest sunsets I ever saw.

It was at Poitiers that our Richard Cœur de
Lion became reconciled to his beautiful and once
fondly-loved Queen Berangaria; and here the royal
pair kept Christmas, and the new year of 1196,
with princely state and hospitality. It was a
year of famine, and the good Queen exerted
her restored influence over Richard in favour of
the poor. He gave them all his superfluous
wealth, and multitudes were saved from star-
vation.

In the time of Edward I., the Earl of Derby
. endeavoured to retake Poitiers from the French,
who had, before the battle of Crecy, conquered many of our English possessions in
France—" But," says Froissart, " it is a large,
straggling city, and he could only, therefore,
lay siege to it on one side, for he had not forces
sufficient to surround it. He immediately made
an assault; but the townsmen of the poorer sort
were so numerous, though little prepared for
such an attack, and defended the town so well,
that the Earl's people gained nothing." Two
days afterwards, however, the English were successful, and upwards of seven hundred of the

inhabitants were slain. "The Earl's people put every one to the sword—men, women, and little children. The city was instantly plundered, and was full of wealth. The army destroyed many churches, committed great waste, and would have done much more, if the Earl had not forbidden, under pain of death, that either church or house should be set on fire; for he was desirous of remaining there ten or twelve days. The army, at its departure, was so laden with the riches they had found there, that they made no account of clothes unless they were of gold and silver, or trimmed with furs."

This gives a sad picture of the humanity of our ancestors in the fourteenth century, as well as of the riches of this old town; and I thought of it to-day as we looked on the mutilated remains of Roman and Gothic antiquities.

But it was with great pleasure we recollected the conduct of our Prince Edward, at the glorious battle of Poitiers which took place some years afterwards, and what he said to his troops before the combat.

"Now, my gallant fellows, what though we be a small body when compared to the army of our enemies; do not let us be cast down on that

134   DEFEAT OF THE FRENCH.

account, for victory does not always follow numbers, but where the Almighty God pleases to
bestow it."

The manner, too, in which he treated John,
King of France, who was taken prisoner that
day, shewed much good feeling and generosity:
" When evening was come, the Prince of Wales
gave a supper in his pavilion to the King of
France, and to the greater part of the princes
and barons who were prisoners. The prince
himself served the king's table, as well as others,
with every mark of humility." He also said to
his royal captive—" Dear sir, do not make a
poor meal because the Almighty God has not
gratified your wishes in the event of this
day."

He said, too: " You have this day acquired
such high renown for prowess, that you have
surpassed all the best knights on your side. I
do not, dear sir, say this to flatter you, for all
those of our side who have seen and observed
the actions of each party, have unanimously
allowed this to be your due, and decree you the
prize and garland for it."

Friday morning.—Fortunately, a blaze of sun-
shine on my bed would not allow of morning

sleep, (there were no outside blinds, nor even curtains,) and a noise of sawing a stone close under my window made me get up, though after a very bad night. I never enjoyed anything more than the early walk it enabled me to take. At six, we went to see ruins of the Amphitheatre, in the centre of the town, and almost the highest part of it. The building is very large, several vomitories are perfect, and we could make out the original entrance through what is now a farm-yard. The arena is occupied by gardens, and full of flowers and luxuriant fruit-trees; poor (not miserable) dwellings are nestled under the ancient archways. We clambered up to the top of the old wall, and there, besides the interesting remains of Roman splendour at our feet, we had a lovely view over the town and surrounding country. The morning air and fresh smell of dewy flowers—the mixture of past and present grandeur, for we overlooked many fine modern buildings—the long train of historical recollections,—all rendered the scene most interesting and delightful. Under the highest part there is a large, arched passage leading downwards—probably the entrance to the arena; this passage is decorated with some

136   CHURCH OF NÔTRE DAME.

ornamented bricks.   Near the Amphitheatre
are the remains of the old church of St. Nicholas, where eight fine old pillars, with a sort
of Roman capital, support the oblong roof of
the choir.   It is now a magazine, and the
effect of the vines which grow round some
of its old columns is very picturesque.   In some
places, the old painting still remains on the roof.
We then crossed the *Place*, and went to St. Pon-
chere: apparently a very ancient church, with
one row of large pillars and round arches in the
centre; its tower and exterior resemble early
Norman.   Afterwards, we proceeded through
the Hotel de Ville, to the market-place.   It was
filled with beautiful fresh flowers and fruit, and
picturesque groups of peasantry, some selling
little cream-cheeses on green leaves, which
looked and smelt very fresh and clean.   In the
midst of all these brilliant colours, and hubbub
of teeming life, stands the venerable church of
Nôtre Dame.

Its facade is crowded with grotesque figures
of a barbaric period ; over the three round arched
entrances, the whole Bible history is sculptured,
from Adam and Eve to the end.   The flower-
women were very anxious we should observe it

all, and pointed out some parts which were most strange: odd faces, with large heads and little arms, strangling serpents.

The interior is regular: two rows of large pillars and round arches, with an oblong choir, like those of St. Nicholas and Radegonde. The whole is very perfect, and apparently all built at the same time, except the little single transept. It contains many old altars, with most curious carved groups of scriptural figures, some as large as life, and coloured in the most grotesque manner. The men (in one group, representing our Saviour being laid in the grave,) wore a sort of broad-brimmed cocked hat, like Spanish banditti, and the women Dutch-looking dresses.

The altars in most of these churches are decorated with flowers—large geraniums, orange-trees, and cactuses, which smell delightfully, and make them appear quite like a garden.

138

CHAPTER VIII.

Journey from Poitiers to Angoulême—Arrival at Bourdeaux — The Castle of Blanquefort — Legend of La
Dame Blanche—Antiquities of Bourdeaux.

Notes in carriage, from Poitiers to Angoulême.—
Just come half way ; the most delightful weather
for travelling I ever experienced. No pavé since
Tours. The roads and posting, too, are excellent ;
and we pass through park-like scenery, which
almost makes us fancy we are not travelling,
but taking a drive for pleasure in the picturesque
grounds of some pretty country place. No dust
—no heat—no cold, and the gentle breezes waft
nothing but delicious smells. We have just
ascended a little hill, which is covered with
wood—very fine chesnut trees; and now we
overlook an extensive woody plain. Passed
some trelliced vines. The peasants are now

busy hay-making, under large walnut and cherry trees covered with fruit.

Half-past two.—Changed horses at Ruffec; a clean and very southern-looking little town, containing several hotels, with gardens and vine-trelliced walks and arbours. We travel very fast. Yesterday, we did 103 kilometres (64 English miles and a half) in eight hours and forty minutes; which, including stops, is at the rate of eight miles the hour. Many of the posts are very short,—some only two English miles.

Very extensive view, going down into Malse, where we crossed the Charente—a sort of Warwickshire country, with red soil and fine trees, and near the bridge are some little woody islands —the water, of a clear and greenish lively colour, I thought peculiar, and much prettier than the yellow, thick Loire.

Angoulême same evening, Friday, May 28, Hôtel de la Poste.—Very good apartments, clean and new; the bed-room looks on a quiet garden, where, I trust, there will be no stone-sawing to wake us to-morrow morning, as we had at Poitiers. The first view we obtained of Angoulême was very imposing. It stands on a considerable height, and, with its old castle, cathedral, terraced gardens, ramparts, and suburbs—which extend all the way up from the plain along the side of the hill, and round whose base winds the river Charente—forms a beautiful picture.

The last two stages, we had very gaily-dressed postillions, — white jackets with large blue sleeves, a bright-red scarf tied round the waist, and a sort of embroidered cap with a long tassel, coquettishly stuck on one side of the head. The peasant women are very handsome. They wear a large white cap of a peculiar form—square at the top, red dresses, blue aprons, and white bodices.

The cathedral here is very curious, and resembles in some measure the architecture which we call Saxon. The nave consists of three large round arches, on massive square pillars, supporting three cupolas; a pointed one supports the more oblong dome of the choir; and beyond there is a row of pillars, like those in the oldest churches at Poitiers—and, like them, it has no side aisles. On the façade, we remarked some very grotesque carving, but the figures are not so crowded or so strange-looking as those of Nôtre Dame, at Poitiers.

We were much pleased with the view from the

promenade on the ramparts. It is of great extent and fine vivid colouring, varied by dark woods on gentle heights, old castles, villages, and garden-like plains, through which the Charente winds in endless mazes, and is terminated by a very distant horizon of undulating heights. I have seldom seen a town which pleased me so much. It is so clean, so high, and commands such very extensive views in all directions —a position which affords uninterrupted and splendid sunsets and sunrises. Then it contains many fine houses, some grey with age and others quite new, and built of a stone so snowy white and in such graceful architecture, that they resemble those white piles of clouds which, on a fine summer evening, awaken all sorts of pleasant thoughts, and make us imagine they are fairy palaces rising high into the blue sky, inhabited by good and happy spirits.

It has also beautiful shady walks all round the old ramparts, and gardens on terraces sloping down the sides of the hill. It seems quite a place to live and be happy in. Not that it is so venerable or original-looking as Poitiers, for that dear old city has the accumulated interest of centuries; it stands also on a fine position, and its ramparts

142   WAITING-MAIDS AT ANGOULEME.

command lovely prospects. But Angoulême has
a greater appearance of modern comfort; its
streets are wider and more drivable, it has
more of present wealth and enjoyment, though
less of aristocratic exclusiveness and past splendour. Angoulême appears the abode of rich
merchants, and Poitiers of ancienne noblesse;
and, for every-day life, the luxury of present
riches, though less interesting, is more enjoyable.

The maids at these inns seem to lead really a
hard life; one here, said she had not been in bed
for four months! But this was nothing compared to the activity of another, who had been
in bed only eighteen times during two years!
Yet they look very healthy, and are full of life
and gaiety. We have had here the best, indeed,
to my mind, the only good bread we have tasted
since we left England. The rolls at breakfast
were exactly like those of a very well managed
English country-house.

At a tournament in Angoulême, King John
of England first saw the beautiful Isabella,
heiress of the Angoumois; and though she was
engaged to Hugh de Lusignan, he contrived to
obtain her hand; but this marriage entailed upon
him much warfare during a long time; and their
son, Henry III., lost the battle of Taillebourg,

on this river Charente, in endeavouring to retain these territories in the possession of England.

Carriage. —Fine view, looking back on the town. Soon afterwards, we passed near a beautiful ruin, the Abbey de la Couronne; it has finely sculptured round arches and traceried windows.

The third stage, Barbezieux, is a nice little town, with a tolerable looking inn, situated in a pretty garden, La Boule d'Or. At Montlieu there is a fine extensive view; the prospects are generally pleasing; vines and corn growing in rows, and interspersed with fruit-trees. Some patches of the most beautiful green herb I ever saw; I cannot discover what it is.

After changing horses at Cubzac, a nice little place, with the ruins of an old castle, we passed the Dordogne by a magnificent suspension bridge; it is 1045 metres, nearly three-quarters of an English mile in length. A large two-masted vessel was sailing under it as we walked over. The eight light and transparent pillars, which support the wire-work of the suspension part, rising to a great height above the bridge, have a beautiful and aerial effect; and the solid arches under the road at each end, terminated by four obelisks, are also very graceful. As we crossed,

144   DISTANT VIEW OF BORDEAUX.

we admired much the extensive and beautiful views on both sides of the bridge.   We are now passing numerous villas, with long shady avenues leading up to them from the road, which is covered with various carriages and diligences. Everything denotes the approach to a large and wealthy city.

Bordeaux.   Hotel de Paris.—We are here, *au second,* in apartments which look over the tops of green trees in the Place Louis XVI.   The first glimpse we had of this magnificent city from the height we descended, was beyond description lovely. We saw the river, with its forest of masts, and the indistinct mazes of buildings, suburb gardens, and villas,—but the near approach, or rather the internal aspect of the town, disappointed us. The houses are dark and gloomy looking, and not much appearance of grandeur or even riches met our eye during the drive to this hotel.   As we drove over the bridge, we could not enjoy its fine views, owing to what appears to be the unnecessary height of its parapets ; but the hotel itself is the most disappointing object of all. Our rooms are less well furnished than any we have met with in France ; and the dinners also are the worst.   To-day, one dish exactly resembled, in look and smell, pieces of old, dirty

beaver hat stewed in castor oil; and this was by
way of vegetables—there were literally no others,
except, indeed, a few plain, half-boiled, black-
looking potatoes, not even so good as those we
had on the coast of Clare, which, strange to say,
were the worst I had ever before met with in
any country. How shameful, in this land of
fine vegetation, and in a dinner of five .francs
a head! But the good humour of the civil, ac-
commodating *fille*, here indeed a maid of all-
work, atones for many defects.

The *Place* in which the hotel is situated is very
grand, the largest I ever saw, and being open, at
the lower end, to the river, commands a splendid
view of the crowded shipping, and of the town
along its banks. which extends in a semicirle on
either side. But what a pity that the centre of
this grand *Place* should be only a flat expanse of
yellow dust, and, like the Frederick's Platz, at
Cassel, a desert in miniature! If it were laid
out in flower-beds, or green alleys, or even
common green grass, how much more beautiful
it would be.

Tuesday, June 1st.—We went yesterday to see
the cathedral. It was built by the English, and
is in the florid Gothic style. The exterior is

richly ornamented, and it has two high spires.
In the interior there is nothing striking, it has
not much painted glass, and it has no side aisles
to the nave.   Its remarkable feature is a high
separate tower, called " La Tour de Peyberlan,"
built in 1492.

St. Michael is a fine old church, with a beautiful
and lofty tower, separated from the building.
In going there from the cathedral, we passed
through a very curious old narrow street, with
verandahs and carved balconies.

Walked on Sunday morning to the Amphitheatre, through the Jardins Publics, which are
very pretty; but the ruins of the Amphitheatre,
called Palais Gallien, are not half so interesting
as those at Poitiers, and I thought not so large
or massive.   The arena is filled with little, dirty
streets and houses, villanous smells abound, and
there is no romance or beauty about it.   We
passed through several fine " *Places,*" as that of
Tourny, Dauphine, &c., and the *Cours,* which
are large, wide streets, with two rows of trees
in them.   These last are beautiful, and smell
very sweet.

I have suffered much from head-ache since we
came here, and did not feel equal to a long

rumbling drive on the pavé, but still I wished to
see either the castle of La Brede, or Blanquefort,
—two excursions on different sides of the town.
Edward the Black Prince passed some of the latter
days of his life at Blanquefort, and Montesquieu
wrote his "Esprit des Lois" at the Château de la
Brede. They are both about two hours' drive from
Bordeaux, but that to La Brede is said to be
the prettier. Now the Black Prince has by far
greater attractions for me, besides it seems a much
less frequented excursion. We should be able
to get an excellent dinner, all the guides said,
at the Restaurant of La Brede; but there was
none they knew of at the little Village de
Blanquefort; and its very name even does not
occur in a guide-book of 570 pages, which we
unluckily bought. Many of the coachmen were
equally ignorant. All this decided us in its
favour; and so off we went in the nicest little
carriage I ever entered, calling itself a fiacre, but
the only thing that betrayed its avocation was its
No. 32. It appeared perfectly new both outside
and in; its form, that of a Brougham, with beautiful silk linings, spring cushions, two handsome
grey horses, in excellent condition, and a smart,

148   CASTLE OF BLANQUEFORT.

gentlemanlike driver—in short, our equipage
was quite perfect, and so was our excursion.

We passed near the pretty villages of Le
Bouscat, Brouges, and Ezzines, and on each
side of the road were innumerable villas, with
gardens full of standard roses and fine orange-
trees in full bloom.

The Castle of Blanquefort is not situated so
high as I had expected from James's description,
for we certainly could not see the windings
of the river from it, but we had a lovely view
over the fertile plains of Bordeaux, with the
striking spires of the cathedral, and the heights
on the opposite bank of the river, covered
with fine woods, villas, and pine-trees.   The
old château itself stands in a little valley below
the village.   How picturesque and interesting
are its ancient walls!   Besides having been a
favourite residence of the Black Prince, Blanquefort is said to be the last place in this part of the
country which held out for the English.   The
whole form may be perfectly traced, with the outward moat and towers.   Some of the rooms
even are in good preservation; the mouldings
of the windows, the corbels, and ceilings

beautifully carved. We could clearly distinguish the English leopard in many places, and, I think, Prince of Wales's feathers on some parts of the walls. The stone is of a yellowish white hue, and looks so fresh and new, that one might almost fancy some of the ornaments to have but just come out of the sculptor's hand; yet the ivy, wild fig, honeysuckles, and vines which over-shadow the ruined towers, and cluster in graceful festoons round the carved windows and broken staircases, give them a venerable appearance. It is, however, so very well and solidly built, that time alone could not have worked the desolation which now reigns. We heard that one of the largest houses at Blanquefort was built of stones taken from our Edward's palace.

A *proprietaire* who was dressed in the blue frock of a peasant, very civilly left his vineyard, where he and his wife were at work, to shew us the way when the road became too bad for the carriage to proceed further.

This intelligent peasant seemed so much pleased with the interest we shewed about the old castle, that I hoped he might know of some tradition relating to its occupancy by my favourite hero, Edward. We therefore asked him who had

originally built it, and whether he had ever heard
of our brave Black Prince.

" No," said he, " I never knew there was
such a person, but I will tell you all about the
castle, and how it came to be called Blanquefort,
for I love the old place as if it was my father,
and often I sit and smell the roses that grow
under the windows till I fancy I see the
beautiful White Lady herself. Indeed, my father
did see her, and I've met with many persons
who have heard her sweet voice imploring the
cruel Baron, her lord, to spare some of the
prisoners that used to be confined in yonder
tower. I could fancy it, indeed, but I never saw
her water those roses with her tears, or breathe
and smile them into bloom on fine mornings, as
some say they have.

" All I know is, that such a person did live,
for the recollection of her good deeds is fresh in
the mind of every cottager for miles and miles
round, though it is upwards of seven centuries
since she died; and that solid tower, which has
stood through all the wars with France, and
against the English, is built over her grave.
Before her time, there was a castle here even
stronger than this one, and it was called Le

Château du Diable. No one could ever take possession of it; indeed, the stone it was built of was so hard that nothing could make the least impression on it. Some said it was inhabited by the devil himself, for not a soul ever appeared on its walls, and yet all assailants were struck down, as if by an invisible force, whenever they approached. The Chatelain du Diable, as he was called, seldom had any intercourse with his neighbours; they had always been a strange family, but the Baron Pierre was worse than any. He proposed for the hand of many a fair chatelaine, but though he offered a great dower, all the neighbouring Barons refused to give him their daughters; so he swore to run off with the most beautiful lady in all Gascony; and so he did, and even forced her parents to be present at the marriage ceremony, and they were married in the chapel within these walls.

" You may imagine the poor lady led a miserable life. She was an angel of goodness, and her whole endeavour was to mitigate the sufferings of her husband's unfortunate vassals. Instead of pining with grief at being separated from her dear parents and the young knight to whom she had been betrothed, and who had won

her love, she earnestly endeavoured to reform
her husband and interest him in favour of his
poor dependents and of the unfortunate prisoners
he took in war.   He used to torture them in the
most horrible manner.   But he was very anxious
to have a son, and after being married three
years, there seemed a prospect of the desired
event.   He then used his wife more gently, and
to please her, he would forego the cruelties in
which he delighted.

" The child was born, and a finer boy was
never seen, but, instead of being grateful, he
treated his poor wife much worse than ever.
So the dear lady began to pine, when she found
she was no use to anybody in the world ; for the
cruel Baron would not even allow her to educate
his boy, but gave it up entirely to a fiend under
the form of a priest, who was certainly in league
with the devil, and who had influenced the Baron
to evil all his life.   At last, the beautiful chatelaine became so ill that her life was despaired of,
and then her husband's heart began to soften,
and he sent for all the doctors in Bordeaux,
and allowed her to see her parents ; but his
kindness came too late.   She got worse and
worse, and soon died in her mother's arms.

ORIGIN OF " BLANQUEFORT." 153

" The baron was in despair, and as if to atone for all the mischief he had done and the misery he had caused, he invited the poor vassals, in whose welfare his wife had taken so much interest, to a great banquet—and when he went to bed that night, she appeared to him dressed in white, and thanked him for having fed his poor vassals. She said her spirit would be always near him so long as he continued to act well. So whenever any poor vassals were afflicted, the Dame Blanche used to appear to the Baron and inform him of their distress, and he always attended to her wishes. He became quite a reformed man, and this castle lost the name of Château du Diable, which it had borne for many generations, and was called Blanche Fort—the fort of La Dame Blanche—and her spirit has presided over all this part of the country ever since, for nothing can be happier than we all are, and whenever we are disposed to quarrel with our wives, we think of La Dame Blanche, and our anger is sure to be turned into kindness."

" And do you really believe that her spirit still lives in this neighbourhood?" inquired W——.

" Indeed I do," said the honest peasant,

154   EDWARD, THE BLACK PRINCE.

" though our good cure says he is sure she did
not die, but it was all a plan concerted with
her mother, and that it was probably herself who
used to appear, and by this means, influence the
Baron to act with kindness to the poor."

Though I was glad to hear about the White
Lady, yet the recollections of our own Black
Prince, were far more interesting, and I imagined
his gay-courtiers and brave warriors hunting in
the beautiful woods which surround the castle.

> " 'Twas near the city of renown'd Bordeaux,
> This goodly company of Edward's court,
> Array'd as archers came their skill to shew,
> And take the pleasure of the sylvan sport.

> " 'Twas in the summer when the leaves were green,
> And birds were quiring in the shady boughs,
> A goodly troop of knights and dames were seen,
> All in a glade where deer had wont to browse,
> Now scatter'd far, or hid in covert screen.

> " And thus, in sport and pastime of delight,
> They wiled away the pleasant busy hours,
> As preparation for the Spanish fight,
> Drew to the Prince his Aquitanian powers.
> At morn the council, and the ball at night,
> By day, the sylvan games and rural bowers."*

* Shepherd's Pedro of Castile.

As we could get no dinner at Blanquefort, we went, on our return, to the Café de Paris, and had a very good one for six francs, and some ice afterwards at a café, in the Place Tourny, by moonlight, under a fine portico filled with orange-trees in full bloom. The view was very pretty,—the lighted shops on either side of the broad *Place*, terminated by that magnificent theatre, the pride of Bordeaux.

The peasants talk a sort of Patois here, which sounds very like Spanish. The shops do not seem particularly good—very few booksellers— at one, however, I have bought several delightful-looking volumes. Guizot's and Thierry's Histories, &c., Plato's Thoughts, and the works of some other Greek philosophers, translated into French. The guide-book of this place is not good, but we got an excellent map of the Gironde.

The dress of the peasantry here is not at all picturesque; the women are by no means handsome, and they wear dingy red and yellow handkerchiefs tied round their heads, or else a very unwieldy kind of stiffened, white cap. They have enormous faces, and rather short, square figures; brown complexions, but hair and eyes not very dark; indeed, some have light blue eyes, which, with a mahogany-coloured skin, is not pretty, and they have, too, a sickly look. At Poitiers the women were beautiful.

W—— has just returned from Mr. S——, the Consul, who has been visiting the old castle of Villandran, where Clement V. was born, between Cerons and Langons; and that of Laroquetaillade, between Langons and Bazas. He was quite delighted with their scenery, and particularly with that of the former.

Wednesday Evening.—We walked over the town to explore, and search for some traces of the old Palace of Aquitaine, the ancient residence of our English kings, and other old buildings. We found several which the long guidebook of Bordeaux does not even hint at. We went first along the quay, and saw the two remaining towers of an old castle, where Richard Cœur de Lion is said to have lived. We then proceeded to the bridge, and went through the old Porte Caillon. It leads to the Place d'Aquitaine, which contains many curious old houses.

The Bourse was here, and though now a wagon office, yet its ornamented façade shews what it once was. We met a most civil and well-

informed man at the office, who very good-
naturedly and cleverly explained the locale to us.
This was one of the chance pieces of good fortune which travellers sometimes meet with.

This building was the old Bourse; but it owes
its magnificence, of which we saw the remains,
to Charles the Ninth.   The old castle of Aquitaine stood on the site which some new houses
on the opposite side of the *Place* now occupy:
this was inhabited by our Richard the First, and
the arms on the top of the Bourse, which seem to
have had leopards for supporters, might have
been of the period.

The old palace of the Dukes of Aquitaine,
our English kings, seems to have been of considerable extent.   Its site is now a strange mass
of old grotesque houses and courts, extending
some way into the Rue d'Enfer.   A dark dirty
street, quite worthy of its name, through which
we waded, holding our noses, but looking up
with great interest at the beautiful carving that·
was here and there to be seen, probably the
debris of England's royal palace, inserted into
the more humble dwellings of a later time.

Our cicerone offered to conduct us to see a
curious entrance to a house, formerly the Evêché,

158   QUAINT DEVICE.

in the neighbourhood, an offer which we willingly accepted. It is in a very narrow, dirty street, but very curious. The entrance to the old Evêché, was highly ornamented; over the door is a quaint device, explanatory of the Trinity. The figure is a triangle, richly decorated, and over it, in a medallion, are three profiles united.

The following sketch, which I made, will give some idea or the original.

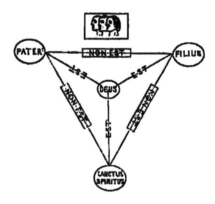

We knocked at the old door, which gave a strange unearthly sound, and a haggard head peeped out from an upper glassless window—all looked dark and mysterious. At last, the same haggard figure opened the door. Our kind friend asked for admittance, and we stumbled among wine casks, through dark passages, which looked as if stained with blood! The woman slammed the door behind us, and disappeared. I own I felt not a little nervous, but our kind friend with the straw hat smiled under its broad brim, and pointed to another archway at the farther end of the court—so we went on and admired the strange building. In a corner of the second court was a large tower, containing a fine old winding-staircase, and some remains of beautiful carvings. It was altogether a very original and strange scene, mixed up with present misery, and some degree of luxury too, for flowers were blooming on some of the old carved balconies.

Our kind cicerone accompanied us back, through the intricate mazes of dirty courts and narrow streets, to the spot from whence we had started, where we expressed the thanks we really felt. Before we parted, he told us that he recollected to have seen the amphitheatre almost entire—and we deplored together the vandalism which could have reduced that interesting monument to its present condition. After leaving our friend, we walked on the bridge, and enjoyed the fine view, and rich sunset.

160   ELEANOR OF PROVENCE.

At Bordeaux, our King John was married to Isabella of Angoulême, in the year 1200; and their son, Henry III., passed much of his time here, and lived in great state with his queen, Eleanor of Provence. This Queen Eleanor was called "La Belle," and possessed great influence over her husband. She was not very popular, and one of her expeditions to Aquitaine is thus noticed by Robert of Gloucester:—

"The Queen went beyond sea, the King's brethren also,
  And ever they strove the Charter to undo;
  They purchased that the Pope should assoil, I wis,
  Of the Oath and the Charter, and the King, and all his."

"It was ever the Queen's thought (as much as she could
      think)
  To break the Charter by some woman's wrench;
  And though Sir Edward was proved a hardy knight and
      good,
  Yet this same Charter was little to his mood."

She was a most active lady, and, in 1254, crossed the Pyrenees, and went with her son, Edward I., to claim the hand of Eleanor of Castile. The young people were married at Burgos, and they all returned to Bordeaux, where Henry III. had prepared grand festivals for the young infanta's reception.

In her latter days, Eleanor la Belle became extremely charitable; and she shewed, too, considerable knowledge of human nature, and gave her son, Edward I., excellent advice, which is recorded in some quaint lines by Piers.

Here, too, many years afterwards, in this old palace,—which, in the thirteenth century, was probably more splendid than ever before or since,—our young king, Edward I., and his queen, Eleanora of Castile, had a wonderful escape, in 1272. They were sitting in royal state on a richly-embroidered couch, in a magnificent room, which had lately been hung with tapestry sent from the luxurious Castile,* when a violent storm came on; terrific lightning flashed through the room, and killed two knights who were standing close behind the royal pair. This Queen Eleanor was called the Faithful, for she always accompanied her warlike husband in all his campaigns; and when her ladies were endeavouring to dissuade her from going with him to Asia, on the crusade, she said, " Nothing ought to part those whom God

* This queen first introduced tapestry hangings for rooms in England.

VOL. I.   M

162   QUEEN ELEANORA'S TOMB.

has joined, and the way to heaven is as near, if
not nearer, from Syria as from England, or my
native Spain."*

* The following epitaph from her tomb is given by Miss
Strickland :—

" Queen Eleanora is here interred,
    A royal, virtuous dame;
Sister unto the Spanish king,
    Of ancient blood and fame :
King Edward's wife, first of that name,
    And Prince of Wales by right,
Whose father, Henry—just the third—
    Was sure an English wight.
He craved her wife unto his son,
    The Prince himself did goe
On that embassage lukily,
    Himself with many moe.
This knot of linked marriage,
    The King Alphonso liked;
And with his sister and this Prince
    The marriage up was striked.
The dowery rich and royal was,
    For such a prince most meet;
For Ponthieu was the marriage gift—
    A dowery rich and great.
A woman both in concil wise,
    Religious, fruitful, meek;
Who did increase her husband's friends,
    And 'larged his honour eke.
                              Learn to die !"

Though · less strikingly beautiful than her royal
mother-in-law and namesake of Provence, who
was surnamed La Belle, she was very lovely, as
her effigy on the monument in Westminster
Abbey still shews. In 1284, she went to Car-
narvon Castle, and there gave birth to Edward II.
I have seen the small dark room where that event
took place, and also the old palace of Conway
Castle, where she lived in state, and where there
is a beautiful arched recess, called Queen Eleanor's Oriel .The old lines I read somewhere
about it, still run in my head :—

> " In her oriel there she was,
> Closed well with royal glass,
> Filled it was with imagery,
> Every window by and by."

Those old palaces give us a favourable idea of
the good taste in architecture of that age, when
even a remote province—as Wales then was—
possessed such splendid residences ; and, therefore, this southern palace at Bordeaux must have
been far more magnificent.

The crosses erected by Edward, in memory of
his beloved wife, are beautiful. I have often
admired the one near Northampton, which still

M 2

164   ORIGIN OF " CHARING CROSS."

remains nearly perfect ; but the most exquisite is
said to have been that at Charing Cross. .It
stood on the spot now occupied by the statue of
Charles I., and the name still commemorates the
affection of .Edward for his faithful queen—
Charing being a corruption of "Chère Reine," as
the good and lovely Eleanor was always called.

It was pleasant to think of all this as we
searched to-day for vestiges of the ancient
royal palace of England, and we talked over the
numerous kings and queens of our land who
passed some of their stateliest hours amidst
these old walls.   Here Edward the Black Prince
came after his glorious victory at Poitiers, in
1356, bringing his royal captive, John, King of
France.*   Some years afterwards, he visited
Bordeaux with his beautiful wife, the Fair Maid
of Kent ; and here, in the year 1367, his son
Richard was born.   Froissart says, " The Prince
and his whole household were very much rejoiced at the event.   On the following Friday,

---

* Froissart says, " It is not possible to relate all the feats
and entertainments which the citizens and clergy of Bordeaux made for the Prince, and with what joy they received
him and the King of France." The Prince remained there
all that winter, and there was much feasting and merriment.

the child was baptized at the holy font of St. Andrew's Church; the Archbishop of Bordeaux performed the ceremony." This was our unfortunate King Richard II. He is said to have been born in the little village of Sormont, not far down the river; and further on, there is a place called Richard, so named from our brave Cœur de Lion.

Soon after the birth of his son, the Black Prince agreed to assist Don Pedro to recover his kingdom of Castile from a usurping brother. The short interval of rest in the active life of the warlike Prince Edward is well described in Shepherd's Poem on Pedro, of Castile.

" The Prince of Wales, from Bourdeaux' peaceful tower,
   With listless eye looks over Aquitaine;
   The black chief droops within his lady's bower,
   And thinks of war, and dreams of Cressy's plain ;

       *   *   *   *   *   *

   Her knights in pleasance match their falcon's speed—
   Or, war's vain image, raise the hunter's cry,
   Or win with idle toil a minstrel's meed,—
   But still for battle breathes the secret sigh.
   Stout Chandos chafes by day his fretted steed—
   By night, the visionary squadrons fly;
   He grasps in startled dreams a shivering spear,
   And wakes with shouts of Guesclin in his ear."

166   DON PEDRO, OF CASTILE.

Soon their wishes are gratified; Don Pedro
and his beautiful wife come to implore for aid,
and then—

" Within a week, the town of old Bordeaux
   Beheld the royal pair; a gallant show
   Of knights and ladies issued from the gate,
   To give them welcome with becoming state;
   And thus the noble heir of England's throne
   Received the monarch who had lost his own."

167

CHAPTER IX.

Journey through Les Landes—Mont de Marsan—Beautiful
scenery approaching Bayonne—Historical recollections
of our early English kings.

*Thursday, June 3. In the carriage, on the road
to Bayonne.*—The country through which we
have passed since we left Bordeaux is pretty,
but we saw nothing remarkable till we had
passed Castres, the second post, and then came
in view the old castle and village of Langoiran,
on the other side of the Garonne.

At Cerons there is a large castle, rather old,
and a good view of the opposite bank of the
river,—which is high and steep, and covered
with vines and wood,—with here and there the
ruins of old castles on projecting heights, and
modern villas below.

Just passed through Barsac, where there is a
respectable-looking chateau, and where our post-

boy wanted us to stop to get " quelques bouteilles
de vin blanc." Enclosed vineyards seemed to announce wine of superior quality. Just before
entering the small town, there is a good-looking
maison de campagne on the right. On the opposite side of the river, St. Croix du Mont has
an old castle in a fine position.

We crossed the river Ciron, a tributary of the
Garonne. Before we reach Preignac is the
turn-off for Villandran, whose ruined castle
Mr. S—— describes as well worthy of a visit.
At Langon,—which is a small town, with, I believe, a tolerable inn,—the road leaves the neighbourhood of the Garonne, and turns south to
Bazas. Langon is the ancient Alingo, where
Paulinus, the celebrated Christian convert, the
friend of Ansonius, had a property. He was
afterwards Bishop of Nola, in the year 408, and
died in 431. Before he devoted his life to religion, he was a scholar and a poet, a man of
large fortune, and high in office, having been
raised to the consulate in 378. He had large
estates in Spain, Gaul, and Italy ; amongst others,
a large property in Alingo (Langon). It was
curious, that just as we were driving through
the town I was reading his Memoirs in the first

number of the " Actes de l'Academie Royale de Bordeaux."

The next post, Bazas, is beautifully situated, with a highly decorated Gothic church upon a height, and an old convent in a garden, which we passed on entering the town. We had pavé to it from Langon, and the road is lined with poplars.

About forty minutes' drive from Bazas, an extensive view over the Pines of the Landes. We again passed the Ciron, near a pretty mill, and soon after entered a fir wood. From Captieux, sandy heath and scattered trees, with houses rather resembling Swiss cottages.

And now we have fairly entered Les Landes, and I have admired the flat interminable plain, and smiled to think how some people would laugh at me for doing so. I am lucky to be able to admire most things in their way; for my internal sensations not being pleasant, it is fortunate to be able to derive enjoyment from external objects in all their varieties. People who have more spirit of inward enjoyment, are often less pleased by what they see, hear, or read.

Very park-like scenery; fine expanse of forest. We had an opportunity of forming some idea of its great extent, as the road occasionally passes over some gentle heights.

Roquefort, famous for its cheeses, is a pretty little town on an abrupt height over a winding, narrow ravine, which is crossed by a bridge. The ruined fortifications round its walls are very picturesque.   On leaving, we crossed a tributary of the Adour, and ascended a hill—the road winding round the town in a picturesque manner. There are some fine trees in these Landes, particularly chesnut and oak.

The little Swiss cottage-like post-house of Caloy, at which we are now changing horses, is overshadowed by a splendid oak.   We met many peasants carrying gracefully-shaped water-pots on their heads, and their dresses of vivid colours have a very good effect.

I understood that, poor as the country is, the peasantry of the Landes are generally wealthy. Their fir-forests are a source of wealth, producing planks, resin, tar, &c.   Until lately, this timber was used abundantly for the production of gas; but the market is now greatly fallen off, from other materials being employed, probably coals.   The practice of bleeding the trees for resin, disfigures them sadly.   The language is a patois resembling Gascon ; and here we saw a

cloth cap in use exactly resembling the Lowland
Scotch cap—generally brown cloth, but blue is
seen also; with this cap, whose acquaintance
was here begun, we were destined to become
very familiar; it is universally worn in the
Basque Provinces and by the Bearnois.

Here we left the department of La Gironde,
and entered that of Les Landes.   Beyond the
Traverses, there occurs a very pretty bit of park-
like scenery. Fine trees—oak, elm, and chesnut;
the latter frequently growing singly in the corn-
fields.

Too hot and dusty, and pavé too jolting to
write many impressions of this long day's
journey, and now I scarcely remember what
they were; but the feelings they have left are
very pleasant.

Friday, 4th. Carriage. — Slept last night at
Mont de Marsan, and found the Hotel des Am-
bassadeurs far better than we expected—a nice
old rambling house, with half-defaced paintings
of Louis XIV.'s time over the doors, and sprawl-
ing shepherdesses and swains languishing in
pale decay over the chimney-pieces. A profusion of sweet heliotrope and flowered creepers
covering the walls of its court-yard, and the
upper windows curtained by jasmines and roses.

172   MONT MARSAN.

In this combination of ancient art and present
blooming nature we slept comfortably, and after
an excellent breakfast, and some Paté de fois de
canard, for which Mont-Marsan is celebrated,
we resumed our journey at half-past eight.

We were also pleased with the look of the
town.   It is situated, like many in the Landes,
on an abrupt height, which overhangs a narrow,
winding ravine, and has various bridges, old and
new, over the little river that runs at the bottom.

An avenue of large plane-trees led us from
the town; and we are passing through a fine
forest, with now and then corn-fields and vines
to break the wild and sylvan scene.   The cottages I admired much.   Their overhanging roofs
of red tile, white walls of mud and timber, and
the open sort of rustic portico in front, look
southern and luxurious.

The peasantry, too, are a much finer race than
near Bordeaux, and the dress far more picturesque.   We often meet carts drawn by white
oxen with sheep skins over their heads, looking
like those I have often seen on ancient bas-reliefs.
The rye is very forward—we saw one field already cut; but the hay harvest is only beginning.

Changing horses at the pretty little town of

Tartas.   The post-house is an old church, and
has a primitive clock-bell over it, which has just
struck eleven twice, with a beautiful venerable-
sounding tone.

A steep descent leads down to the river before
us, and I see the road winding up the other side,
through the rustic buildings, and can trace it
afterwards for some distance in the woods beyond.   It all looks and feels peaceful, and the
prospect of a shady forest drive, where the
smells are delicious, is very pleasant.

Four o'clock.—Something happened to one of
the wheels, and we were obliged to stop for some
time. We came here at a foot's pace, and found
a fair going on in this little village ; and the
maimed carriage (in which I am writing,) is surrounded by numbers of peasants, and some
soldiers, staring at every part of it.

The women in broad-brimmed straw hats,
which serve also as umbrellas, and men in blue
or brown caps, like Scotch bonnets.   The goods
selling in stalls are chiefly crockery, or rather
earthenware, which is very pretty : pans of every
variety of shape and colour, pale-green, buff,
red of every shade, and umber.   The other
goods are the broad-brimmed hats, (one of which

I think I ought to buy,) nails, dried fish, and ropes. The people look gay and kind-hearted, and very anxious about the operation our wheel is undergoing, and probably rather wondering at my writing so unconcernedly all the time. Few of the windows are glazed, but they have all green shutters; the little " Hôtel des Voyageurs," can boast of only one glazed window.

Before the present fine Chaussée was made— one permanent advantage at least of Napoleon's expedition into Spain—the sand was here so deep as to make travelling very tedious; my informant, an old postillion, told me that with eight horses our carriage could hardly have been dragged along; now the malle de poste does the distance between Bayonne and Mont de Marsan in six hours—98 kilometres, 61¼ English miles; upwards of 10 miles the hour.

Bayonne.—Evening.—Hôtel St. Etienne.—The last three hours of our drive was through very lovely scenery. The Pyrenees were but dimly visible in the distant haze; but here and there a blue summit peeped above the light clouds, and still further, a snow-capped peak glistened through them. There was something in these mysterious outlines which enchanted me, even

more than if we had obtained a clear and uninterrupted view of our new friends—friends I
trust they will be, for I know of nothing in
inanimate nature to which we get so much attached as mountains. We soon learn their forms
and names by heart.

Then the distinct and near views were beautiful—the sea, the Bay of Biscay was on our
right, bounding a woody plain, and on each side
of the road, the plane, the tulip, and cork-
tree frequently occur, telling of new regions,
and southern lands ; and vines, treliced over
whole fields, form an umbrageous roof to Indian
corn, which grows beneath. Then we passed
by little clear lakes, and dells, and abrupt heights,
and scenes which suddenly transferred us in
imagination to an old English park, with its
giant oaks and lordly fern, looking wild, yet so
aristocratic, that we gazed through a break in
the forest, almost expecting to see the old
manor house: but a distant mountain appeared
instead, and the eye travelled far over vine-clad
plains ; and Spanish-featured peasants, carts
drawn by oxen, and the smell of wild heliotrope,
told us that we were far south.

And in this town everything tells that we are
very near Spain. The shops, the hotels, have

176 VISIT TO THE CONSUL.

Spanish as well as French signs, and the old
arcades and highly-ornamented houses have
quite a Spanish air. · The low, old-fashioned
arcades, the dress and look of the people—the
language, all announce a frontier town.

After a visit to our consul here, Mr. H——,
and making inquiries, we started in a most
jolting kind of cabriolet to look out for a house
at Biaritts, where we intend to remain some time
for the advantage of sea-bathing. It turned out
a more attractive looking-place than I expected.
There is a noble expanse of sea, and some
warm-baths have been lately constructed. We
saw a great number of houses; and at length
fixed upon one near the Vieux Port, Madame
Espernon, proprietaire, where we shall be
" grandement logés," but oddly. Our landlady
assured us she contrived to stow away eighteen
persons in it last year. The houses are singu-
larly placed, and the interior arrangements of
the greatest number far from attractive. We
did not get back till six o'clock.

We started this morning to visit the Cimetière Anglaise, and had much difficulty to find it,
owing to being misinformed as to the place.
We thought it lay in the valley beneath the fortress ; but after continuing for some time along

the road, a peasant told us we were quite wrong, and that we must return to Saint Esprit, and take the Paris road : instead of doing so, we ascended the height beneath the citadel, and as the morning was clear and delightful, we had an opportunity of seeing the beautiful environs of Bayonne, and the fine chain of mountains, which seem to bound the broken and varied basin where the town lies.

The town is of small extent; but, as in most fortified places, the houses are built very close to each other. It lies at the point where the Nive falls into the Adour, and consists of three divisions. Saint Esprit, lying below the citadel on the right bank of the Adour, is connected by a bridge of boats with La Petite Bayonne, which occupies the tongue of land between the two rivers. Three bridges, one of them a suspension bridge, connect it with La Grande Bayonne : in the latter is the cathedral, which, though its dilapidated tower, with a slated roof, is far from what it ought to be, still has a fine effect, and so has the Château Vieux. The military hospital, the Château Neuf, and the arsenal, said to be worth seeing, are in La Petite Bayonne. I heard the population stated at

VOL. I.   N

178   BAYONNE.

23,000.   The view from the glacis of the citadel
is very fine.   The Pic du Midi and La Maladetta
are said to be visible from it, but we did not
see them

Our way continued round the citadel, until we
came near the Paris road, where additional fortifications, on an extensive scale, are carrying on.
The object is, to erect higher works in front of
the citadel, which is here much exposed; and I
afterwards heard that it is the intention to raise
Bayonne to a fortress of the first class; to do so
will be the work of years.

Having reached the Paris road, a little beyond
the office of l'Octroi, we turned to the left, and
got into a pleasant lane, shaded with trees.   We
then reached a nice campagne, which belongs,
I heard, to M. Gomez, a Jew.   From a point
near it, there is a charming view in every direction, particularly towards the mouth of the river,
and the high land on the left bank studded with
villas.   Had we turned to the right, through a
farm opposite to M. Gomez's villa, we should
have saved ourselves much time and trouble;
but a girl sent us considerably further along the
road, till we came to its termination, at the
bottom of a steep hill, near the river.   Here, on
inquiring at a farm-house, we discovered our

mistake, and a girl came to set us right, without whose assistance we should certainly have had great difficulty to find the place.

The Cimetière Anglaise lies near the bottom of a ravine, covered with oaks ; a very wild se-questered spot. The Consul told me, that in the enclosure there once stood an old tree which had been struck by a ball, which still remained in the tree : this circumstance would have told the tale of death admirably; but unfortunately the tree no longer exists.   It was probably removed to make way for the present arrangement, which is as common-place as four high walls and some twenty or thirty poplars can make it.

The space allotted to the memory of those brave fellows, whose lives were so uselessly sacrificed, is about fifty feet square.   Some steps fixed in the wall, lead to the interior ; near these steps is a tablet, with the following inscription :—" Burial-place of British Officers, espe-cially of the Coldstream Guards, who fell in action near to this spot, on the 14th of April, 1814.   The night of the sortie from the citadel of Bayonne."   This, as I have said, was a use-less expenditure of life, to a melancholy extent. I believe the treaty of Paris was already signed,

180   SORTIE FROM THE CITADEL.

and consequently the blockade was but carelessly kept up.

On that night, whilst the officer who commanded the pickets was taking a bottle of sherry with a brother officer, a deserter came in, who informed them of the intended sortie ; the man, probably without much credit being given to him, was forwarded to head quarters. The French account is, that the disappearance of the deserter was perceived, and that the sortie was hastened in consequence. The result was, that the British were taken by surprise, and the whole affair fell upon the pickets. Support was not sent with sufficient promptitude, or the French might have been cut off. As it was, they succeeded in driving the British from the position they occupied, which the French kept during the night ; but attempted nothing further. The next morning they were driven in ; and this affair, not creditable to either party, cost the French upwards of 1000 men, and the British 3000 and a great number of officers. Sir John Hope was made prisoner.

We got home much quicker than we went, and after a very agreeable walk, arrived at the hotel in half a hour. After breakfast, we lounged about this interesting old town, and its low, uncouth arcades, which are dirty, curious, and useful. We then ascended the tower of the cathedral, and had a very fine view over Bayonne, and of the chain of Pyrenees, with which we hope to become better acquainted! At this end, La Rhune—between four and five thousand feet high (800 toises)—and Les Quatre Colonnes, are the most conspicuous mountains.

The interior of the church is handsome, the architecture of the windows curious, like the circles of a girandole. I copied one of those at the west end of the aisles. The church has a very lofty nave, with two ranges of highly ornamented windows. The arms of England on the roof, shew that it was built during the reigns of our early English kings. It has two side aisles, inconsiderable in height, with a range of chapels on the north side, but none on the south, owing probably to the cloisters, which adjoin the church on that side.

While I was drawing, a good-looking portly priest came up to us : he had excellent manners, talked much of England, and expressed his joy at the manifestations now making of the return of the English to the bosom of the church,

182   LIBERAL INSCRIPTION.

which he had no doubt would be accomplished, and which he said was the object of their daily prayers.

We then bought some flowers in the Marché, the small and dirty " Place," near the church. On the west side, is another small place, where a sarcophagus has been erected, with a *rather* liberal inscription. After a fine panegyric on a tailor and an Etudiant de Médécine, qui " Succomberent glorieusement à Paris, le 29 Juillet, 1830, pour la defense de nos droits, et le triomphe de la liberté," it ends by the following maxim :—

> " Les revolutions justes
> Sont le chatiment
> Des mauvais rois."

After the inspection of some shops, and the purchase of some cakes from one in the arcade for our expedition to-morrow, we made an excursion into Petite Bayonne, which has, I think, cleaner streets than the other; we got out of the town near the Château Neuf, and, from a height on the road to St. Jean Pied du Port, had a beautiful view of the rich country towards the mountains, the course of the Nive, and the range of mountains beyond.

INTERIOR OF THE CATHEDRAL.   183

In this direction lies Cambo, about three leagues from Bayonne — a mineral watering-place, worth a visit. We met a civil man here, who told us that the works of the fortress are to be greatly strengthened on this side also. We returned home to our excellent dinner at four, after a very agreeable walk.

Yesterday we went and heard mass in the old church. It is pleasant to see the arms of England still adorning the ceiling of the cathedral, and to think of the numerous kings of our land who have in different centuries sojourned here.

Richard Cœur de Lion, when Count of Poitou, came here in 1177, and went to a splendid tournament, given by Sancho the Strong, King of Navarre, at Pampeluna. It was there our brave king first saw the beautiful Berengaria, Sancho's sister, and was so captivated by her loveliness, that he broke his engagement with Alice of France, and never rested till he had obtained her hand. Richard was obliged to wait many years; but as soon as he became King of England, he sent his mother, Eleanor, to the court of Navarre. And here that imperious dame must have come on her road to

184   THE PRINCESS JOANNA.

Pampeluna, and soon returned with the fair
Berengaria, whom she had obtained for her son.
These royal dames, no doubt, came to make
their devotion in this old cathedral, and were
nobly entertained by the bishop, in his palace,
which adjoins. This same bishop afterwards
pronounced the marriage benediction on the
valiant Richard and fair Berengaria in the Isle
of Cyprus, in 1191. An old chronicler thus
describes it:—

> " To Limoussa the lady was led,
>   His feast the king did cry,
>   Berengère will be wed,
>   And sojourn thereby
>   The third day of the feast;
>   Bishop Bernard, of Bayonne,
>   Newed oft the geste—
>   To the Queen he gave the crown."

Here, two centuries later, came a fair descendant of old Queen Eleanor's, Princess Joanna
of England, daughter to Edward III. It was in
1348 she came to wed Don Pedro, of Castile, afterwards called the Cruel. Her beauty and grace
have been sung by many a minstrel; she was
escorted here by all the wealthiest citizens of
Bordeaux, and in this cathedral the marriage
ceremony was to be performed. I can imagine

this old building gorgeously adorned, and the Spanish Prince impatiently awaiting the arrival of his lovely bride — the streets hung with tapestry, and all the splendour of Spain exhibited on the occasion. The cortège approaches the city, and the trembling Joanna, who was only fifteen years of age, meets her royal lover. They are delighted with each other, for Don Pedro was a handsome and accomplished prince, and no traces of those violent passions afterwards imputed to him, could then be traced on his noble countenance. They pass through the town amid the exclamations of multitudes, and Joanna beholds the beautiful cathedral, where on the morrow her fate is to be sealed; never had she appeared more lovely, the glow of joy beaming in her eyes, and heightening the colour on her cheeks. They enter the Bishop's palace, and after a splendid banquet, the Princess retires to rest. From that richly-embroidered bed of state, which it had been the pride of many a Spanish lady to prepare for her, she never rose again! A fearful plague called the Black Death, at that time ravaged Europe, and, on the morning of her bridal day, seized the beautiful Joanna. Vain was the skill of medicine, vain

the tears and prayers of the distracted bridegroom—before the hour appointed for the joyful
nuptials, she was dead !

Soon after a mournful cortège approaches the
cathedral, the King of Castile and his miserable
son follow, with slow and solemn steps. They
place the body of that fair English Princess
near the altar where the nuptial roses still
bloom. But the song of joy was turned to woe,
and the grave closed over the remains of her
who, twelve short hours before, had gazed on
these walls full of joyful expectation of a long,
blissful future.

Saturday.—The promenades by the river side
are beautiful; and last night we walked all through
the town, over the two bridges, and upon the
ramparts of the fortress at the other side. They
command a most splendid view over a great extent
and variety of country. We looked on the town
and rivers beneath, and could see the windings of
the broad and united streams as far as the ocean,
on our right: before us was the coast of Spain,
stretching far away into the distant horizon;
and, on our left, the Pyrenees. Then the town
itself, with its numerous bridges and old buildings, surmounted by the fine cathedral, which

stands on a height—the junction of two broad rivers (the Adour and Gave) in its centre,—the woody country beyond, with many graceful villaed heights and fertile plains, which occupy the space between the town and the far-off Pyrenees; all this formed a succession of pictures too varied and numerous for description,—but lovely in the extreme.

Tuesday, June 8.—Still at Bayonne, and more delighted with it every day. Splendid panorama from the summit of the cathedral tower, which we again ascended to-day. The mountains were all clear, and the sea beautifully blue. Explored afterwards the oldest part of the town, and the curious old arcade by the river, shut in with canvas. We then walked out on the road to St. Jean Pied de Port, and went into the fields beyond the rope-walk, where we found one of the most lovely views imaginable, terminated by the heights near Cambo and mountain range. All the walks and drives round the town, in every direction, are interesting and beautiful.

188

CHAPTER X.

Excursion into Spain—St. Sebastian—The River Bidasoa—
Fine scenery—Irun and its church—Hernani—Independence of the Basques.

Biaritts, Saturday, 11th.—Since I last wrote, we
have been in Spain ! I find that, as great beauty
of scenery seems to paralyse my powers of
sketching, so great interest in a subject inter-
feres with description.   On approaching the
Pyrenees, in walking in the beautiful environs
of Bayonne, I never took out my sketch-book ;
and during those three most delightful days of
our excursion to St. Sebastian, I could scarcely
note down any of the various charming impressions left on my mind.   We were very
fortunate in every respect.   My first trial of
travelling by diligence proved more satisfactory
than I expected.   The greatest disadvantage of

it was, the extreme roughness of the carriage,
and the rate of travelling over some of the most
uneven pavements I ever saw—not the slightest
regard for dips or inequalities,—to write or draw
when in motion was impossible.   The roads in
some places, however, were excellent—bordered
sometimes by large coping stones, and sometimes by raised trottoirs with parapet walls.

We decided to make our little expedition into
Spain by the diligence, and had every reason to
rejoice at our decision; so far as our experience
goes, it confirms what I have heard, that the
diligence is the only comfortable way of travelling in Spain.

We started exactly at six, with a most talkative and obliging *conducteur*. W——, Frisk, and
I occupied the coupé.   We thought of having
my maid with us; but we were too crowded to
be comfortable, and therefore transferred her to
a place in the body of the vehicle, and thus,
with our courier on the roof, we made an excellent journey.   The road to the French frontier
(the Bidasoa) is excellent, nothing can be better
kept.   The material used seemed a hard lime-.
stone; heaps of it, small and evenly broken,
were ready for repair; the roads scraped, hedges

190   SPANISH FARM-HOUSES.

trimmed—in short, the most minute attention
paid by the numerous cantonniers employed.

Before we reached the first stage, (Baidar,)
which we did in an hour, we ascended, having
the sea at some little distance on the right, and
came to a lake separated by a narrow range of
sand-hills from the sea.   Is this the Duck Lake
Inglis speaks of?   From Baidar we had a steep
and long descent, with a fine view of the mountains: La Rhune (Larrun) shewing its table
height, and, more to the west, the bold and
rocky summit of Les Quatre Colonnes, or, as it
is sometimes called, les Trois Couronnes.

Guetter, and the country round, is scattered
over with excellent farm-houses, built something
like the Swiss. The timbers, of which the walls
are partly composed, are painted black, while
the rest is white-washed, so they looked very
neat. We changed horses at Baidar, in about
two minutes, and coachman also; each drives
his own team, which, though inferior to post
horses, went very well.

St. John de Luz is a very curious old place,
in a charming position, but liable to encroach-
ments from the sea, to which its decadence is
attributed.   Its population, in 1718, was 4800;

now, not more than half that number. The fisheries were then the source of wealth with all the towns on the coast, but they have now much fallen off.

St. Jean de Luz was the place where the marriage of Louis XIV. with the daughter of Philippe IV., Marie Therèse, took place. The house is pointed out where he lived, at the corner of the " Place." We crossed a narrow arm of the sea by a wooden bridge, and afterwards the Nivelle. From the bridge, we ascended through the rough and very narrow street of a faubourg, called Ciboure ; where numerous gipsies (the gitanos of Spain) are to be found.

Before reaching Urrunge, we came to the old Château de Urtubi, which seems kept up quite in its antique state ; and, according to the conducteur, is a " très belle propriété." It appears well worth seeing, and has considerable historical interest, as the place of interview between Louis XI. and the Kings of Arragon and Castile, in 1462. Of this interview, and the romantic legend connected with the castle, I will say more on our return. Urrunge was, in former days, celebrated for the contests between two factions, with the comical designations of Sabelchouri (Ventres-blancs) and Sabel-gorri (Ventres-rouges).

Soon afterwards we reached Behobie, a small place on the French side of the Bidasoa. Here our passports were viséd, and, whilst our courier was arranging about them, we walked on the bridge. I believe the passage of the river, in 1814, was effected some distance below, nearer to Fontarabia, which is built at the mouth of the river, and was a fortress of some importance; but now, I understand, fallen away. It has some old houses, the remains of an ancient Moorish palace, re-built by the Emperor Charles V.; and a church, well worthy of a visit.

Its French neighbour, Hendaie, on the opposite side of the river, and Fontarabia—" ont péri," as M. Morel, in his description of Bayonne, says, " l'une par l'autre." In 1793, the Spaniards destroyed Hendaie by a bombardment from Fontarabia; and, in the year following, the revolutionary army of France returned the compliment. Neither town recovered.

From the bridge of the Bidasoa, we saw close to us the miserable remains of the once celebrated " Isle des Faisans." What a falling off!

—it is now a narrow strip of ground, on which a cow was feeding; much of the earth has been removed by the peasants; the river does its work also; so that in a few years it will have totally disappeared. And yet, in the days of its glory, what a fine place it must have been! Cardinal Mazarin, and the Spanish minister, Louis de Haro, here negotiated the marriage of Louis XIV. to the daughter of Philip IV.: a magnificent pavilion was then erected on the island, and bridges connected it with the shore on either side. Afterwards Philip and Louis met here.

During the delay occasioned by an examination of passengers and packages at the Custom House, W—— and I crossed the bridge, and strolled along the road on the Spanish side of the Bidasoa. Besides the delight of feeling that we were in Spain, we were surrounded with interesting memorials of historical events; and I hurried on to an elevation which commanded a view of the once celebrated old town of Fontarabia, to make the sketch which forms the frontispiece of this volume.

This spot seems, from the earliest to the latest times, to have been peculiarly consecrated

VOL. I.   O

194   THE PALADINS.

to war.   Here Roland passed with his brave
paladins :—

> " Ah ! for a blast of that same horn,
> On Fontarabian echoes borne,
>   That to King Charles did come ;
> When Roland brave, and Olivier,
> And every paladin and peer,
>   On Roncesvalles died."

Our nimble conducteur, who runs about his
lumbering charge like a cat, soon joined us, and
we entered Spain.   The height above the river,
with its church (St. Martial ?) was the main
position of the British at the battle of Bidasoa.

Irun is a very interesting old place; we
stopped to breakfast there, and made an excellent
meal under the auspices of a very pretty Spanish
" moza ;" so that our first trial of a Spanish
posada gave us a most favourable impression.
The decorations of the houses and beautiful
carving of the projecting balconies announce a
splendour which no longer exists ; and in the
" Plaza" there is a fine old column, on which
the arms of Charles V. are inscribed.   I tried to
take the view from that spot, but was soon
ordered to desist by some Spanish soldiers.   We
then went to the church, which is very striking,

particularly under the circumstances in which
we saw it.   It is of considerable size, and of a
mixed architecture, half Gothic, half Roman:
its groined roof is supported by four massive
pillars.   The altar is very fine—its ornaments
occupy the entire end of the church, and reach
to the ceiling, and the whole is richly gilt.   Mass
was celebrating; no chairs or divisions encum-
bered the floor, which made the congregation in
the dim light more striking.   It consisted almost
entirely of women, dressed in black, with their
mantillas; they were grouped in lines of five or
six, and knelt upright, with small tapers burning on the floor before them; their immovable
figures, apparently absorbed in devotion, gave a
peculiar solemnity to the scene.

The narrow street of Irun is very steep, and
so miserably paved, that we blessed our stars we
were not induced to take our carriage; it would
have fallen in the struggle.   Irun (the *I run* of
electioneering jokes) was one of the remarkable
scenes of the late war; indeed, all the country
through which we passed has an additional
interest from the same cause.

At Ouyarzon is a fort built by the Spanish
Legion; before we reached it, the scenery is

196   HERNANI.

very fine, and the road very hilly, through defiles
covered with fern. The rocky height of the
Trois Couronnes still continues to be the leading
feature among the mountains: we continued
ascending and descending, and thus reached
Astigarraga, which was the head-quarters of the
Carlists, we then came to Hernani, so celebrated
during the war; the Fort St. Barbara, on a very
steep hill near it, was built by the English under
Evans, and is still kept up.

We were much struck with the noble air of
every peasant we saw, and their majestic bearing
reminded me of what I lately read in Lord C——'s
interesting work. He says—" When, formerly,
I crossed the frontier of the Basque Provinces, I
felt myself at once in a free land, amid a race of
men possessing and deserving freedom. The
erect, not haughty carriage, the buoyant step,
the frank and manly, yet respectful greeting, and
the whole bearing, spoke of liberty long enjoyed,
well understood, and not abused."*

---

* He says, in another place—" Every Biscayan is noble,
and is acknowledged as such by the law in every province
in Spain.   A perfect equality of civil rights prevails in
Biscay.

" The house of the Biscayan is his castle, in the most em-

Sketched by Lady Chatterton and drawn on stone by Bichebois.

Printed by Lemercier, Benard and C.^o

HERNANI.

And the fortress of Santa Barbara (Spain)

This consciousness of their nobility, and the peculiar feeling it produces on the minds of the Basques, is shewn by an anecdote I heard of a peasant in the little village of Astigarraga.

It was a lowering afternoon, when a traveller— a rich Andalusian merchant,—returning from the completion of an enterprise which had brought a plentifully golden harvest into his coffers, arrived at an inn at Astigarraga. The very best that the house afforded was ordered for his repast; but our luxurious traveller was not dependent for refreshment upon such chance fare as could be procured on the road; his own baggage contained an ample store of dainty cates

phatic sense of the word. No magistrate can violate that sanctuary; no execution can be put into it, nor can his arms or his horse be seized; he cannot be arrested for debt, or subjected to imprisonment upon any pretext whatever, without a previous summons to appear under the old tree of Guernica, where he is acquainted with the offence imputed to him, and called upon for his defence; he is then discharged on the spot, or bailed, or committed, according to the crime imputed to him. This, the most glorious privilege that freemen can possess — this, the most effectual safeguard against the wanton abuse of power—this, a custom more determinately in favour of the subject than even our own cherished habeas corpus, was enjoyed by the Basques for centuries before that far-famed guarantee of British liberty had existence in our islands."

and choice wines wherewith to supply all de-
ficiencies.

The merchant had not completed his savoury
meal, when the rain began to descend. The
evening looked black and threatening, but he
was obliged to proceed; and summoning the
landlord, he desired him to provide a guide
and to order out the mules forthwith. The
latter were soon at the door, and before many
minutes the guide too had made his appearance.
He wore the high, conical hat of the country—
his thread-bare cloak, which was gracefully
thrown around him, but partially concealed the
jacket beneath, whose embroidery of stamped
leather was evidently the worse for wear; but
the lofty bearing of the man shewed a nobility of
nature far superior to outward ornament, an
opinion in which it was clear the man himself
entirely participated.

The merchant proceeded to prepare himself
for the road, and some little time did it take
before his fat, comfortable person was encased
in a pile of cloaks, mantles, and furs enough to
render it impervious to the most untoward elements. At last, being duly packed up, and
established on a mule, as well fed and well

covered as his wealthy master, the little procession moved off.

The rain continued to pour on in drenching
torrents. The merchant, after jogging along
for some time, suddenly woke up out of a nap
into which he had been soothed by the effects of
a luxurious dinner, and by the warmth and
comfort of his present position. He put his
head out of his snug nest of cloaks, and his eyes
fell upon his guide.   The young man was
drenched to the skin; indeed, it would not have
taken much to penetrate his scanty garments.
His broad-brimmed hat, however, was perched
on the side of his head with the same air as
before; and he walked on, beside the traveller's
mule, with his usual haughty carriage, evincing
conscious dignity in every movement.

The good-natured little merchant was touched
by the dripping figure beside him. He drew a
contrast between his own wealthy, successful,
and luxurious condition, and that of his ill-fed,
half-clad, and penniless guide.   At last, these
thoughts so worked within him, that he could
not avoid breaking out into a compassionate
exclamation :—

"My poor friend, how wet you are! and

how lean and thinly clad! I do, indeed, pity you!"

" Pity *me!*" exclaimed the guide, erecting his stately figure to its full height, while every vein swelled with the proud blood of the Zurias —" Pity *me!* a noble Biscayan!" and, his dark eyes flashing haughtily, he darted a look of supreme scorn at the clod of plebeian earth enveloped in its costly coverings. " It is I who pity you, sir merchant," he cried; " for I am a noble!"

At Hernani we left the Tolosa road, and turned to the left, towards St. Sebastian. A new road is said to be in contemplation, direct from Irun to St. Sebastian, passing up the valley, which would lead by Passages, be almost level, and shorten the distance two hours. Near Oriamendi is another fort, which was abandoned by the English; and near it, the scene of action of the 5th of May, 1837, where the allies, though superior in numbers, and strongly posted, were defeated by the Carlists. I heard, that had it not been for the firing from the steamer—I think the "Phœnix," under the direction of Lord John Hay, —the British would have hardly regained St. Sebastian : as it was, their loss is said to have been very great—nearly two thousand men, and sixty five officers. Lord John Hay was much liked; he and his brave detachment supported the British reputation, and greatly contributed to the success of the war.

After passing Hernani, the view back on the little town is very picturesque. The country becomes less interesting until near St. Sebastian, where it improves; but the immediate neighbourhood of the town shews melancholy traces of the war. The Queenites destroyed every house: some have been repaired, but numbers, still in ruins, shew how impartially the work of destruction was done. It explains why the Basques were such zealous Carlists; indeed, so strong was this feeling, though shewn to a weak and worthless object, and so strong was the country, that had not Maroto been a traitor, the war would still be raging.

We reached San Sebastian about three. It is a well-built town, containing but few remains of its ancient greatness: an Englishman must blush when he hears that this was caused by the war of 1813. The English took it by storm, and destroyed the greater part of the town; so that since that date it has been rebuilt: this has been done very regularly, and the streets, though narrow, are good. The " Plaza" is also perfectly regular, surrounded by arcades ; all the windows are numbered, with a view to letting them out at bull-fights ; the municipality, on letting the houses, reserve the windows on these occasions, when the occupiers must vacate.

We went to the Hôtel Français, kept by a Frenchman, named La Fille, who, involved in some affaire d'opinion at Brest, established himself here : the promises held out by the approach were anything but attractive. The entrance was occupied by a cobbler, with all the sweet-smelling accompaniments of his trade ; this led to a dark and dirty staircase, and on the second floor we found the apartments, which did not look at all inviting, and yet, on trial, they turned out far more comfortable than we expected, and the living very good.

Immediately after our arrival, we went to deliver the letters the Consul of Bayonne had given us : one was for Mr. B——, the English vice-consul, who was not at home ; but we found Mr. Ybar, a young man speaking English very well. We were fortunate in meeting him, for he most obligingly devoted himself to us, and to his attention we are indebted for our pleasant visit to San Sebastian.

He accompanied us in our walk to the citadel. It occupies the summit of the rock, at the foot of which the town is built; the view from this point is very fine — a magnificent extent of sea. The town and its little harbour stand below — beyond, an extensive view over the country, bounded by heights and wood, and studded with ruined houses—the tender recollection of *Christian* occupation. The commanding height, on which is an old tower, formerly used as a light-house, and up which Lord John Hay contrived to drag one or two guns during the war, forms the southern boundary of the bay, where the bathing is admirable, and whose smooth strand makes St. Sebastian a favourite watering place.

We then visited the church, which in its interior is handsome—in the same style as that of Irun, but not so rich: it stands in that little slip of houses which were not destroyed by the English, being reserved for lodgings. We saw afterwards, the part of the works near the river, where the English stormed the town, and continued our walk until dinner time, which meal

204   ACCOMMODATION.

was, unluckily, a bad attempt at a " diner à
l'Anglaise," that is, a tough, under-done, bad
beef-steak : however, we had other things, and
so fared tolerably well ; and our beds proved far
better than we expected.

205

CHAPTER XI.

Splendid Fête at St. Sebastian — Good Music — Spanish
Hospitality—Walk to Passages—Evening Promenade—
The Fandango.

Thursday, June 10.—Was a great day at San
Sebastian, La Fête Dieu, and we were lucky to
come in for it. In Spain, the fêtes are still
held on the days they occur; in France, they are
postponed to the following Sunday: it is in
contemplation to introduce the same practice
into Spain. Women are no longer permitted to
become nuns in Spain, and all the monasteries
have been done away with. Mr. Ybar, and his
pretty sister Candida, called on us, and we
went to the church. The gentlemen sat in a
gallery, arranged with stalls, like a cathedral;
the ladies were all in the aisle, and the universal
mantilla, worn over, in many instances, gaily-
embroidered shawls of Merino, looked very well.

206   LA FÊTE DIEU.

Last night I bought one, and therefore took my place in due form.

The choir and organ, with some amateur musicians, vocal and instrumental, were in the gallery where the men sat, and we had a good deal of Rossini's music, some airs from his most beautiful operas being performed in the instrumental parts. The chants, however, were sacred; and a young man, a pupil of Rubini's, who had been for three years in London, sang a solo, with a fine voice.

The church ceremony lasted about an hour, and then the procession began: the streets through which it passed were strewed with rushes, and the balconies ornamented with hangings, some of tapestry, some of silk, some of simple white cotton, but altogether producing a gay effect.

Troops lined the streets, and at intervals the guns of the citadel fired. The procession opened with three men, in full-dress liveries; two of them played on a pipe, which they stopped with one hand, and beat the drum with the other; the third played on a larger drum; the air, a kind of plaintive march, the music and instruments purely Basques, and of the most remote antiquity.

A number of the Bourgeois, walking two and two, were followed by a company of the Engineers and their band, very fine-looking troops. To these succeeded a company of Grenadiers; and then came the holy part of the procession, the leading dignitary under an embroidered canopy, upon which the spectators threw rose-leaves from the windows; he carried the Host, and was supported by two priests, others walking by the side, and two incense bearers before him. He was preceded by a priest, bearing a standard of embroidered yellow silk, of high antiquity, and in the form of half a cross: a lamb was embroidered on it; the priest was supported by two gentlemen in full dress.

Immediately after the canopy, came the general commanding the district, supported by the mayor and his adjunct. We got excellent places in the house of Mr. Caillié, who had been for some time in the United States: near his house stood the colonel of the regiment, who kept the lines and the colours of the regiment: they were laid flat on the ground before the priest, when the procession halted, the priest came forward, and whilst all the assistants were on their knees, he blessed the colours, by moving the Host over them, and afterwards walked upon them, to shew the superiority of the church over everything : he then returned to the canopy, and the procession proceeded.

Opposite to Mr. Caillié's house a piece of carpet was spread; and a little lower in the street, the procession stopped, that the people might receive a blessing : this was very striking ; every soul, troops and all, were on their knees, and a feeling of the deepest reverence seemed universal.   At Mr. Caillié's there was a large assembly, the ladies well dressed, all wearing the becoming mantilla, and among them were some very pretty girls.   We had, for refreshments, strawberries, cakes, and sweet wine.

We then went to Mr. Ybar's house, to see the procession on its return : here were other ladies assembled, and more refreshments, and afterwards we had some good music.   Two gentlemen sang some beautiful Spanish airs to a guitar accompaniment, and then some ladies alternately took the instrument, and delighted us by the graceful and plaintive manner in which they sang.   I understood that the greatest equality exists in society.   Every person in the town, high and low, is known to his neighbour, and rich and poor are on a certain footing of intimacy: amongst those at Mr. Ybar's to-day, were two pretty girls who earned their livelihood with their needle. There is not a carriage in the town.

The ceremony over, we went home, and the town was so quiet, that it was evident every one did the same thing. W—— afterwards called on Mr. B——, and from his handsome wife got some intelligence about Spain. She has just returned from Madrid and Valencia, and said the diligence is the only mode of travelling—and the hotels are wretched, even at Madrid.

About six o'clock, Mr. Ybar called to walk with us towards Passages ; and it was a charming expedition. We crossed the bridge over the Irumea, where excellent salmon are taken ; and, ascending a hill of some height, had a fine view of the rich valley of Loyola, through which the river flows.

This valley gave birth to the great founder of the order of the Jesuits, and the view is very beautiful. I find that land is high in Guispuzcoa, not yielding in general more than $2\frac{1}{2}$ per cent. Tenants are very seldom dispossessed, and generally hold on for generations, from father to son : a common mode of letting, is for the landlord

210   SPANISH COSTUME.

to give the house and seed—the farmer tills the
ground, and they divide the crop.

It is supposed that the " Fueros" will be
confirmed,—except that the contribution to the
state, instead of being, as under the old regime,
in name at least, voluntary, will be fixed;
but the mode of taxation left to the states.
We and our obliging cicerone crossed over
to the new road leading to Passages, and
from a high part of it, called, I think, " the View
of two Crosses," we saw it, or rather the steep
heights which form its narrow entrance. On
the top, is the fort, still called Lord John Hay;
the harbour is excellent, but of difficult access.
We hastened back to see the promenade, which
was very interesting; the ladies still wearing
their mantillas, and the peasantry attired in
their holiday costume, but contrary to the usual
habits of other nations, the dress of the men
was far more brilliant and varied than that of
the women.   Many had embroidered waistcoats,
and short blue cloth jackets, ornamented with
patterns of different coloured leather on the
sleeves and back; the high conical-shaped hat,
which gives such a picturesque, as well as
aristocratic look to the Basque peasantry, was

adorned with feathers, and the cloak, thrown over one shoulder, was worn with true Spanish grace.

Some of the women of the lower orders, had, indeed, petticoats of a bright-red, or yellow cloth; the black mantillas, however, invariably covered the neck and shoulders—and the most common colour amongst the older women was black.

In several different parts of the promenade, dancing was going on. Sometimes the fandango, with its lively accompaniment of castanets, was in full force, but the favourite seemed to be an old Basque dance, something resembling a gavotte I remember learning as a child, in which the graceful pas de Basque occurs constantly; and this they executed with much ease and grace.

I was amused at the stately and decorous distance at which the gentlemen and ladies, (of the higher orders, I mean,) walked from each other. The moment we returned from Passages, and approached the promenade, Mr. Y——'s pretty sisters came and took me with them, and we paraded up and down, leaving W——, and their brother, and one or two other friends to walk up and down at a respectful distance; and this lasted during the whole evening, no words passing between the different sexes, though to judge by the eloquent language of the dark eyes, which glanced from under the graceful folds of black-lace mantillas, and the gratified smile which lighted up the handsome features of some of the aristocratic-looking youths as the fair ones passed by, they were well known to each other.

" When do you ever speak to those gentlemen, who appear so delighted to see you?" I inquired of a pretty blushing young girl who had joined our party.

" Only when we dance," she replied. " Yonder caballero was my partner last Sunday at the ball; he is my cousin too, but he never spoke to me till we danced together that evening, which was my first ball."

Friday, June 11.—Though we started exactly at six, on our return to Bayonne, our attentive friend M. Ybar was at the office to see us off. After leaving the ruined church, and the walls which shew how much the neighbourhood of St. Sebastian suffered during the late war, we ascended the steep hill which leads to Hernani.

Sketched by Lady Chatterton

G.Rowe, lith. Chelts.

THE FORT and LIGHT-HOUSE of St SEBASTIAN, SPAIN.

On the summit of the next height I sketched the view here given. Met a number of carts loaded with barrel staves, a great export from San Sebastian. Cocoa-nut shells are also exported to Dublin, to make for the Irish that preparation of cocoa, known by the attractive appellation of "miserable." Barrels are sent to Bilboa, I think, which has a considerable export trade in flour.

The cart drawn by two oxen is universal in the Basque Provinces — here the carts have wooden-wheels, crossed and shod with iron. The oxen are all of the same colour, a dingy yellow, and have the same curious covering of sheep-skin on their heads. On approaching the old town of Ouyarzon, or Ourgunzun, I made the sketch which is given at page 251.

The peasants are now occupied with their maize. We had a rapid descent to Hernani, changed horses, as before, at Astigaragga, and about ten, reached Behobie, on the French side of the Bidasoa. Here we breakfasted, and went through the ordeal of the French Custom-House, which is very strict. The Spanish bread is so much better than the French that we bought a loaf at Irun; it was only by courtesy that it

214   ARRIVAL AT BIARRITTS.

passed duty free.   I wore my mantilla, otherwise it would have paid duty.

We reached Bayonne at three, and after
making our arrangements, packing up, &c.,
proceeded by post to Biaritts, where we took
possession of Madame Esperon's house, which
promises to suit us very well.   How we have
since enjoyed the charming air from the heights
overlooking the sea !   The unceremonious, independent life we lead, is delightful.   We have
the place almost to ourselves.

215

CHAPTER XII.

Legend of Urtubi Castle—Louis XI. and Beltran de Cueva.

THERE is a story connected with so many of the beautiful and interesting places on the borders of Spain and France, that I must relate it.

Towards the end of the fifteenth century, the Castle of Urtubi, which we passed on the road to St. Sebastian, belonged to Count de Montreal. He was a valiant knight, and, like most others in those times, devoted to war, but he also enjoyed the short intervals of peace which border strife, and internal feuds and dissensions, sometimes afforded. The Count de Montreal's daughter was universally acknowledged to be the most lovely girl in all Pays Basque. Even many Spanish knights, whose eyes had been rejoiced by a sight of her loveliness during a short visit she once paid to her aunt, at Hernani, maintained that Spain itself could not boast of such a beauty. Elvira de Montreal was, besides, sole heiress to all her father's broad lands and feudal castles; and of course her hand was eagerly sought by many a valiant knight and powerful noble. But her father loved her better than anything in the world, and, contrary to the usual habit of those times, he declared that he would never control her choice, but allow her full power to select according to her fancy, provided the family of her husband was noble. Elvira's lot, then, appeared most enviable; yet, in the midst of all this apparent happiness, a cloud was often noticed on her fair brow, and it was evident that not one of all her admirers had power to awaken a feeling of interest in her heart. Some persons whispered that a favourite page of her mother's, whose birth was of low degree, had secretly won her affections; others observed that it was only since the short visit to Spain, when she attended a tournament at Hernani, that the cheerful buoyancy of spirits seemed gone.

That visit was made during one of the short truces which very rarely occurred in those days of border warfare. Since then a regular war had broken out between France and Spain, and

daily skirmishes took place between the chiefs
on either side of the Bidasoa. This state of
things had continued about a year, when a
rumour arose that peace was about to be established between the two countries. It was even
said that Louis XI., who had lately made a pilgrimage to Nôtre Dame de Sarrance, in the Valley d'Aspe, was coming to visit Urtubi, for the
purpose of carrying on negotiations; and that
the Kings of Aragon and Castile had quitted
their kingdoms, and, confiding in the honour of
Louis XI., were about to trust themselves within
the French territory.

Little was said on these important subjects at
the Castle of Urtubi, but preparations were
made, as if for the reception of guests of distinction. The state chamber was hung with
new arras, and broiderers were busily employed
to adorn the satin hangings and bed-furniture
with new and cunning devices, and even the fair
hands of Elvira and her stately lady mother were
occupied in embroidering a prie-dieu of unusual
magnificence. In short, all was bustle and
anxious expectation amid the numerous inhabitants of Urtubi, and the neighbouring town of
Urugne.

Elvira, too, seemed in expectation of some joyful event; her step became lighter, and often, during the long hours she sate at work, she would sing the wild airs of her country with all her former glee.

The only person who did not seem to participate in the bustle and joyous anticipation was Rudolf, the favourite page of the Countess de Montreal. He wandered about the castle with a listless air; his voice, which was wont to cheer the maidens at their work, was now silent, and his lute unstrung. Yet Elvira spoke kindly as usual to him, and even once inquired the reason of his depressed spirits. Rudolf answered with a pettish, haughty air, which called forth a rebuke from the stately Countess. But she was a kind dame, though somewhat proud, and so full of respect for her own and husband's family, and so occupied in the maintenance of state, that she had little time to think of anything else. Yet, when she saw the look of deep sorrow her rebuke had caused on the handsome countenance of her favourite page, she said—

" Well, I suppose it is all my own fault. I have spoilt you by allowing one of such low degree to associate with ourselves, and by praising your singing and verses. There, never

mind it, now.   Go and send Madelaine to me, I
want to tell her about the new toilette table in
the purple chamber."

Rudolf obeyed her commands, but the kind
words of his mistress failed to clear up the dark
cloud that lowered on his brow.   Muttering
some inaudible words, he hurried through the
long corridors, and as soon as he found Madelaine, and commanded her with a haughty air
to attend the Countess, he left the castle by a
small postern gate on the south side, and proceeded through the thick woods, which covered
then, as they do now, the height where the
castle stands.   Rudolf had hitherto been considered an amiable as well as clever youth ; but as
yet the world had gone well with him—he had
been successful far beyond his expectations ;
but he was of those characters whose qualities,
both good and bad, seem only to become fully
developed by misfortune.   And perhaps he had
been till now as ignorant as most other people
of his own real character.   He was foster-
brother to Elvira, and from earliest childhood
had lived in the castle, and been loved and
caressed by its inmates.   He was now surprised
at the bitterness and violence of his own feelings
as he paced up and down the dark recesses of the

forest.   He may have thought, like Words-
worth's Borderer :—

> " Action is transitory—a step, a blow,
>   The motion of a muscle, this way or that ;
>   'Tis done, and in the after-vacancy
>   We wonder at ourselves like men betrayed :
>   Suffering is permanent, obscure and dark,
>   And shares the nature of infinity."

After some moments of deep thought, he
muttered — " Yes, I will accept their offer.
Those vile, presumptuous Spaniards shall be en-
snared, for she loves one of those dark nobles of
Castile : I have marked her well.   But she
shall be mine, though millions perish—though
this fair land be again deluged in blood, and
those proud towers consumed with fire ; and the
poor serf of low degree, to whom even the use of
arms is forbidden—the despised page, shall excite
the discord, and kindle the flame. "

That night Rudolf was absent from the castle,
and no one knew where ; but the next morning
he resumed his usual duties with unwonted
alacrity, and received, in consequence, the com-
mendations of his mistress, and even an approving smile from the Lady Elvira.   The following evening, King Louis, attended by a

brilliant retinue, was expected to arrive. The
Countess, who delighted in state and grandeur,
was beyond measure pleased at the prospect of a
visit from her sovereign. Though the last fortnight had been occupied in preparing for his
reception, yet she had scarcely believed it possible such a glorious and joyful event would
actually occur. She had never before seen the
King—for the Count, who was aware of the
dangers of the capital, would never consent to
gratify her ardent desire to visit Paris and attend
the court. He did not now look upon the intended visit of Louis with so much joy—on the
contrary, he dreaded the approach of such a wily
politician as the King, surrounded too, as he
was, by lawless followers and unprincipled
divines; but he scarcely expected that such a
timid man as Louis XI. would think of venturing
so near the confines of Spain—that country which
had been so long at war with France, and Urtubi
Castle being only about two hours march from
the Bidasoa, which was then, as it is still, the
narrow boundary between the two countries.

As the hour of the King's expected arrival approached, the principal inmates of the castle
went up to the battlements, and gazed in the

222   THE FATHER'S FEARS.

direction of St. Jean de Luz. The Count appeared unusually thoughtful, and he looked with
some uneasiness on the beautiful countenance
of his daughter. The father and child both
seemed as if oppressed by some apprehension.
They soon forgot to gaze on the road where
the gorgeous retinue of Louis was to appear,
and moved slowly towards the other side of the
battlements.   When they had reached the
western turret, which commanded a view of the
road to Spain, Elvira said—

" I see, my dearest father, you are apprehensive about this visit. What are your fears ?"

" Dearest child, it is only on your account
that I dread it. I well know Louis would not
venture here without some powerful motive;
and still less do I think it likely that the sovereigns of Spain would trust themselves in
France, the country of their bitter enemy. The
alleged reason that Louis gives for coming here
to meet them is, I think, only a pretext. All
I fear is, that he may covet the rich heritage to
which you will succeed, for some of his favou-
rites ; and thus the anxiety I have always
felt, that my darling child may marry a man she
can really love may be frustrated. I now almost

wish I had persuaded you to accept the Lord of Orthez. He, at least, would have loved and protected you."

" Ah ! do not regret it, dearest father, I could never have loved him ; and I would rather die than——"

" Yet, my dear child, remember that all damsels but yourself are disposed of by their parents, and they often have not even seen their intended husband. Thus your mother, darling, was betrothed to me, and we never saw each other till the day before our marriage."

" It is very true ; but you, dear father, have taught me better things, and—and——"

" Wherefore that blush ? I sometimes think you have seen the person you would like to wed. Yet, of all the noblesse I have seen, there is not one who is worthy of you."

The Count cast a scrutinizing glance towards the Page Rudolf, who stood with the Countess at the further end of the battlements.

" Tell me the truth, dear child," said the Count.

Elvira blushed still more deeply, she trembled, and was about to reply ; but at that moment a shout was heard.

" They are coming !" exclaimed the Countess, clapping her hands.—" Joy ! joy !—we shall indeed have the honour of receiving our sovereign within these walls. See how gracefully he sits on his palfrey !—and what a handsome knight that is on his right! See how gallantly he manages his charger ! But come, let us hasten down to greet them."

A splendid banquet had been prepared, and, soon after the King's arrival, the whole party sat down in the knights' hall. A table at the upper end, on a raised dais, was reserved for those highest in rank ; and there the King, with a few of his favourite followers, was placed.

" I find that fame has for once spoken the truth,—or, rather, not said enough," exclaimed the King, whose penetrating eyes had been riveted on the fair countenance of Elvira. " Your daughter is even more lovely than I expected ; though nothing seems to be talked of in these parts but her beauty. It is a pity, Count, you have concealed such a rich jewel so long from our gaze. And how comes it, too, that she is still unmarried ? Are there no valiant knights in Bearn or Foix worthy of such a prize ?"

Poor Elvira was much embarrassed.   The

King perceived it, and endeavoured to relieve her, by saying, " Well, blush not, fair one, I do not seek to penetrate the secret of your heart. Nay, look up," he whispered, in a lower tone; " be not afraid! I do not come to control your feelings or act the tyrant, though I know your father suspects me of such a design. But," he continued, in a gayer though still low tone, " it is the faculty of kings to see further than others ; and what if I knew, better than even your father himself, the real wishes of that little heart?"

Louis paused to see the effect of his words, and then, bending still nearer, he whispered one single word in her ear which made her start, and overspread her countenance with blushes. She raised her eyes in astonishment, and gazed with joy and hope into the face of Louis.

" Ha, I am right!" said he, with a low, chuckling laugh, " I see the blessed Lady of Sarrance has granted my prayers, and enables me to be the good genius of my people, to see into their hearts and gratify their wishes. Well, say nothing of this to any one,* but trust with confi-

---

* It is not at all improbable that Louis XI. may have been well informed on the apparently trivial subject of the fair heiress of Montreal's secret feelings, for he maintained spies

dence in the future. My lord Count," continued Louis, turning towards his host, and speaking in a loud voice, " I fear we must be further
burdensome on your hospitality. To-morrow,
at noon, I expect that our renowned cousins of
Castile and Aragon will come to speak with me
on some important matters,—say, can your
hospitable halls receive them? You start!—per-

in every part of his dominions ; and so great was his anxiety
to obtain information from different parts of his kingdom,
that one of the first acts of his reign was the establishment of
the post. That blessing, an offset to the many evils of that
cruel king's reign, was first established, in France, in 1464.

He moved about, too, with wonderful speed and secrecy ;
in order to ascertain, by personal observation, whether the
information he received was correct, or to negotiate in
person some treaty with foreign nations. His visit to
Urtubi Castle was probably soon after his brother's death,
whom he is said to have poisoned; and his departure from
Tours, on this southern expedition, is thus described by the
old historian, Monstrelet :—

" On Saturday morning, the 14th of March, the king,
who then resided at Plessis du Parc, formerly called Montils
les Tours, set off very early, and with a few attendants,
for Bordeaux and Bayonne. That no person living might
follow him, he ordered the gates of Tours to be closed until
ten o'clock had struck ; and had a bridge broken down near
to Tours, to prevent any one crossing the river. For further
security, he commanded the Lord de Gaucourt, the captain
of the gentlemen in his household, to remain in Tours, for
the same purpose."

haps you dread the approach of those who have
been hitherto always our enemies. Yet, fear
nothing ; this interview will, under our Lady of
Clery's blessed protection, prove of inestimable
benefit to our beloved country."

The Count replied that nothing would give him
more pleasure than to receive such illustrious
guests. " But I knew not that they were
within many days' journey of the frontier," he
added.

" Last night they reached Hernani, and were
graciously entertained by its duke, the Prince of
Leon,—who is, as you may know, a near kinsman of the King of Castile, and whose son,
Don Garcia de Leon, will accompany their majesties here to-morrow."

The King cast a hasty glance towards Elvira,
who endeavoured to conceal the embarrassment
she felt.

" This night," continued the King, without
noticing her blushes, " their majesties pass at
Fontarabia, in the royal palace of the sovereigns
of Castile ; and to-morrow, about the hour of
noon, they will reach this place."

" We shall, indeed, be most honoured !" exclaimed the Countess. " I well remember Don

Garcia, who won the chief prize at the Hernani tournament, and received it from my daughter's hands. We shall be most highly honoured by a visit from their august majesties."

But the pleasure she felt at the expected honour was contending in her mind, with some embarrassment, as to how such a numerous host could be lodged. The King had already brought more than double the number of· followers she had expected; and besides those lodged at the castle, she learnt that the adjoining towns of Urugne and St. Jean de Luz were filled with his guards and retinue.

" Do not be uneasy, Lady," said the King, who instantly divined her thoughts; " our noble cousins will only take their mid-day banquet within these walls, and, after conferring with me on the welfare of our dear countries, will depart, and return to Fontarabia."

" But surely they will bring a large force with them," said the Count. " No Spaniard has been known to cross the Bidasoa unarmed since the expiration of the last truce; and surely the Kings——"

" Fear not, brave Count, they come with peaceful intentions, attended only by twenty followers. They wisely put faith in their brother's kindly feelings, who is anxious to restore that peace which my poor brother of Guienne was the unfortunate means of troubling. Peace be to his blessed soul!" continued the King, with a deep sigh, as he devoutly crossed himself.

When the banquet was ended, the minstrels, who as usual were stationed in the gallery above, struck up a lively air, and the dance began. The handsome knight, the Duke of Alençon, led forth Elvira ; and her mother remarked, with a triumphant smile, to her lord— " Well, I think at last our child has found a noble worthy of her hand. See how joyous she looks ; I have not seen her so happy for a long time. And, indeed, the noble Duke of Alençon would be a princely match !"

" I like not his countenance," said the Count, with some anxiety, " and am surprised to see that Elvira smiles so graciously, and listens with any patience to his foolish discourse."

" And so she ought ! Surely the King's near relative is not to be despised."

Elvira did, indeed, appear radiant with happiness, and smiled graciously at all the compliments the young Duke poured into her ear ; but

230   THE KING AND THE PAGE.

her thoughts were far away, and she several
times betrayed by her answers that she did not
even hear his enthusiastic praises.

In the mean time the page, Rudolf, watched
everything that passed. This handsome youth
had not escaped the King's notice. He had stood
behind Elvira's chair during the banquet; and
once, when he approached to present a golden
salver to the Count, Louis said something to
him in a low tone, which had such an effect that
he turned deadly pale, and nearly let the salver
fall.

———

"How strange," thought Elvira, as she leaned
over the battlements the following morning,
and anxiously watched the road from Spain,
along which the sovereigns were expected,
"that this King Louis, whose very name always
made me tremble, should be acquainted with my
most secret thoughts—should know what I have
never breathed to a human being, not even to
my dear father. Indeed, it is only lately that
I have suspected it myself, for Don Garcia did
not say anything." And here Elvira fell into a

reverie,—one of those deep fits of musing in which thoughts are too vague to be expressed by words.

The whole scene of that memorable tournament at Hernani passed before her eyes. She saw the broad arena, filled with splendid warriors in their gayest attire, distinct and vivid as when the May-day sun illumined those richly-carved balconies, and glistened on the jewelled circlets of many a Spanish fair; she saw the heights of Santa Barbara, with its ancient fortress, defined against the clear blue sky, and heard the flourish of trumpets and the touching tones of the Basque pipes playing the old national air.* But among all the noble knights and brilliant dames which she recalled to her memory, a single form was most conspicuous. She remembered the exact spot where he first arrested her attention. She followed his every movement; again her heart beat high with agitation,—for at one time he swerved in his saddle, and the followers of his opponent uttered a shout of exultation; but fear was turned into

---

* This air is still played on all state occasions, and we heard it the other day in the processions at St. Sebastian.

joy when she beheld him vanquish every ob-
stacle, and gracefully approach to receive from
her hands the prize awarded to the conqueror.

Elvira was on the battlements alone, yet she
covered her face with her hands, to conceal the
blushes which a recollection of the pressure of
his hand occasioned.   Then every word he uttered during the banquet and the dance was
again repeated—every look pondered over ; and
her own impressions of the eventful day, on
retiring to rest.   Then those sweet, thrilling
tones which brought her to the window.   The
blissful recognition of his voice, the air, the
words he sang, are ever present to her mind,
and she clasps her hands in an ecstasy of delight.

But the morrow : alas! he had not appeared,
she never heard anything more of him.   Poor
Elvira !—a tear has replaced that beaming glance
which so lately danced in her eyes.   Hark !—a
trumpet is heard.   They come !   Yes, there
is the banner of Castile waving over the height
behind Urungne ; that of Aragon, too; and—oh,
joy ! there follows the White Lion—that well-
known emblem which had so often appeared in
her happiest dreams, the banner of Don Garcia
de Leon.

King Louis was right: the train consisted exactly of twenty men, not one more; and it arrived at the very hour he said. Strange that these two rival kings should venture together, and with so few followers, into the country of their bitter enemy.

" He is a wonderful man !" thought Elvira ; and a feeling of hope was again awakened in her heart.

" Your presence is required. The Lady Countess bade me inform you that their majesties are arrived," said Rudolf, gazing on her with an expression of more ardent and determined admiration than his speaking eyes had ever yet expressed. Elvira shuddered as she met his glance—why, she knew not, for she had always loved the page almost as a brother.

" You are much changed, Rudolf," she said, with a gentle tone.

" So is the Lady Elvira ; and the whole world is changed !" he exclaimed, with a bitter laugh, as he followed her down the winding turret stair.

The Kings had retired to a private conference before Elvira reached the reception hall ; but

234 GARCIA'S DISAPPEARANCE EXPLAINED.

among their followers she descried Don Garcia, in earnest conversation with her mother. But I will not describe their meeting, the blushes of Elvira, or the delight of Garcia—I will only say that her image had never been absent from his mind during the year which had passed since their first and last meeting.

The reason of his sudden disappearance the morning of her departure was soon explained. His cousin, the Lord of Pampeluna, had sent to crave his assistance against an attack of the Count of Armagnac. Not an instant was to be lost, but he trusted in a few days to have been able to return to Hernani, and never contemplated the possibility of any occurrence that would then prevent his proceeding at once to Elvira's castle, and endeavour to obtain her hand. But before he was able to leave Pampeluna, war again broke out between the two countries, and the Bidasoa became an insurmountable barrier to any approach to Urtubi. Thus passed a year; and it may be imagined that Don Garcia received the summons of his sovereign to attend him to Elvira's abode with no small joy. Yet still he feared the Count of Montreal might not consent to the marriage of his daughter with the native of a country so often at war with France; and even now, as he stood with Elvira in the deep recess of a bay window that looked on the river, he feared that their blissful meeting would soon be brought to an end; but the beautiful girl looked so beaming with delight, and she spoke so confidently of her father's wish for her happiness, that he gave himself up to joy.

In less than an hour, during which the politic Louis had contrived to conclude a treaty with Spain greatly advantageous to France, the door opened, and Louis, followed by Count Montreal, entered the room.

" I have no objection, Sire, provided my daughter consents; on the contrary, I well know that a more valiant and amiable knight than Don Garcia does not exist in all Spain."

" Well, we shall see !" said Louis, with a malicious smile, approaching the window where Elvira stood. " Fair vassal, we have determined to exercise our royal privilege, and dispose of this pretty hand in marriage. The treaty between our country and Spain is ready for signature ; but one condition remains to be ful-

filled, and I trust you will not prevent the desired peace by any unruly objection."

While Louis was saying this, Don Garcia,
who had never seen the King of France till that
morning, and who knew not that he had any
kindly feelings towards himself, gazed with horror and apprehension on his sinister countenance, and was about to interfere with some
warm assertion of the lady's right to dispose of
herself in marriage, when the King, turning to
him, and taking his hand, said—

" Stay, Sir Knight, I guess what you are
going to say. I know your thoughts ; but I shall
soon see these haughty looks brought low. Ay,
and on your bended knee you will do homage to
me as your lawful sovereign. Nay, do not seize
the handle of your sword ! Your own King of
Castile is safe, and will presently appear. But
kneel, Sir Knight, kneel at this fair lady's feet,
and crave her hand ; and if you cannot win her
heart, you are no true knight. Ah ! I knew
how it would be. Well, well, I forgive you ;
and may you both be happy ! Such a sight
as that really makes me feel almost young
again ? Well, Sir Count, does your daughter
look very miserable ? Have I put a tyrannical

force on her inclinations ?   Shall we need the aid of dungeons and iron cages to enforce obedience ?"

***

The royal guests had departed from Urtubi. Don Garcia remained for a few days with his intended bride, and then proceeded to Hernani, to make preparations for her reception.. The marriage was to take place in less than a month. The estates of Count Montreal and those of Don Garcia's father were both of great extent, and formed, for many miles, the border between France and Spain,—the Duke of Leon's extending as far as the ancient town of Fontarabia, and those of Montreal to Hendaye; thus, the union of these two houses by marriage was a measure very likely to ensure a continuance of peace between the countries. Louis, who by means of the new plan of posts, obtained what appeared then to be a miraculous knowledge of all that was going on in his dominions, had calculated right, and returned to his favourite residence of Plessis les Tours, in high spirits at the success of his negotiations. But in this turbu-

238   BELTRAN DE CUEVA.

lent world, and particularly in the restless and
unprincipled fifteenth century, the best formed
schemes for peace were often overturned.

Henry IV., of Castile, had been accompanied
to Urtubi by his favourite Beltran de Cueva, a
man who, originally a page, had risen to the most
important offices in the kingdom. Wily and
politic as King Louis himself, Beltran had long
been in correspondence with that monarch, and
he had suggested the expediency of cementing
the peace by a marriage between the great
border houses.

Full of his own projects of aggrandizement,
and dreading the faction which upheld the Infanta
Isabella, the King's sister, in her rights of succession to the crown, he was anxiously desirous
to obtain the assistance of France. He had not,
however, seen the lovely heiress of Montreal
before the peace was concluded, and the marriage
contract signed; but ere the kings left the castle,
he was presented to Elvira. She had heard
many sinister reports about him, and therefore
it was with a shudder that she replied to his
whispered compliments, and she looked on him
with a cold haughtiness which made a deep and
lasting impression on the upstart Duke.

During the time of preparation for the marriage, Rudolf was often absent from the castle. Elvira, who observed with sorrow the great change in his disposition, began to fear that the surmises of her attendant Barbara were right, and that the poor youth had indulged a foolish love for herself. Several times she was on the point of speaking about him to her father, or Don Garcia, but a feeling of timidity always kept her silent. There was at times a ferocity in his looks which made her tremble, and she felt a vague kind of apprehension when his melancholy eyes were fixed on her, as if there was some fearful spell in their ardent gaze.

A few evenings before the day fixed for the marriage, and after Elvira had retired to rest, Barbara rushed into her room, with looks of horror :

" Oh, dearest lady !" she exclaimed, " may St. Jean and all the saints protect us !—the country is up in arms again ! They say, Don Garcia's people have been attacked, by some of our own lord's vassals, at Behobie ; and all Hernani is up in arms, and thousands of Spaniards are crossing the Bidasoa, to come and besiege us."

Elvira, in great alarm, ran to her father's

room.   The strange tidings had already reached
him, and he was hastily buckling on his armour.

"Fear not, my child," he exclaimed; "it is
doubtless only an outbreak of our lawless
peasantry of the Bastan.   They were ever a
turbulent set, and difficult to keep in order.
They have been discontented ever since peace
was declared.   Nay, do not tremble, dearest
girl—I have already dispatched a messenger to
the Lord of Orthez, for more assistance to quell
this rebellion."

"To the Lord of Orthez, father!   Surely,
were it not better to send for Don Garcia?"
said Elvira, whose fears were increased by hearing of the approach of a rejected and disappointed
suitor.   "Surely, since——"

"Foolish girl! know you not that the moment these border feuds break out there is no
possibility of sending a messenger across the
Bidasoa? and if the Spaniards attack us——
but hark! what do I hear?—an armed force approaching on the road from Spain?"

"Joy—joy! it must be Don Garcia himself,"
thought Elvira.

The Count had hurried down to the barbican,
and Elvira and her mother ran to the window

that looked towards the road from Spain. It was a clear moonlight—one of those warm, glowing nights which the southern atmosphere alone can give; and they could see the armed force which had approached—but, alas, Elvira looked in vain for the well-known banner of Don Garcia! The standard of Castile was indeed there, but no White Lion could be seen.

"Let me see," exclaimed the Countess, "three boars' heads, gules, in a field, azure—whose device can it be? That banner was here on the day of the conference—I noticed it well. Yes, now I remember—it is that of the King's favourite, Beltran de Cueva."

"Beltran de Cueva!" said Elvira, shuddering with horror. "Oh, that Don Garcia were here! See, he has crossed the drawbridge—oh, God, protect us! Ah! thank Heaven, the others are not admitted! I trust my father will not accede to his proposal, whatever it may be—he can mean us no good."

"Foolish girl! what do you fear?" said the Countess, who liked excitement and change. She had been much struck with the handsome favourite; and his honeyed compliments had made a deep impression on a disposition some-

242   CUEVA'S INSOLENT DEMAND.

what vain. " I am sure all will be well now that the noble Chancellor of Castile is come himself to visit us. But bless me, what do I see—he is departing again so soon! Gracious Heaven ! see, his troops surround the castle !"

Elvira breathed more freely. With the instinctive feeling of dislike which innocence and purity often has for vice, she dreaded the presence and apparent friendship of that lawless noble more · than the formidable army which now surrounded the castle.

At this moment the Count entered the room, with a hurried air and disturbed countenance.

" You must prepare for instant flight; there is no hope of maintaining peace with Spain but on conditions too ignominious to accept. The base-born Cueva has had the audacity to demand your hand in marriage, my darling child, and insolently to bid me to break my faith with your betrothed husband."

" But where is Don Garcia !—oh, tell me,—is he safe ? Surely they must have used base stratagem and violence to prevent his coming to our assistance."

" All is ready," exclaimed the Page Rudolf,

rushing into the room; "and not a moment to be lost. They are forcing the barbacan, and in five minutes they may have entered the castle if we do not receive a reinforcement."

"Go, then, my darling child—my dearest wife! I trust we shall soon meet again; in the meantime, Rudolf and Pierre will conduct you by the secret passage to Bayonne, where you will be quite secure till this sad outbreak be quelled. But why do you tremble so, my darling child?"

Elvira was indeed terrified. She dreaded falling into the hands of the base Cueva—but to fly under the protection of Rudolf filled her with other and vague apprehensions of a scarcely less painful nature. However, there seemed no alternative. She endeavoured, indeed, to persuade her father to accompany them, but his sense of honour was so great that nothing would induce him to quit the castle.

The party proceeded in silence through the long, dark, subterranean passage, which led towards St. Jean de Luz. Besides Rudolf, the ladies were attended by two men at arms; and the Countess, who had several times before been obliged to fly by this passage from the hostile troops of Spain, felt much less apprehension than her daughter. Her love, too, for excitement and adventure nearly equalled her fondness for splendour and display; therefore she proceeded almost gaily along the dismal passage. Not so Elvira; for the last time they had been obliged to fly she was quite a child, and her heart now sank as she quitted the abode of her youth.

Rudolf rode by her side, and endeavoured, with more tenderness in his manner than she at all liked, to cheer her drooping spirits. She saw, too, now and then, by the flickering light of the torches, that a smile of triumph played on the Page's handsome countenance, and she began bitterly to regret that she had never mentioned her suspicions about him to her dear father. But it was now too late even to return, they had reached the mouth of the subterranean passage. The ponderous iron gate turned on its rusty hinges, and closed behind them with a clang that sounded to poor Elvira like the death-knell of her hopes. The torches were extinguished, they emerged into the thick forest which, in those days, spread over the mountain's side and extended down to the gates of St. Jean de Luz. The bright moon-beams scarcely penetrated the thick chesnut and cork trees, and gave the

travellers much less light than the torches had
afforded ; yet, here and there, the spectral moonbeams gleamed on the white twisted roots
and speckled stems of the beeches, making
them shine like huge serpents, and adding to
the horrors of the path.

" Are you certain of the road ?" inquired
Elvira of Rudolf, " do not we pass through St.
Jean de Luz ?"

" We must avoid it, lady, for the towns-peo-
ple are ill-affected towards us, and a report
reached the castle that they had given it up to
the Spaniards.   We shall be obliged to make a
detour to the north."

" Then how are we to cross the water ?"
inquired Elvira ; " surely would it not be better
to traverse the high-road, and proceed some way
up the stream where it is narrow ?"

" Fear not, lady, we shall find a boat to
take us over—for, believe me, the high-road is
beset with Spanish troops.   We could not cross
it without danger."

Elvira saw it was useless to remonstrate, and
therefore resigned herself to her fate, and proceeded in silence through the dismal forest.
Their progress was slow, for there was no road,
and the underwood in some places was so thick,

246   ELVIRA'S FEARS REALIZED.

that it was with great difficulty they could find
a passage.   After some time, the Countess became quite tired, and she began to regret having
left her comfortable room at Urtubi.

At last, after proceeding two hours, without
reaching the river, she said—" Surely we must
have lost ourselves !"

" We are going towards the west," whispered
Elvira; " I saw it by the last slanting moonbeams
that illumined yonder height !   We are going
quite in a contrary direction from Bayonne."
And she added, in a lower tone—" I much sus-
pect the Page is playing us false—I feel sure we
must now be near Hendaye."

" Rudolf play us false, child !—what can you
mean ?   I would as soon trust him, the son of our
poor nurse Margaret, as your own father !   To
Hendaye, indeed !   That would, truly, be to lead
us close to the lion's den.   Besides, how can you
know we are going towards it ?   I have seen
nothing this last hour."

It was indeed now quite dark.   The moon
had long gone down.   Elvira fancied that
the Page had dismounted, and was leading her
palfrey over a stony road, for the horse occasionally stumbled, but she could not distinguish
any object.   Soon afterwards, the horse stopped

for a few minutes; and then she heard an iron gate close behind them, and the sound echoed as if they were riding on pavement, under an arch. " Here we must dismount, dear lady," said Rudolf, while he gently drew her from her palfrey.

" Where are we ? Let me go, I command you ! Oh, help ! help, dearest mother !—come to me ! Save—oh, save your child !"

" You are alone with me, adored being," said Rudolf, passionately embracing her—" no one is near—you are at last in my power ! Mine now and for ever !"

I will not describe the horror and dismay of Elvira. She screamed for assistance, but the hollow echoes of the passage alone answered her cry. Rudolf was touched by her distress, and suddenly changing his demeanour, he implored forgiveness. He promised to restore her to her father.

But Elvira's worst suspicions were now confirmed, and her heart sank as she remembered the look of deep determination and earnest resolve which had of late so often startled her to observe on his countenance. Any fate now seemed preferable to that of remaining in his

power—even to fall into the hands of the base
Cuevà appeared less dreadful; and bitterly she
regretted having quitted her father. These
thoughts and apprehensions overpowered her
so completely, that she could scarcely stand.
Almost senseless, she was borne along the dark
passage by Rudolf, who now became seriously
alarmed at having terrified her so much. At
last, they reached the end of it, and a faint light
was visible. They pass through another gate,
up a flight of winding stairs, and enter a small
turret chamber.

"Here I will leave you, dearest lady," he said,
in a more respectful tone. "I leave you for one
hour, to consider. In the adjoining chapel, a
servant of God is ready to unite us. Be mine,
or from that window you shall see Don Garcia
murdered!—yes, he—that favoured rival—is in
my power."

On hearing this, Elvira uttered a piercing
shriek, and sank senseless on the ground. In
vain Rudolf endeavoured to restore her to consciousness, and in an agony of self-reproach, he
exclaimed—

"I have killed her—my foolish threat has
destroyed the being I would give worlds to save.

Yes, I now find that my love for her is so great that I could sacrifice my own passion to see her happy."

He now perceived it was utterly impossible she could ever love him. He had made her miserable—he had destroyed the happiness of a creature who had never treated him with anything but kindness.

Thus, as Rudolf contemplated with agony the apparently lifeless form of Elvira, the better feelings of his wild and ill-regulated, yet affectionate heart revived, and he bitterly reproached himself for having destroyed her peace.

———

The night preceding that on which Urtubi Castle had been attacked by Beltran de Cueva, Don Garcia, who had no suspicion of any disturbance, was indulging in delightful anticipations of approaching happiness. His father had given up his magnificent palace at Hernani to the young people, and retired to his castle at Fontarabia, after causing the former to be fitted up with the greatest splendour.

Spain in those days was far advanced in civilization. Its inhabitants had imbibed a taste for

magnificence and luxury from the Moors, whom
they sometimes equalled in the beauty of their
architecture and decoration.   Hernani still contains some remains of its ancient magnificence.
A ruined building in the highest part of the
town particularly attracted my attention, and I
fancied it might have been the dwelling of the
Dukes of Leon.*

On that eventful night, Don Garcia was suddenly arrested in his palace, accused of high
treason, and conducted by a strong body of the
King of Castile's troops to Ourgunzun.

Don Garcia immediately felt convinced this
was Cueva's doing.   The insolent favourite had,
in several instances, ventured to arrest Castilian
nobles, men of the highest rank, who had endeavoured to withstand his growing power; and
now Don Garcia bitterly reproached himself for
not having been more upon his guard.   He remembered, too, with horror, that he had observed
the impression Elvira's beauty had produced on
the profligate Chamberlain. On being forced from
his own palace, he hastily wrote a few lines, and
contrived to give them to his Page, with orders
to take the paper at once to his father at Font-

* See the view of Hernani, at page 196.

Sketched by Lady Chatterton and Drawn on stone by Bichebois.   Printed by Lemercier Benard and C.⁰

OURGUNZUN CASTLE AND TOWN IN SPAIN.

arabia. The family of Leon was rich and powerful, and had such numerous friends, that Don
Garcia had no doubt the news of his arrest would
raise the whole neighbourhood in his favour, and
soon liberate him from even the King's power.
But it was for Elvira he trembled; he knew
not how to rescue her; and all that night and
the next day he paced up and down the narrow
limits of his cell in an agony of apprehension.

It was near the summit of the highest tower of
the ancient palace of the Kings of Castile—that
stately edifice which was afterwards rendered
still more magnificent by the Emperor Charles V.,
and some remains of it may even now be seen
in the view here given of Ourgunzun.   Don
Garcia gazed through the iron bars of his narrow window which commanded a view of the
road from Hernani, but in vain he watched for
the approach of any troops—all was quiet; no
sound indicated the coming of his father's feudal
vassals.   The second day passed slowly away;
the shade of evening fell, and Don Garcia gave
himself up to despair.   Towards midnight a
sound was heard.   " That was certainly the
clang of arms !" thought the captive; " the
place is stormed !"   Yes, that is the war-cry of

his race—"San Giovanni for Hernani!" A long hour of suspense ensued, during which either party seemed alternately to have the advantage. The door is forced open, and Don Garcia is clasped in his father's arms.

"Is she safe?—is my beloved Elvira rescued?" was Don Garcia's first inquiry.

The old Duke shook his head, mournfully, and replied—" I fear this outbreak is worse than we first imagined. The base-born Cueva has been joined by the French ; and it appears there were traitors even in the Castle of Urtubi. The ladies escaped, but were accompanied by a page, who, instead of conducting them to Bayonne, as he was ordered, carried off the Lady Elvira to Hendaye. Whether this was done by Cueva's orders or not I cannot learn. A report has just arrived, which says the Page proved false to all parties, and wished to retain the fair captive in his own hands, and that Cueva was about to march against him in order to obtain possession of the beautiful lady. But let us hope for the best ; and we will now proceed at once to Fontarabia, where we shall soon be joined by a strong reinforcement from Pampeluna, and from thence we can watch the proceedings at Hendaye, and be near at hand to take advantage of whatever may occur.*

We left poor Elvira in the power of Rudolf, who was beginning to relent on witnessing her distress. His heart smote him for having indulged the selfish passion that had plunged the whole country in war. At last, his good feeling prevailed, and Rudolf vowed to save her; but fate seemed to have decreed that his iniquitous designs should succeed. He had no sooner resolved to give himself up, and endeavour to unite her with Don Garcia, than he descried Beltran de Cueva's forces approaching. In a moment they surrounded the town, and all chance of escape was cut off. His agony may then be imagined. He had sacrificed his own love in vain, for she must inevitably fall into the hands of one so utterly unworthy to possess such a treasure. In despair, he went and threw himself at her feet, and avowed all his diabolical designs.

The room in which he had imprisoned her

---

* The position of Fontarabia and Hendaye can be seen in the view I have given in the Frontispiece, and the following part of this story will then be better understood.

overlooked the river, and from the window they
could plainly distinguish the town of Fontarabia
on the opposite side of the Bidasoa, and saw the
banners of Garcia waving over his father's castle.

" Is there no means of sending a messenger
across the water ?" inquired the horror-stricken
Elvira ; " or could we not escape there ourselves ?"

" The quay is already in possession of the
rebels," said Rudolf ; " and the current is so
strong, that no one has ever been known to
swim across at high water."

Poor Elvira, in the midst of all this distress,
felt some consolation in seeing Don Garcia's
banner on the opposite bank of the river, and to
know that he at least was safe.

" They are battering down the outer gate !"
exclaimed Rudolf, almost frantic with terror ;
" and, oh, agony ! what is worse, there is
treachery among us ; for I see our people have
opened the inner entrance to the base Cueva,
and I alone am here to defend you from his
odious presence !

Elvira implored him to plunge a dagger in her
heart sooner than allow her to fall into Cueva's
hands.

ESCAPE OF ELVIRA AND THE PAGE. 255

" It shall pass through my own heart first !"
said the unfortunate Page. " Yet, stay; I will
make one last, though I fear hopeless, attempt
to save thee !" So saying, with an almost supernatural strength, which despair gave him, he
wrenched from the window the iron bars, exclaiming, " God grant I may yet be able to save thee !"
The next moment he took her in his arms, and
jumped into the water below; it was a fearful
height. No traces of them appeared; but Rudolf still retained a firm hold of Elvira, and they
soon rose to the surface of the water. " Thank
Heaven !" he thought, " no one has discovered
us," though the battlements above were crowded
with troops.

In the meantime Beltran de Cueva had entered the prison, and was furious at not finding
the prize for whose possession he had plunged
the whole country in war.

" Ha ! the bars gone ! They must have
drowned themselves in the river below. No !
What is that I see in the water ? Ha ! there
are two heads !—fire—fire from the battlements !
Point every weapon against them ! She shall
die rather than fall again into Don Garcia's
power. And he, too, has escaped ! His cursed

banner is waving over his castle. Fire—fire for
your lives, base villains! What! has not your
shot yet reached the fugitives?" Then, running up to the battlements, Cueva, whose aim
had never been known to fail, himself pointed a
cannon.

In the mean time Don Garcia, who had
anxiously watched the castle at Hendaye, which
he knew contained his beloved Elvira, perceived
what had taken place. " Quick—a boat !" he
exclaimed; " let us hasten to save them!"
In a few moments Don Garcia was rowing towards the Page, who with his precious burden
had hitherto escaped the shots, but he was
almost exhausted in contending against the
strong current. It was then that Cueva fired
the fatal cannon; the shot reached the heroic
Page.

" They sink !" exclaimed Don Garcia, whose
boat had now approached near. " Yet see, they
rise again! He holds her still—but, alas! the
water is stained with blood; and that base
Cueva is firing still! Pull—pull for your lives!
See, he is sinking again !"

Rudolf was indeed mortally wounded; but
with that superhuman energy which a strong

and, above all, a good motive gives, he was able still to keep his lovely burden above the water. Firmly he holds her—but now he can scarcely stem the current. More shots fall in the water close around him. At that moment he descried the boat. One more effort, gallant Page! It was his last!—but at that moment the boat reaches him. He feels that Elvira is taken from his feeble grasp—he sees her clasped in Don Garcia's arms. She is safe—she opens her eyes.

"Forgive me!—and may you both be happy!" were the last words uttered by the dying Page.

All efforts to restore him to consciousness were fruitless, but his countenance looked in death more calm than it had for many a day: it bore even a blissful expression, for he had seen that Elvira was happy. And long she remained so, and enjoyed perhaps more positive bliss than falls to the lot of most mortals.

Count Montreal lived long enough to see the sons of his beloved daughter take a glorious part in the successful war against the Moors under Ferdinand and Isabella, the united sovereigns of Aragon and Castile. The mild yet firm sway

258   LEGEND OF URTUBI CASTLE CONCLUDED.

of these wise rulers soon restored peace to the countries along the frontiers of France; and Urtubi Castle was no more molested by hostile bands, nor the country desolated by border warfare.

259

CHAPTER XIII.

Historical account of Bayonne—Excursion to Çambo—
Roland and his exploits.

JUST returned from a pretty walk to the old
church at the little inland village of Biaritts,
which is detached from the sea-port. The church
is said to have been built by the English, when
they had possession of Bayonne, and the interior
is in a good style of Gothic. On one of the
clustered columns is a projection, with date 1541,
which was probably added afterwards. From
the church-yard there is a beautiful inland view
of the Pyrenees ; near it are some pretty country
houses, with their groves and gardens—their
southern-looking green balconies and their flat
and terraced roofs. Nothing can be cleaner or
more cheerful than the appearance of the houses
and cottages in this part of the country : the

s 2

walls are as white as snow, and the blinds, balustrades, and under-part of the broad projecting roofs are painted a fresh and vivid green. In those which are partly built of timber, the wood is painted of a rich brown, and the roofs of all are covered with reddish tiles.

We often drive over to Bayonne, and we have been reading, with great interest, some histories of that curious old place.

Bayonne was the ancient Lapurdum. Here St. Leon, having with his breath overthrown the statue of Mars, converted, by this miracle, the Basques to Christianity: he was put to death by the Norman pirates, whose depredations he attempted to suppress. They beheaded him. " But," says the legend, " like St. Denis, Sainte Valerie, and others, his body remained standing, and he even took up his head, and walked with it in his hand, for eighty paces." This took place in the beginning of the tenth century.

In 1132, William, Duke of Guienne, enlarged the town, and changed its name to Baia-on-a. (Bonne-baie.) By the marriage of Elinor of Guienne with King Henry II., Duc d'Anjou, afterwards King of England, it fell into the hands of the English. It was greatly favoured by our monarchs, and attained to a state of great prosperity; its war contingent was twenty vessels and ten galleys, and it is recorded that a fleet of Bayonnais, English, and Irish ships, gained a victory over the Normans.   In 1451, Count Dunois drove out the English, and thus completed the conquests of Charles VII.

Francis I. slept here on the 15th March, 1526, on his return from captivity in Spain.   On the 22nd of March, 1529, Anne de Montmorency, Grand Maitre et Marechal de France, arrived at Bayonne, to pay to the deputies of Charles V. 1,200,000 crowns in gold, the ransom agreed on for Francis I.   It was discovered that the crowns were not of the weight agreed upon, "onze deniers et seize grains."   This was a trick attributed to the Chancellor Duprat.   Montmorency had, in consequence, to add 40,000 crowns.

When all was arranged, and the treasure exchanged for the hostages, the sons of Francis, accompanied by Eleanor the Queen Dowager of Portugal, and eldest sister of Charles V., the fiancée of Francis, arrived at Bayonne, on the 2nd of July, 1530, and a magnificent fête was given, for their reception.

The history of the massacre of St. Bartholo-

262   THE MASSACRE OF ST. BARTHOLOMEW.

mew is curiously connected with Bayonne. The idea is said to have had its rise from a conversation between Catherine de Medici and the famous Duke of Alba, during a magnificent fête given on a visit of Charles IX., who was making a progress through the southern provinces of the kingdom.

Catherine took this opportunity to have an interview with her daughter, Elizabeth, Queen of Spain, and whilst the gentlemen and ladies of the two courts, disguised as shepherds and shepherdesses, were making a promenade en bateau on the Adour, to the Isle de Rol, Catherine and the Duke were thinking of the means of destroying the Huguenots,—when the Duke made use of the celebrated words, seven years afterwards remembered by Catherine—" Dix mille grenouilles ne valent pas la tête d'un saumon."

The massacre took place on the 23rd June, 1565. But if the horrible thought had its origin here, so here, also, its execution first received a check, in the fine answer given by the Governor, Viscount Orthez, when he received instructions for the murder of the Protestants of Bayonne—

" Sire, I conveyed your majesty's commands

to the inhabitants and garrison of Bayonne. I have found amongst them only good citizens, and brave soldiers; but not one executioner." ("Pas un bourreau.")

In 1706, Bayonne afforded an asylum to the exiled widow of Charles II., King of Spain; she lived here till 1738, and expended her pension of 400,000 ducats. She built the Château of Marrac, afterwards celebrated as the residence of Napoleon.

Bayonne was the scene of revolutionary occurrences, and suffered much under Robespierre. After the elevation of Napoleon, it became the passage of his troops into Spain. In talking of Napoleon, M. Morel has a good remark, I rather think I have seen it before; but here it is well put—" Dans les époques de lutte et de travail social, la fortune et la puissance appartiennent à celui qui a choisi un but, *qui en à conscience*, et qui dévoue à ce but son intelligence et son énergie. Voyez Rome, Mahomet, Charlemagne, Napoleon, s'ils n'avaient pas tous un but, et une croyance en quelque sorte fataliste dans ce but?"

This is very true, particularly the necessity of being aware of the motive; I believe many who have a motive fail, from want of the consciousness of it.

On the 14th April, 1808, Napoleon arrived at Bayonne, and soon after, took up his residence at the Chateau de Marrac, which he purchased, with some land adjoining. Ferdinand VII. and his brother, Don Carlos, arrived at Bayonne on the 26th April. He soon found the result of his foolish confidence; he was offered the crown of Etruria in exchange for that of Spain, which he refused. Godoy, the Prince of Peace, arrived on the 26th, and four days afterwards, Charles IV. and his queen, Marie-Louise.

Immediately after his arrival, Charles paid Napoleon a visit at Marrac; an interesting anecdote is related concerning this visit. Charles had a sore leg, which made him lame. As he ascended the staircase, leaning on Napoleon's arm, he said—" Soutenez-moi, mon frère, j'en ai besoin." Napoleon answered, with a smile—" Appuyez-vous, et ne craignez rien, je suis fort." The 6th of May, Ferdinand restored the crown of Spain to his father, Charles IV., who, by a treaty executed the day before, disposed of it in favour of Napoleon.

On the 6th of June, Napoleon proclaimed his

brother Joseph King of Spain. Charles IV. retired to Compiegne, with a pension of £300,000 a-year. Ferdinand to Valençay, with an allowance of £40,000. Joseph arrived from his kingdom of Naples on the 7th. At his interview with Napoleon, the latter concluded his reasons for the change, by saying — " D'ailleurs ces arrangemens terminent nos querelles de ménage, je donne Naples à Lucien."

On our way to Cambo, we passed the ruins of Marrac, once the scene of so much splendour, and of so many important events,—now, the remains of the shell gives some idea of what it was. Our coachman was gardener there, and says it was fitted up with great magnificence. On the restoration of the Bourbons, the handsomest part of the furniture was removed, and the castle, according to the gardener's account, set fire to and destroyed. Napoleon was a great patron of Bayonne, and many of its embellishments owe their origin to him.

Thursday, 17.—We made an excursion yesterday to Cambo, a pretty little mineral watering place in the mountains, about two hours and a half's drive on the other side of Bayonne. The road lies through a rich and woody country,

full of fig-trees and Indian corn, and the smell
of hay, which the peasants were making under
and between high trelliced vines, was delicious.
The bright red petticoats and blue jackets of the
women, with the yellow handkerchief worn by
some on the head, looked very picturesque, as
seen through the green vines. The village of
Cambo stands partly on a high terrace overlooking the river Nive, and an irregular street
of broad-roofed and balconied houses slopes
down to a wooden bridge.

The house which contains the spring and
baths (and where there is also, I believe, a good
hotel) is at some distance from the town, and we
walked to it through a wood of fine chesnut trees.
The mountain range behind is very beautiful,
but the houses have their backs turned to it, and
only look down upon the little narrow valley,
which is indeed adorned by the river Nive
winding through fertile fields, but does not possess much feature or beauty.

We had a very good dinner at a little, clean,
homely sort of inn, and brought home a loaf of
excellent household bread—a very rare luxury
in France.

In the mountains beyond Cambo is a place

called Le Pas de Roland, where there is a rock marked by a gigantic foot-print, said by the peasants to be that of Roland.   How all these sort of superstitions resemble each other in different countries !   A little beyond it, on the Spanish side of the mountain, is the celebrated vale of Roncesvalles.   This was the road by which the famous Roland led the hitherto victorious army of France towards the fatal plain of Roncesvalles.   I could fancy the brilliant cortège winding through these romantic defiles, and thought of the various songs and legends which describes the battle :—

" Say, whither are bound these illustrious knights,
    The pride and the glory of France ?
In defence of his country, its laws, and its rights,
    Each paladin takes up his lance.
And foremost is Roland, whose scimitar keen
    The harvest of war prostrate leaves ;
While, led to the slain by its glittering sheen,
    Death gathers them up in his sheaves.
            Shout, comrades, shout !
                Roland, famous in story ;
            And your war-cry give out
                For our country and glory !

" On our frontier the Saracen armies extend
    Their legions in splendid array ;
The unnumber'd bands, from the hills that descend,
    Their menacing banners display.

268   THE WAR-SONG.

'Tis the foe!—'tis the foe! Sons of France, spring to arms
    And drive back the barbarous horde!
To them, not to us, will the fight bring alarms;
    Brave Roland has ask'd for his sword.
        Shout, comrades, shout! &c.

" On, onward with Roland, to honour and fame—
    Glory's waving her flag by his side,
And those who would gain an illustrious name
    Must follow his plume as their guide.
On—onward, to share in his glorious career!
    He stops not to number the foe;
Till, cleft by his sabre, or pierced by his spear,
    Their bravest and best are laid low.
        Shout, comrades, shout! &c.

" How many? how many? the coward may ask,
    As he lurks in his covert secure;
But perilous odds urge the brave to their task,
    And danger itself is a lure.
To Roland the number of foes is unknown;
    To count them he never is found,
Until, at the close, by his might overthrown,
    They lie stark and stiff on the ground.
        Shout, comrades, shout! &c.

" Once more rings the blast of the paladin's horn,
    As he rallies our wavering bands;
But, pierced by a shaft, to the earth he is borne—
    His life-blood is clotting the sands.
Still faithful to honour, he heeds not the pain,
    But smiles with a welcome to death;
While high o'er the tumult is heard the proud strain,
    Which he shouts with unfaltering breath :—

> Swell, comrades, swell
>   The loud chant of my story;
> Sing how nobly I fell
>   For my country and glory !*

In later days, too, these narrow defiles were trod, and with better success, by a warrior not less illustrious than Roland. It was through the passes leading to Roncesvalles that our valiant Black Prince went to assist Don Pedro of Castile against his usurping brother, Henry,† and shortly afterwards gained the victory of Navarète. In that glorious battle, which reinstated Don Pedro on his throne, Prince Edward took the brave Du Guesclin prisoner :—

> " 'Twas on the field of Navarète,
>   When Trestamare has sought
> From English arms a safe retreat,
>   Du Guesclin stood and fought :
> And to the brave Black Prince alone
>   He yielded up his sword."‡

The victorious prince and his celebrated captive returned by the same road, accompanied

---

* From Bentley's Miscellany.

† It was the same Don Pedro whose marriage with Edward's beautiful sister Joanna, had been so fearfully interrupted by her sudden death at Bayonne.

‡ From Milnes's Breton ballad, which describes the interesting manner in which Du Guesclin was ransomed.

by the King of Navarre as far as Roncesvalles;
"whence," says Froissart, "the Black Prince
continued his march to Bayonne, where he was
received with great joy. He remained there
four days to repose and recruit himself."

La Grotte d'Isturitz and the church at Itxat-
sou, further among the mountains, are said to
be worth seeing.

The little church-yard of Cambo is beautifully adorned with flowers—each grave surrounded by a well-kept little garden; and its
position on the terrace at the entrance of the
village is very pretty. On a woody height at
our right going there, the driver pointed out a
little rustic chapel, where, he says, a hermit has
lived for a great many years.

Sunday, 20th June,—Biaritts.—There is a fair
here to-day, and a number of peasants are come
from different parts of the country, dressed in
their gayest attire—many in white; with the red
bands on their heads arranged with much taste,
and two long curls of dark hair on each side of
the face. Several are now sitting under our
windows; and I observed that here, as at St.
Sebastian, the men and women keep in separate
groups, and seldom speak to each other.

Nothing can be more beautiful than the view from the old light-house here, when the mountains are clear. At sun-set this evening we could distinguish the coast of Spain as far as Bilbao.

" Serene and sweet the lovely landscape lay
  Outstretch'd beneath a summer's glancing ray ;
  And from blue skies a fost'ring sun like ours,
  Swell'd in the fruits, and glitter'd in the flow'rs.
  Above, the silent mountains stood on high,
  Their outline graved distinct along the sky ;
  And forests stretch'd their undulating wreath,
  Above the vales that smiling slept beneath ;
  While far away the breath of fresh perfume
  Pass'd on the breeze which rose from western caves,
  And o'er the glow of summer's form and bloom,
  Calm ocean's voice came up from slowly-moving waves."*

* From "V's" beautiful poem—" I watched the Heavens."

272

CHAPTER XIV.

Journey to Pau—Orthez—The court of Gaston de Foix—
Pleasant society at Pau—The Moon of the South.

Pau, Saturday, June 26.—A sad event has happened since I last opened this diary—we have
lost our darling little dog Frisk. One moment
deprived us of our dear companion—that creature of life and joy, the very essence of affection,—and all centered in us ; but it is too
painful to write or think of. This loss has
upset all our plans ; it induced us to leave
Biaritts suddenly, and here we are seeking for
distraction and excitement in new scenes. The
lovely scenery we passed through yesterday
on our way from Bayonne, the range of snow
mountains, the old towns of Peyrehorade,
Puyoo, and Orthez, even the first glimpse of
the old chateau of Henri IV., failed to excite
as much pleasure as they otherwise would have

done. But I will try to relate some of the par-
ticulars of our journey, for it was through a
country too interesting not to be noticed.

We started from Bayonne for Pau at ten minutes before eight, and reached it at five; thus
doing the 105 kilometres, upwards of sixty-eight
miles, in nine hours and ten minutes. Heavy
showers occasionally occurred, and the weather
became so cloudy as to shut up the view of the
higher mountains, and thus deprive the landscape of its chief attraction: still, enough was
left to make it very beautiful, and occasional
glimpses shewed us what the scenery would
be with the high chain exposed. We had an
opportunity of judging of the fine position of
Bayonne this morning, with the mountains
clear. The view, soon after leaving the town,
from the Pau road, was very beautiful, and, for the
first time, the snow mountains were distinctly
visible; they soon became clouded. We passed a
nice campagne commanding this fine view: the
river is an interesting feature in the foreground
—as is the Pic du Midi in the distance. Before
descending to the Adour the view must be fine;
it was in a great measure hidden from us. The
river, which is crossed by a good modern bridge,

VOL. I.   T

is here, as it appeared to me, a broader stream than at Bayonne.

At Peyrehorade, which is on the Gave, there is a bridge over the river, here a fine stream, and near it is an interesting old castle, now, I believe, a poor-house. Its position is good, over the river; and the terrace of a little garden we walked to, commands a fine view. On the height above, are the remains of an ancient castle. All this country is very highly cultivated, and the rich green of the Indian corn contrasts well with the yellow tints of the wheat, fast advancing to maturity. After ascending a côte beyond Peyrehorade, we came to a pretty maison de campagne, commanding a rich and extensive view of the course of the Gave and the range of mountains. In the villages, the St. John garlands are universal : these garlands are made of flowers gathered on St. John's eve, and, being blessed by the priest, are suspended to the barn-door, where they remain until replaced by a fresh one on the following year, and are supposed to have the effect of protecting the crop.

The little town of Orthez, famous for its ancient splendour when the residence of the Counts of Foix, and for its battle in 1814, may claim for

its neighbourhood the character of peculiar rich-
ness, even in this highly cultivated country. It
looks very prosperous and happy.

At Orthez, Froissart, that historian whose romantic pages increase so much the interest of
this lovely country, put up at the Hotel of the
Moon; and he gives a most lively description of
the splendour of Gaston, Count de Foix's residence in this town. He remained twelve weeks
at the court of the celebrated warrior, and says
he had never seen so handsome a prince, " either
in the form of his limbs and shape, or in countenance, which was fair and ruddy, with grey
amorous eyes, that gave delight whenever he
chose to express affection. . . . . He loved
earnestly the things he ought to love, and hated
those which it was becoming of him to hate, and
was a prudent knight, full of enterprise and wisdom." And yet this same valiant and magnificent prince did some things which are rather at
variance with our modern ideas of prudence and
wisdom. But I will not quote any more of my
friend Froissart till we arrive at some of the
other places he describes, and reserve the most
striking act of Gaston's powerful reign till we

T 2

reach the old town of Foix, which we hope to visit.

Indeed, the whole drive was beyond description lovely. No wonder the romantic Froissart should be enchanted with such scenes. He says, in a pastoral composed in honour of Count de Foix, the handsome Gaston Phebus, that being—

> " En beau Pré sert et plaisant
> Par dessus Gave la rivière
> Entre Pau et Ortais seant,"

he saw shepherds and shepherdesses who were conversing of different lords, and the arms they bore. He adroitly makes use of this fiction to name with praise all those from whom he had received any marks of liberality, and terminates his list with the Count de Foix.

The position of Pau deserves its reputation, and in crossing the bridge, we had a good view of its interesting castle. We are lodged here in great comfort. Our rooms (in the Hôtel de France) look upon the promenade and terrace-walk, with the valley beyond—through which the Gave winds—and which is bounded by a range of woody heights; above these are the splendid snow mountains, but they have scarcely been visible since we came, and it has rained

in torrents. This evening, we walked out between the showers, to the old castle, and saw
its venerable walls illumined with the rosy hue
of sunset. It put me in mind of the old castle
at Blois; the form of the upper windows and
some of the stone ornaments being very like
those of Francis the First's buildings there. The
situation, too, is something similar; but this
has the advantage of possessing a splendid view
from its windows, as well as being a beautiful
object in itself. Repairs are going on; and
the Duke de Montpensier, who passed here the
other day, is said to have expressed disappro-
bation at their backward state. One great
charm of a tour in the Pyrenees to me is, that
everything is lovely, but there is not much to
be seen—at least, the beautiful spots seem to
lie in such a small compass that, with every
advantage of variety, there cannot be a great
deal of fatigue; and then people do not appear
to have such a rage for mountain expeditions
here as in Switzerland.* Oh, how painfully
I used to be impressed, and reminded of my

---

* We did not find it so afterwards; on the contrary, the
distances are great, there is a great deal to be seen, and the
expeditions, too, are numerous and very fatiguing.

278   PENSIVE REFLECTIONS.

bodily weakness, by hearing of all the mountain
walks and rides over and through the various
cols! The giant feats of delicate-looking women,
who were said to be consumptive, and travelling
for their health! But I believe consumptive
people *can* do more than any others.

Bought a real capuchin and ordered a capulet,
as we thought it would be very useful in the
mountain tour. We had a beautiful drive to
visit the Compte de M—— and M. de C——, at
Taillefer. Lovely view back upon the town.

Thursday, July 1st.—Mountains continue invisible, so we are still here. Every year and
every day that I live on amid beautiful scenes,
and love, and prosperity, convince me more and
more how inadequate are all apparent blessings
to endue us with a spirit of happiness where
there is a sort of bodily *malaise*, causing a
sickness of the soul, which darkens our enjoyment of life's fairest scenes. Ah, what
would I give for that sort of buoyant health of
mind and body that I see glancing in the eyes,
and animating every gesture, of those peasant-
girls beneath our windows !

Saturday, July 3.—After writing the foregoing

melancholy bit, I went to call on the Marquesa de N——, a most interesting person. Her husband is nephew to the brave Palafox, Duke of Saragossa. She is very beautiful, and has had a long and severe illness, which seems to have left her more like a creature of a better world than an inhabitant of this. She appears full of the good and beautiful thoughts with which a long life of suffering in this world prepares the favoured children of God's love for the enjoyment of a glorious eternity; and yet she has all the playful cheerfulness of a young child whose mirth has never been dimmed by a shadow of grief. She gave me a most interesting description of her illness, and what miseries her friends underwent when travelling with her in Spain, in the midst of the war. She did not suffer, she said, with great naïveté, because she felt already half in the next world, and therefore was indifferent to all the temporal dangers which surrounded them.

We were at her house last night, and met there her handsome and charming sister, the Marquesa Q——, and many other Spaniards, who seemed to be very original and captivating. Round the room were groups of pretty women—

some at work, some sitting near the windows,
looking out on the beautiful moon, and lovely
view which it illumined.   One was standing out
on the balcony, leaning over it in a truly Spanish
attitude, and holding her fan with the peculiar
grace which belongs to that country of romance.
The whole scene recalled to my mind the stories
I have read, and the pleasant dreams I have
imagined, of serenades and romantic lovers, of
cruel parents and cross duennas.   Then we had
music, too : modinhas and boleros sung by beautiful voices, and with that peculiar union of
grace and force so striking in the national airs
of Spain, but an expression which strangers
can seldom give.

  There is a sort of confiding affection shewn
almost at first sight by most of the Spaniards I
have seen which is very captivating, and further
removed from our English reserve than what we
see in other foreigners. Any and every day, from
twelve o'clock till two, or from eight in the evening till half-past ten, will that fascinating creature be glad, she says, to see us. How few
English would say as much to their dearest
friends !   The society of Pau is very agreeable :
the beautiful Madame de M—— called on us

the day before yesterday, and Madame de C—— and her pretty daughter yesterday.

Sunday, 4th.—The mountains here are like dear friends, to which we can run when in sorrow,—sure to find consolation and peace in contemplating their mysterious and dreamy recesses, and pure, eternal-looking summits.

Last night, they were illuminated by the brightest and most glowing moon I have ever seen. Its colour was much warmer as well as more brilliant, but I am not sure that I liked it so well as the pure white, and perhaps spectral-looking rays, it gives us in the north, and which are hallowed by early associations, and by the remembrance of Gothic arches and ruined cloisters. In our land, the moonbeams have certainly a more solemn air; they seem to me to be the light of the dead, and I always feel that the spirits of those dear ones who are gone visit me in their rays.

The last two days have been very hot, but our apartment has, fortunately, rooms looking on three different aspects; so we contrive to run away from the sun as it comes round the house. Our south windows command lovely views over gardens, valleys, and mountains, which we can

enjoy, free from sun, mornings and evenings;
those to the west look on the promenade, and
are shaded by its lime-trees, now in full bloom,
so that we are not obliged to close the outer
blinds, and have thus the uninterrupted enjoyment of fresh air, delicious perfumes, and besides, the amusement of looking at the various
groups of promenaders, who luxuriate beneath
the shade.   Fortunately, few carriages come
there, so we are free from any noise but the
pleasant sounds of children at play, or, now and
then, that of a guitar or strolling musician.

Then our dining room is to the north, and
looks upon the large court and other buildings
of the hotel; there we see the arrivals and de-
partures of all sorts of vehicles, from the well-
appointed carriage to the little rickety car,
destined for bad roads, and mountain expeditions; and the curious little vinaigrettes in
which people drive about the streets of Pau.
Here, too, we see the various operations that go
on in the out-of-door life of these climates, and
which afford an endless variety of interesting
pictures.   Peasants, in their mountain costume,
bringing vegetables and milk to sell; the hotel-
girls in their less national, but equally pretty

and coquettish attire ; and couriers, with their consequential air, and approving nods of condescension, are the leading features of the scene. This morning there was an inspection of a regiment, and we had the enjoyment of hearing its band under the lime-trees. To-morrow we are to start for the mountains, and dive into the blue recesses of those lovely forms we have admired so much.

> " Go, travel 'mid the hills ! The summer's hand
> Hath shaken pleasant freshness o'er them all.
> Go, travel 'mid the hills ! There, tuneful streams
> Are touching myriad stops invisible ;
> And winds, and leaves, and birds, and your own
>   thoughts,
> (Not the least glad) in wordless chorus, crowd
> Around the thymele* of Nature."†

* The central point of the choral movements in the Greek theatre.

† Miss Barrett. Beginning of a sea-side meditation.

284

CHAPTER XV.

Journey to Bagnères de Bigorre—Lourdes and its Castle—
Montrejean—Bagnères de Luchon—Terrific storm and
fire.

Tuesday, 6th July,—Bagnères de Bigorre.—Hotel de
France, the nicest we have been in since Angoulême ; and, oh, how much happiness—at least, to
an invalid—depends upon the hotel ! The English
are reckoned by foreigners foolishly fastidious
and particular about their comforts at hotels.
" It is so odd," said a pretty little French lady,
the other day, " that the English, who travel more
than any other nation, should be so much more
particular about their comforts."   But it strikes
me that this is the very reason.   The Englishman travels for pleasure, and therefore comforts
are essential.   The usual object of foreigners
when they travel, is to reach some particular
place ; and the short duration of their journeys

makes inconveniences of less consequence. But when we come to pass a year or two on the road, when we *live* at hotels, it is of much greater importance that they should be good.

Another universal advantage of good inns arises from the fact that we are much more affected at first by the aspect of the rooms we inhabit, than we ever are afterwards; we soon get accustomed to, and almost cease to *see*, the objects which surround us; but the first two or three days we are positively influenced by them.

Long life then, to good inns, and prosperity to the Hotel de France, at Bagnères de Bigorre, with its pretty garden and sweet flowers, and its cheerful corner-room, where I am now sitting. Near me are two windows—one looks up a little street containing a few detached neat houses, with green blinds, terraced roofs, and little pinnacled towers, which have a pleasant, luxuriant air; above them, and at the end of the street, is the mountain. It rises abruptly, close to the town, and is covered with large chesnuts and beeches; I see walks and narrow paths winding up in various directions, inviting one to explore the cool and umbrageous recesses, and enjoy the beautiful view they must command.

286   LAUNDRESSES.

All this sounds cheerful, and so it is, in spite
of a heavy rain which keeps us at home, and
affords me the delicious repose of a soft, red
velvet chair, worked footstool, and polished
mahogany table, covered with some new Spanish
books, and some favourite old volumes, which I
love better than most things.   Now and then, I
have an idle peep out of the window on the
various groups of peasants, with their red
capulets or brown capuchins.   A stream rushes
down through this said little street—a mountain torrent, fresh, sparkling, and wild, as the
scenes from which it comes, but here enclosed
within two walls, with an opening near each
end, where the laundresses of the town pursue
their avocation, and a little further on the stream
becomes a bath for horses and pigs.

My bed-room opens into this apartment, and
looks out on the garden, at the end of which is a
curious and beautiful tower, slender and lofty
as a minaret; of architecture, half Gothic and
half Moorish, with a light, airy gallery at the
top, and a large bell, supported by wrought iron,
over it, forming a sort of transparent crown,
and striking the hours with a sound peculiarly
melodious and strange.

It would appear from all this that I was very
much pleased with Bagnères—yet, on the contrary, I am rather disappointed; for a French
gentleman described it to me as " une petite
Athenes—une ville si mignonne, tout pleine de
jolies maisons." In vain we have tried to discover any resemblance to Athens. The approach,
indeed, is very pretty; for the minaret sort of
tower I have just mentioned, and the tall spire of
the Gothic church, are two striking features;
these, with a splendid background of mountains,
a fertile plain in front, and woody hills on either
side, form a beautiful picture; but once entered,
Bagnères resembles most common French towns
in its narrow streets and not very gay shops.

It has two or three small irregular *places*. In
the centre of one is a nice promenade, shaded by
trees. It contains some good houses; those on
one side have little terraced gardens before them,
under which are shops the gayest in the place—
most of them being devoted to the sale of the
tricoterie de Bagnères, a worsted-work of fine
texture, and great variety of pattern and colour,
aprons, shawls, coverlids, caps, are worked in
flowered patterns of great beauty.

We walked round and through the town. A

remarkably pretty girl, the daughter of a bookseller, tempted us to add to our stock of Spanish
books.

The road we travelled to-day, on our way
from Pau, lies, as far as Lourdes, through
scenery the perfection of loveliness. At Les-
telle, the first post, we went into the church.
It is well situated, at the foot of a woody
height, near a rushing stream, and a bridge,
whose single arch is adorned with festoons
of the most luxuriant ivy. The interior of the
church is very gorgeous. The altars richly gilt,
and galleries resembling those we saw in the
Spanish churches. The outside is odd and
grotesque, adorned with statues in niches,
Roman columns, and an old French roof, something like that of the Tuileries.

The approach to Lourdes is very beautiful,
and its old castle is a striking object. On the
heights behind are considerable quarries of slate
and marble.

An interesting anecdote of fidelity in the com-
mandant of this castle is related. It belonged
to the English until the treaty of Bretigny, and
was besieged by the Duc d'Anjou, in 1374. It
was valiantly defended by Armand de Bearn,

whose liege lord was the Count de Foix, and who
sent for Armand to induce him to surrender the
castle. He obeyed the summons, and, as commanded, went to Orthez, the residence of the
Count.

On the third day after his arrival, the Count,
before his assembled court, urged Armand to
give up the castle; but he remained firm in his
refusal, saying that its defence had been committed to him by the King of England, and for
him he would retain it as long as he was able.
Upon this, the Count drew his dagger, and,
before the assembled nobility, who dared not
interfere, he struck him with it five times.
Upon which Armand exclaimed—" Oh, Mon-
seigneur, vous ne faites pas gentillesse;" and
soon after died.

A drive by a capital road, through a rich plain,
brought us to Bagnères de Bigorre. In fine
weather, when the mountains can be seen, it
must be beautiful.

After quitting Lourdes, we had no more
mountainous roads and steep precipices, much
to the delight of my rebellious nerves. I quite
agree with the little French woman who said—
" La vue des precipices me fait mal;" therefore,

290   VALLEY OF CAMPAN.

I pay very dearly for the pleasure of beautiful scenery.

Bagnères, at first sight, is very disappointing : why its architecture should be extolled I cannot conceive.   I fancy an Athenian would find some difficulty to discover any resemblance to his celebrated city ; and even metaphorically, the " Athens of the Pyrenees" has so little claim to be called so, that one reading establishment, and a very poor bookseller's shop, seem to be its only literary resources.

The costumes are very pretty.   The capulets at Pau are white—here they are usually red, and bordered with black velvet.   They look very comfortable, and serve as parasol or umbrella, according to the weather.

Wednesday, July 7.—Still cloudy, with frequent showers ; but we have had a delightful walk round about the town, and on the heights above it.   We looked up the Valley of Campan, and explored some narrow paths in fine chesnut woods and through fields, up the steep sides of the rocky heights towards the Elysée Cotin and the Grotto.   We paid some visits, and inspected the baths.   In the evening, accompanied by our friends Le Vicomte and Vicomtesse de St. I——, we went to the marble works, and saw some beautiful specimens of Pyrenean marble : the works are well executed, though we thought them inferior to those at Matlock.

Bagnères de Luchon, July 8, Hotel du Commerce.— How much one suffers in trying to be comfortable ! Of all miseries, house or lodging-hunting is the greatest. We arrived here after a charming drive through scenery so exquisitely lovely as to baffle description by words or pencil— scenery that makes one feel perfectly happy, imparting a delicious calm—a thorough feeling of contentment, as if in fact nothing could ever again ruffle the temper or excite bad thoughts. Alas, how soon does this blessed frame of mind vanish !—put to flight by the sight of wretched dirty rooms, the noise and bustle of eager washer-women, horse-dealers, guides, &c., all crowding round us ! We agreed that it was impossible to sleep at the inn, so, in an evil moment, commenced the laborious and most embarrassing work of hunting for lodgings. We saw a great number—the price nearly the same—from ten to twelve francs a-day. Most of them looked good, and tolerably well furnished; but we could not

292　　WELL-FURNISHED APARTMENTS.

make up our minds, and so here we are in the dirty Hotel du Commerce.

The first aspect of this town is unpromising—dark, unpainted shutters, glassless windows, and narrow streets ; but soon the scene changes on arriving at the modern part, where the lodging-houses are : these are really very pretty dwellings, of tasteful architecture, and with the avenue of fine lime-trees between them, must have, in sun-shine, a cheerful and inviting air.

Friday, 9.—After all our trouble, we have succeeded in getting a most comfortable, well-furnished new apartment, and I am sitting on a red velvet sofa, near a polished satin-wood table, with my feet on an embroidered footstool. I try to read, but the splendid mountain views our windows command, keep my eyes continually turned towards them, and fill my mind with indolent delight. Our bed-room, adjoining this salon, has three large windows, opening on a wide balcony, or rather portico, with an orna-mented iron balustrade. The pediment above is supported by four Ionic columns of white stone ; blue striped curtains are suspended between them, which have a luxurious and southern look, and, when closed, form another cool and most delicious room, into which the lime blossoms of the adjoining avenue, d'Etigny, seem to send their sweetest perfumes. This house has also a garden of its own, partly in front of the house and partly running up the steep base of the adjoining mountain, with terraced walks, rows of fruit-trees, and borders of flowers.

Luchon seems to me to possess all the beauties of Bagnères de Bigorre, but on a much grander scale : the mountains, which rise up close behind the town, are of great height, and covered with wood : then the majestic snow mountains of the Port de Venasque are seen in most of the views ; indeed, they are visible from almost every house we have been in. Yet, with all this beauty, I have met with two or three people who were disappointed in Luchon, and maintain that the environs of Bigorre are more beautiful. I cannot imagine how any one can find the scenery of Luchon less beautiful than they expected, unless it be that its valley is perhaps still more lovely, about three or four miles before one arrives at the town. There are more old castles and villages perched on apparently inaccessible and detached heights ; the gigantic masses of rock are thrown about in more picturesque groups ; there is, in fact, more variety, and the scenery has a more peculiar and striking character.   But here, too, it is beyond description lovely and grand; and I never met with a comfortable dwelling in such beautiful scenery before.   It puts me more in mind of the finest parts of the Tyrol—of the scenery between Innspruch and Bolzen—than of any other place.

The costume of the peasantry is very pretty. The women wear light blue capuchons, lined with red ; the men, scarlet caps and embroidered jackets, with a red scarf tied round the waist, and the ends hanging down on one side.   We first saw this scarf some posts on the other side of Bordeaux, and I have seen it often in all the places we have since visited.

But I must say something of our journey to this place.   We left Bigorres about seven yesterday morning, and wound up the heights leading to Escalledieu (the first post) in brilliant sunshine. We had a fine view over the town and up the valley of Campan, and of the range of snow mountains crowned by the Pic du Midi.   After passing Escalledieu—a curious old convent, now a comfortable chateau—the road is through a

more bare and uninteresting country; but we had
splendid views of the snow mountains—often of
the whole range, from the distant heights near
Pau, in the north, to the Maledetta range and
other mountains of Spain in the south.   Montrejean is a curious Spanish-looking old town, full
of carved black timber; roads all excellent, and
posting good.

We passed, near St. Bertrand de Comminges,
on our right, a curious old town, with a fine
church nestled under the higher mountains.

The drive from Montrejean here is through
scenery much more beautiful than any I have
seen in the Pyrenees; indeed, I think it was the
most lovely drive I ever had.   The views up the
valley, to Luchon, are terminated by the Port de
Venasque and part of the Spanish range of
mountains about the Maledetta, the highest and
most snowy of all the Pyrenees; then the woody
heights, or rather mountains, on each side of the
road, are covered with trees to the very summit,—
old castles, standing on rocky points, command
narrow passes, or overlook wilder parts of the
valley; and the rushing Garonne, already a fine
river, plays no inconsiderable part in the landscape.

296   CONFLAGRATION.

Saturday, 10.—A dreadful storm of thunder
and lightning yesterday evening—and just as the
sky began to clear and the thunder only growled
among distant mountains, we were alarmed by
the cry of *fire*, and saw flames rising up behind
the houses which face this.   The large establishment of baths was burning, and for three or
four hours the sight was magnificent.   The
woods and rocks on either side of the valley
were brilliantly illuminated, a lurid glare shone
even upon the more distant snow mountains,
and sparks flew up to an immense height, and
came down like showers of rubies among the
green trees and gardens.   But the fatigue of
house-hunting, unpacking, making ourselves uncomfortable, &c., so fatigued me, and the thunderstorm had already made me rather nervous, so
that fear and awe were the predominant feelings
excited by the splendid conflagration—and I
could scarcely admire it.

Fortunately, a heavy rain had fallen during
the storm, and there was no wind, or the ponderous wooden roofs and balconies of the older
houses in the town might have caught fire.
We remained at the windows, fascinated by the

·awful sight, till about twelve o'clock, when it was nearly spent, and there was no excuse for not going to bed. But I could not sleep : the thunder again began to growl, and the lightning was so vivid, that I started up from bed several times with the frightful impression that our very rooms were on fire.

I like to live on a height. Valleys, however high in themselves, if bounded by very lofty mountains, are rather gloomy, and give one the feeling of imprisonment. Hence it is that Bigorres, though far less beautiful, is no doubt a more cheerful residence than Luchon. We certainly see this place under every disadvantage, owing to wet weather and awful storms; and, strange to say, our mountain expeditions are as much impeded by bad weather here as in Scotland or Ireland. The beau ideal of a southern climate is not often realized, and we are disposed to find far too much fault with our own, and particularly with that of poor dear Ireland. I can state as a positive fact that, during the various wild and mountain expeditions we made in the south and west of Ireland, during the year 1838, there were not more than six days in which the

298   WET WEATHER.

bad weather at all incommoded us ; whereas, in
this greatly-extolled south of France, we have
had almost constant rain or storms ever since our
arrival at Bayonne, about six weeks ago.

During our expedition in Spain to St. Sebastian,
we had rain.   In our fortnight's residence at
Biaritts, the mountains were very seldom visible,
and it was so cold, that I was obliged to have
recourse to some of my winter clothing.   During
the eleven days we were at Pau, the mountains
were only clear during a part of one, and in our
day's journey from Bayonne to Pau, and the day
from Pau to Bigorre, no mountain-tops were
visible.   The days we spent at Bigorre were like-
wise showery and dark, and it was only on the
morning we left it that the snow mountains appeared.

Two o'clock.—We thought the rain had ceased,
and so sallied forth, armed luckily with umbrellas.   I had a great longing to explore one of
those inviting little paths we see from our windows, and which run in all directions along the
precipitous sides of the mountain.   To reach it,
we went through the old part of the town, which
is very gloomy, and soon after we began to
clamber, the rain came on.   The path was rugged

and disagreeable, here and there washed away by mountain torrents, so that sometimes we could scarcely find any footing; in short, this my beau ideal of a pleasant walk evaporated, like most others, in clouds, which prevented our seeing anything but the brambles and walls of rock on one side, and on the other they veiled the depths of the precipice, down which not to tumble required all our attention, (what a German-sounding sentence!) Thus we got a good wetting, lost the path, and a black-lace colleret, which hitched in the brambles, without my perceiving it. However, a dear, honest boy ran after us with it, and shewed us the shortest way to get down from our unpleasant situation. I came home very cross, and covered with mud.

I am so thankful to have had pleasant letters this gloomy day! How much do our impressions of places, as well as our real happiness abroad, depend upon the bad or good news we receive in them from our friends at home!

In these parts of the country there is no such thing as "making bargains." I find that the shopkeepers here, unlike those we have often met with in the northern parts of France, never ask more than they mean to take; but they have

300   IMPOSITION MADE AGREEABLE.

a very pretty habit of coaxing their customers,
and reconciling them to the price demanded, by
adding some little thing as a present to the object in question. Thus I bought some shawls
to-day of the Bagnères tricoterie, and the woman
in the shop presented me with a pair of very
prettily embroidered mittens.

301

CHAPTER XVI.

Legend of Castel Biel and St. Bertrand de Comminges.

Luchon, Saturday.—Every country has its tale
of the influence of ill wishes, and of the destruction of some neighbouring family or castle from
the curse of an offended old woman or gipsy;
and the romantic valley of Luchon is no exception
to the general rule. I rejoiced to find that the
legend here relates to my two favourite places,
the ruined Castel Bielle, and that beautiful old
town, St. Bertrand de Comminges, we saw on
our road from Montrejean. I had a long talk
with the lady who told it, during our walk to-
day, on the effect of ill wishes. She maintains
that a strong will or wish *has* an effect—that
curses or blessings invoked by a powerful mind
have a decided influence on the fate of those who
are the objects of them. She believes, too, in

the power of magnetism, and thinks that the fervent prayer of devotees, the will of magnetisers, and the imprecations of violent characters, in past ages, are all of the same nature, and have equal power. She says—" May there not be good and bad spirits always hovering near us, who assist all our strong wishes, either for evil or good ?"

As to the truth or falsehood of this theory I shall say nothing, but proceed to relate the lady's romantic   tale before it fades from my mind.

CASTEL BIELLE, OR THE EFFECTS OF ILL WISHES.

In the latter part of the eleventh century, when the good St. Bertrand de Comminges caused happiness and peace to reign in this land, this Castel Bielle was the abode of the Lord of Montauban.   He was one of those turbulent barons whose evil deeds still dwell in the minds of the surrounding peasantry.   His only child, Gonilda, was unlike her father in every respect, being highly revered throughout all the land for her piety and goodness.

It so happened, that in one of her yearly visits

to an old aunt who lived at Leon de Comminges, the fair Gonilda became acquainted with the young Bertrand, who afterwards gave the name of St. Bertrand to that ancient town. He was, indeed, distantly related to her, and though not yet dignified with the title of Saint, he evinced that devoted admiration for whatever is lovely and good which is the first step to perfection. Now the most perfect being he had ever seen was Gonilda, therefore it was no wonder that she should gain his affections, and that his happiest moments were spent in her society.

But all Gonilda's actions were watched by an evil eye. Strange it was that one so fair, so devoted to the happiness of all around, should have excited the ill will of any one. But so it was. The lady of Fronsac hated her, for her father's sake, who had, with the utmost perfidy, won her affections, and then cruelly abandoned her; and she hated Gonilda still more when she saw her in the enjoyment of requited affection.

From her turret chamber, that overlooked the palace inhabited by Gonilda's aunt, she could see the beautiful girl with Bertrand, walking in the gardens, and the Lady of Fronsac was made almost frantic by the sight, and vowed she would

be revenged on the father in his child.   She determined that both the lovers should be miserable.
There must be a strong power in hate, for as
that wicked woman's eyes were fixed upon the
young pair, and she muttered curses on their
heads, Gonilda trembled, though she saw and
heard nothing but the sweet tones of her lover's
voice.

" This bliss cannot last!" she said; " our
world would be too delightful; it would be—it is
even now, heaven to me!   No, Bertrand, I feel
I never can be yours!"

The young man shuddered as she spoke, and
yet endeavoured to cheer her spirits.   " Why
do you tremble, dearest Gonilda—what is there
to fear?   Your aunt favours our suit, and your
father is too much occupied with war and feasting to make any objection to our wishes."

And so Bertrand tried to reason her fears
away; for man ever clings to reason, and is
fortunately less influenced by those vague apprehensions or presentiments to which woman is
more liable, perhaps from the superior sensitive-
ness of her nature. Besides, his character, though
full of feeling, was prone to look on the sunny
side of everything.

"Much mirth he hath, and yet less mirth than fancy;
His is that nature of humanity
Which both ways does redound, rejoicing now,
With soarings of the soul anon brought low:
For such the law that rules the larger spirits.

The richest mirth—the richest sadness, too—
Stands from a groundwork of its opposite;
For these extremes, upon the way to meet,
Take a wide sweep of Nature, gathering in
Harvests of sundry seasons."

Gonilda's fears did indeed seem groundless, for days and weeks passed on, and nothing occurred to interrupt the young people's happiness; on the contrary, the old aunt approved of the match, the father's consent was obtained, and a day fixed for the marriage. It was to be celebrated at Castel Bielle, and the old Baron of Montauban seemed so overjoyed at his daughter's prospects, that he invited all the neighbouring nobles to a grand feast for the occasion.

On the evening before the eventful day, Gonilda went to pray in her oratory. It was still early, but the castle was so full of noise and revelry, that she wished to spend a few hours in retirement, to implore the blessing of God on her approaching nuptials.

The last rays of evening sun shone through

the open casement, and tinged her white dress
with its golden hue.   Never had she appeared
more lovely, and yet no human eye beheld her;
no, not even Bertrand's, for he would not venture to intrude.   Besides, there was no entrance
to this little oratory except through her own
sleeping-room; it was, in fact, one of those little
projecting oriels we often see in old buildings.
All vestiges of it are now gone, but the tower
still remains which contained the great staircase
leading up to Gonilda's apartments, and a distant
view of it is here given.   I can imagine the oriel
window resembled the one so beautifully described by Keats, in the " Eve of St. Agnes."—

> " A casement high and triple-arched there was,
>   All garlanded with carven imageries
>   Of fruits, and flowers, and bunches of knot-grass,
>   And diamonded with panes of quaint device,
>   Innumerable of stains and splendid dyes,
>   As are the tiger-moth's deep-damask'd wings;
>   And in the midst, 'mong thousand heraldries,
>   And twilight saints, and dim emblazonings,
>   A shielded 'scutcheon blush'd with blood of queens
>   and kings."

Gonilda prayed fervently, and was so absorbed
that the sun had set, and the short twilight was
nearly gone without her perceiving the change.
No doubt, vivid images of the bliss for which she

Sketched by Lady Chatterton and drawn on Stone by Biedebois.

Printed by Lemercier, Benard and C⁰

CASTEL - BIELLE WITH THE PORT DE VENASQUE MOUNTAINS
from the promenade of Bagnerres de Luchon.

implored, passed before her, and so bright and
all-engrossing were these visions of futurity that
she would probably have remained still longer,
but that she was startled by the fall of something on her dress, and to her surprise she found
it was a letter.   How could it have come there?
The door was closed and the window high.
She looked out through the casement; it was too
dark to see any object, yet she thought she
heard something rustle in the branches of a tree
which overshadowed that part of the castle,
and she shuddered as if some evil eye were upon
her.   The sensation reminded her of that day in
the garden at Comminges, when she had told
Bertrand of her fears.   "How very foolish!"
thought she; "perhaps it is some sport of Bertrand's, who may be annoyed at my long absence.
The moon will soon appear above yonder mountain; I shall then see what this mysterious letter
contains."   So Gonilda waited; for her thoughts
and prayers, in that little oratory, had been so
pleasant that she did not like to leave the hallowed spot.

But now the spell of happiness seemed broken.
She tried to pray again, and knelt before the
Virgin's shrine, and implored more fervently than

x 2

ever the blessings of her heavenly Mother, for
a vague sense of terror oppressed her heart.
Soon afterwards the moon rose, and, to use the
words of Keats—

> " Full on this casement shone the wintry moon,
>   And threw warm gules on Madeline's fair breast,
>   As down she knelt for Heaven's grace and boon ;
>   Rose-bloom fell on her hands, together prest ;
>   And on her silver cross soft amethyst,
>   And on her hair a glory, like a saint.
>   She seemed a splendid angel, newly drest,
>   Save wings, for heaven."

Then Gonilda hastily unfolded the letter.   It
was fastened with a braid of dark hair, and contained these words :—

" ADORED GONILDA,—Danger lurks within
the castle; your rejected suitors have vowed that
you shall not be mine.   On approaching it, I
found the gates closed.   Breathe not a word of
this to any one ; but instantly quit the castle by
the postern gate, and hasten down to the lowest
terrace : there you will find your devoted

                              BERTRAND."

Gonilda had never seen Bertrand's writing,
for in those days young people did not keep up
much correspondence with each other ; but not

a doubt crossed her mind that it could have been written by any one else. It was strange ; but still she resolved to obey his wishes, well knowing that her father could scarcely be depended on ; and so, without further deliberation, she put on her mantilla, and hastily left the castle. No sooner had she passed through the postern gate, than the bright moonbeams became obscured by heavy clouds, and Gonilda trembled as she descended in darkness to the southern terrace.

In the meantime, Bertrand's visions of future happiness were no less blissful than those of his lovely bride. He did not retire, indeed, to an oratory, but he quitted the boisterous mirth of the banqueting hall, and walked along the forest paths that led up the valley towards Spain. There he prayed, and gave thanks to God for his approaching happiness. He lingered for some time at a lovely spot where the three valleys of Luchon, Lys, and Portalet branch off. There was in those days a lake in the Vallée du Lys of considerable size, whose waters were fed by the fine cascade that may still be seen at its upper end. On the side nearest Castle Bielle the stream emerged from it through a narrow

310   THE CASTEL BIELLE.

aperture, where a gigantic rock kept them from overflowing even in winter.

As the young Bertrand stood on the height which overlooked this spot, the thought occurred to him that in case of one of those sudden invasions of the Spaniards that sometimes devastated the valley of Luchon, it might be possible to remove this rock, and thus allow the entire lake of Lys to inundate the plain of Luchon, and make an island of the height on which Castel Bielle was situated.   He was the more pleased at this thought as the Baron had expressed an intention of giving up the castle to him, and retiring to pass his old age in peace at Montauban.

Castel Bielle was one of the most unsafe fortresses on the border ; and it often occurred that Gonilda was obliged in the utmost haste to seek for safety with her aunt, at Comminges. Of late, a truce had been proclaimed with the King of Aragon ; but it might not last long, therefore Bertrand thought, with extreme satisfaction, that the labour of one hundred vassals for some days might remove that rock, and render Bielle quite secure.   While he was busied with this project, to ensure the happiness and security of his bride, the shades of evening fell—the short twilight soon ceased, and veiled every object from his view. Soon afterwards, a violent storm came on, and those heavy clouds which had veiled the moonbeams from Gonilda, as she approached the lonely terrace, now came rolling into the valley. The thunder growled in the distance, and then—

" From nearer clouds bright burst more vivid gleams,
  As instantly in closing darkness lost;
      *   *   *   *   *   *
Then swells the rolling peal, full, deep'ning, grand;
And in its strength lifts the tremendous roar,
With mingling discord, rattling, hissing, growling,
Crashing, like rocky fragments downward hurled—
Like the upbreaking of a ruined world;
In awful majesty the explosion bursts,
Wide and astounding o'er the trembling land."*

Bertrand sought shelter in one of those little châlets which abound in the Valley du Lys, till he fancied the storm was somewhat abated; he then hurried homewards ; but had not proceeded far when a sound, as of many voices, met his ear.

" Hush !" said one of them ; " do not make so much noise."

" How foolish !" said another.· " What can

---

* Joanna Baillie:

you fear ?   The whole castle is buried in merriment and wine, and she will soon arrive.   What a glorious plan it was ! And how our Prince Louis will thank me for bringing him such a prize—for she is the most beautiful girl in all the four cantons !   Ha ! ha ! how the young bridegroom will storm ! But we shall all be safe in Venasque, far out of reach of his fury ; besides, even if he discover it, what can he do against a hundred and fifty of us ? 'Tis a good number to carry off one poor young girl."

" But are you sure she will fall so easily into our hands ?   Perhaps, after all, we may have to attack the castle."

" No, no ; the old hag of Fronsac knows better what she is about.   She has sent a letter, signed by the lover himself, to lure her into our nets.   Santa Maria, what a night it is !"

Bertrand listened with dismay.   His first impulse was to fly towards the castle, but the flashes of lightning shewed that it would be impossible to traverse the flat open space without being seen by the Spaniards.   There was, indeed, a circuit of a mile by which he might reach Bielle ; but he reflected with horror that before he could go round all that way, Gonilda might fall into the hands of the enemy.   Whilst paus-

ing, irresolute how to act, a sudden thought
flashed through his brain. He rushed back to
the spot where the huge rock kept in the waters
of the lake. " Oh, for the strength of a thousand arms!" thought Bertrand, as, with the
energy of despair, he endeavoured to move the
huge stone; but he might as well have tried to
move the Maledetta itself. " Alas!" thought
he, " I can do nothing; and my bride will fall
into the hands of those lawless men!"

Bertrand had always been remarkable for his
piety and firm belief in the power and goodness
of God; and though, at first, despair and apprehension for his loved Gonilda had made him
almost blaspheme the Almighty, yet at length
better feelings prevailed, and he suddenly threw
himself on his knees, and prayed fervently for
assistance. In the meantime the storm went on
increasing; the thunder roared still nearer and
nearer among the mountain tops, and the rocks
shook beneath his feet:—

> " Upon the lofty mountain's side,
>   The kindled forest blazes wide;
>   Huge fragments of the rugged steep
>   Are tumbled to the lashing deep;
>   Firm rooted in his cloven rock,
>   Crashing falls the stubborn oak."*

> * Joanna Baillie.

314   BERTRAND'S PRAYER ANSWERED.

"Oh, that the rocks may fall and crush those base Spaniards!" exclaimed Bertrand, during one of the short pauses of this awful storm. "Oh, that God would cause the lake to break down its barrier and overwhelm them!"

He had no sooner breathed this last prayer, than a noise louder than the thunder was heard, and Bertrand saw the gigantic rock give way. The next moment, the waters rushed out, and Bertrand was hurled along in their impetuous course.

For some instants he lost all consciousness; but, being an experienced swimmer, he soon rose, and the first sound which met his ear were the plaintive tones of Gonilda's voice. The vivid lightning shewed a wide expanse of water, and Bertrand could plainly see that it covered the entire plain between the former lake and Castel Bielle; and therefore the Spaniards, en-cumbered as they were with heavy coats of mail, must have been crushed to death beneath the rocks, or hurled along by the overflowing lake.

But, alas! had the waters also engulfed his beautiful bride? and whence came those touch-ing accents? Again he hears her voice! Nearer and nearer it sounds as the impetuous current bears him along. He approaches the western terrace of the castle, which, though formerly on a considerable height, is now very little elevated above the surface of the water. Again all is dark, and he can only hear a low, moaning sound ; but certainly it is Gonilda ! Another and a louder voice meets his ear : " Thank God," thought he, " she has received assistance from the castle! Yet, hark ! what are those angry tones ? A woman's voice, too !"

He redoubles his efforts to reach the terrace. Another flash of lightning shews him the fair form of Gonilda, on the brink of the flood, and near her stands the tall figure of the Lady of Fronsac.

Bertrand sees no more—darkness again conceals every object from his view ; but angry voices are heard, then a piercing shriek, and a heavy plunge into the water — another flash shews the Lady of Fronsac standing alone upon the brink, a ghastly smile of triumphant malice on her countenance. She gazes on the unbroken surface of the now more tranquil water ; no vestige of Gonilda is seen ; but Bertrand gains the shore. In a moment he is standing by the Lady of Fronsac.

316 DEATH OF GONILDA.

" Ha!—are you come to seek your bride? Ha! ha!"—and the stern Lady laughed wildly —as she beheld his despair!

But Bertrand heeds her not—a low wailing sound has reached his ear, and he sees a white object at some distance, borne along by the current. Pushing away the Lady of Fronsac, who endeavoured, with all the fury of revenge, to detain him, he rushes again into the lake. In an instant he has reached the spot, and clasps in his arms the beloved object.

" Speak to me, dearest Gonilda! Oh, she is cold—oh, horror, she does not breathe!" He bears her to the terrace, and endeavours by every tender endearment to restore her to life. In vain!

" She is dead!" exclaims the Lady; " and I am revenged; and rejoiced am I that you did not perish too, for now I shall have the gratification of knowing you will be miserable all your life."

Bertrand was indeed miserable — but not through life, for he served God, and devoted all the energies of his powerful mind to the good of his fellow-creatures. He entered into holy orders, and so high was his reputation for piety and devotion, that, in 1076, he was made Bishop of Comminges; he still continued to live only for others, and to devote the increased means his high position afforded to the happiness of those around him. He died in 1126, and was afterwards canonized. There is scarcely a town or village for miles round whose inhabitants do not still bless his memory. Numerous miracles were performed at his shrine; and it is a well-known fact, that our English Saint Thomas à Becket had such a high opinion of St. Bertrand's powers, that he sent a lady of high rank, who was afflicted with some incurable malady, to visit his tomb at Comminges. The journey, in those days, must have been an affair of no small toil and fatigue; yet the poor lady arrived here safely, was completely cured, and returned home to England, full of gratitude to the pious St. Bertrand.*

The person who suffered most by this sad event was the very one whose early crimes had entailed such a dire vengeance on his child. The unfortunate Baron of Montauban never recovered

---

* See the History of St. Bertrand de Comminges, p. 26.

318   DEATH OF THE LADY OF FRONSAC.

the loss of Gonilda.   She had been the only thing which seemed to link him with the better part of human nature—in fact, the only object he really loved.   From the moment of her tragic end, he gave himself up to despair.   Sometimes heading his vassals against the Spaniards, in which he would burn and pillage without mercy; at others, he indulged in wild debauchery with dissolute companions.

He is said to have perished, at last, in the lake, in the very spot where his daughter was drowned, but whether he destroyed himself, or fell in during a fit of intoxication, is not known.

On his death, the Lady of Fronsac seized on his possessions, for which, as he died without an heir, she obtained a grant from the King, and she instantly proceeded to pull down the castle, and destroy the fine terraced gardens which formerly adorned it.   So great was her anxiety to leave no vestige of the proud abode of her enemy, that she laboured herself at the work of destruction; and, despising the cautions that were given her by the workmen, she proceeded to undermine the southern tower, the only one which now remains.   On she toiled, with a savage smile on her haggard countenance, when suddenly, a stone on which she stood gave way, and she was precipitated into the lake below.

Her body was never found, and no wonder, for some of the Baron's old vassals whom she had expelled from the castle, and who had been obliged to seek refuge with their former enemies in Spain, maintained, that on the evening she perished, they saw her carried along by the devil, who rode on one of those dark mists which sometimes shroud the mountain-tops. They plainly saw him drag her by the heels as far as the base of the Maledetta, and, with a hideous laugh, cast her into the Trou de Toron, that spot where the Garonne commences its underground course.

In proof of this, they said that the river, even as far as Bordeaux, was black for a whole year afterwards, and would have remained so for ever, had it not been for the fervent prayers of the young man she had so deeply injured. St. Bertrand, at the head of his clergy, made a pilgrimage up the valley of Luchon, rowed along the surface of the new lake, and blessed the Garonne. From this blessing arose the prosperity of those numerous fine towns which are situated on that queen of rivers; but he said nothing of the

320   LA MALEDETTA.

mountain from whence the river has its source,
and therefore it has ever since borne the name,
both in France and Spain, of La Maledetta. It
is, then, probably owing to the machinations of
the wicked Lady of Fronsac, that the mountain
still abounds in evil spirits, that no one has
ever reached the summit without meeting with
some signal misfortune, and that so many luck-
less travellers perish in the daring attempt to
invade its gloomy solitude.

321

CHAPTER XVII.

Visit to the Lac d'Oo, or Seculejo—Cascade of Montauban—Ride to the Vallée du Lys—Hopelessly bad
weather.

July the 11*th.*—A bright sun cheered us early
this morning, and shewed the valley and mountains in all their beauty.　We walked across the
valley to Montauban, a little village, with its ancient church, and vine-clad cottages, which is situated a short way up the mountain.　The church-
bell was ringing as we passed, and a procession,
headed by the priest, emerged from the rude old
porch: the men walked on one side, and the
women on the other ; each sex making the tour
of the church, and meeting again at a cross on the
opposite side, where the priest knelt down, and
read some prayers, and sang, the people joining
in the chant.　The music of their voices, and the

bright colouring of their costume in that wild
spot were very striking and beautiful : most of
the women had small lace caps under their red
or white capulets—the old ones only wearing the
large and rather heavy capuchin : the predominant colours were red and yellow.

The object of the procession was to place some
stones round the foot of an old wooden cross,
which seemed in a tottering condition, its founda-
tion having probably been loosened by a storm,
or mountain torrent. After the ceremony was
over, we ascended a steep path leading up the
height towards Spain, which on that side cannot
be very far distant, and rambled among the
woods far above, resting occasionally, and enjoying the view over Luchon, and the valley on
both sides.

Evening.—The town of Luchon is certainly situated in the least pretty part of its lovely valley.
This evening, we walked some way up the valley,
passing close to its highest village, St. Mamet,
and up as far as Castel Bielle, along the road to
the Port de Venasque, and talked to a worn and
interesting-looking peasant woman, who said she
was now so "*maigre*," from grief for her only son,
who had been drawn in the Conscription, and was

obliged to join the army. Poor thing! she looked as if she would not have long to deplore her loss. Castel Bielle is certainly a lovely spot, and the old castle, formerly belonging, like all others in these parts, to the English, in a very fine position, evidently placed to protect the fertile plain from incursions of the Spaniards, and, in even earlier times, has stood, as we heard in the legend, many an assault from Moorish warriors, and seen the proud crescent driven back from its walls.

Monday evening, 12th.—Started this morning, at nine, for the Lac d'Oo, or Seculejo. W——on foot, and I on a nice little mountain horse, which carried me very successfully up the steep, and sometimes very narrow paths, and along the sides of awful precipices. The sky was not very clear, but sometimes the clouds rolled up and disclosed large fields of ice among the upper heights, and, I believe, rendered the wild scenes still more grand, from imparting to them an air of mystery, and casting here and there dark masses of shade.

Some of the old castles and villages near which we passed are situated in most romantic and striking positions, particularly that of

324   ACTIVITY OF ST. AVENTIN.

Blanquet. It stands on the summit of a stu-
pendous rock, which is detached, near the top,
from the mountain, and rises perpendicularly
from the valley below. This castle belonged to
the English, and must have been most important
in old border wars, for it commands the narrow
passes into three valleys : as a military post, it
occupied a position between the Castel Bielle
of the valley of Luchon and the Castel d'Oo.
It defended the valley of Guille, which is on the
road to Montné, and well worthy of a visit; the
village Corviel, which we saw, is upon the road.
We passed the chapel of St. Aventin, who must
have been an active fellow, for he jumped,
according to tradition, from the Castle Blanquet
to the spot where the chapel is built, as the mark
of his feet on the rock outside the chapel bears
testimony !

This country is thickly inhabited. After three-
quarters of an hour, we reached the village of St.
Aventin, which contains three hundred inhabitants ; in another quarter of an hour, we passed
near Castellon—three hundred and fifty inhabitants ; and then passed through the old village of
Cazon ; the guide said part of its church was built
by the Romans. We saw some rude carving on

a house, a coat-of-arms, with a stag and hare as supporters; the arms were designedly effaced; they looked like fleurs-de-lis.

We descended its very narrow and ill-paved street, and soon after passed on the right, the direction of the intended new road to Bigorre, and to the Port of La Pierre Sourde. We continued descending in a smiling valley, with carefully-cultivated fields, greatly subdivided— the probable result of the French law of inheritance; they grow, in little patches—sarazin, millet, rye, wheat, hemp, and potatoes. The little village d'Oo, with its picturesque old castle, is an interesting object.

After passing an open space near the now quiet little river Oo, but which gives evidence of what it can sometimes do, we crossed the bridge d'Astos, or Lasto, to enter the very pretty valley of the same name, and here we had a beautiful view of the Glacier de la Vache, where the stream takes its rise. The peasants are busily occupied with their hay, and as we advanced, we passed through meadows for some distance.

We ascended gradually, but constantly, and at length, leaving beauty and cultivation behind, we approached scenery of a stern character.

326   TAX UPON HORSES.

At the extremity of the valley, the road has been
re-constructed within a fortnight, in consequence
of the remonstrance of the guides to the renter
of the little inn at the Lac d'Oo: a tax of ten
sous is now levied upon every horse, and the
guides claimed in return this new road; and, to
judge of the old one by some parts we crossed,
they have not made a bad bargain.   Yet the
new part looks and feels as if the first shower of
rain would wash the loose stones and earth, of
which it has been hastily composed, down into
the roaring torrent far below.

The valley is now bare and wild, and at its
extremity a zig-zag road leads up the mountain :
a further steep ascent of this considerable height,
which grows some good fir-trees, leads to the
summit of the pass.   From it, a descent of ten
minutes brought us to the wooden bridge thrown
across the stream soon after its exit from the
lake, but the lake itself was still invisible.   During this descent, the scenery was very wild ;
by the side of a deep ravine, round projecting
rocks, and through a dark wood of firs, the
gloomy and mysterious effect of which was
greatly heightened by the heavy distant roar of
the waterfall, the sight of which we expected to

burst upon us at every turn, but in vain; it was
not until we reached the bridge that we saw it
on the side of the distant mountain. As yet, no
lake had made its appearance, but on ascending
the rock which forms its southern boundary, we
saw it lying below.

The scene is very peculiar: all around, except
at the point where we approached, the bare and
stern rock rises, perpendicularly, upwards of a
thousand feet above the lake, forming a complete cirque, and apparently inaccessible; the
lake lies in the bottom of this bowl; strongly
contrasting, by its peaceful appearance, with
the stern character of the rocks around it. Immediately before us was the great fall, pouring
down a large body of water, with a thundering
noise, a perpendicular height of, according to
our guide, 950 feet. I counted seven other cascades contributing their supplies to the lake;
the extent of which is stated to be thirty-seven
hectares, about ninety-two acres; its depth, in
the centre, 300 feet; its form, oval.

These cirques terminate many of the higher
valleys of the Pyrenees, and are, I believe, quite
peculiar to them. The same character is impressed upon them all; and it looks as if, to form

328 BEAUTIFUL FORMATION OF ROCKS.

them, the mountains which bound the valley receded at the extremity, and presented a semicircular barrier to further progress. How these cirques have been formed ·is not an easy question to decide ; there is nothing which indicates volcanic action. Whether the softer calcareous rocks have melted away under the influence of water and the elements, leaving more of the harder rocks exposed to view, or whether the yielding of the lower strata has formed these concavities, I know not—this point I leave for geologists to determine—but the result is a very grand and beautiful formation.

Many of them occur in these mountains ; that of Gavarnie is, and I believe justly, the most celebrated. That of Heas is remarkable for its vast extent ; its grand amphitheatre would afford easy accommodation for millions : this of the Lac d'Oo, is, as we have now experienced, very fine ; so is that of the Valley du Lys and many others.

We were fortunate in arriving so early, for the clouds, though collecting, still enabled us to see the lofty summit of the Quarate towering above the fringed outline of the rocks above the lake : our enjoyment, however, was but short-lived, for the Quarate was soon hid by the increasing mist. Near these heights, by the Glacier de la Vache, is a foot passage to Venasque by the Port d'Oo.

We took some provisions with us, but the old woman who lives at the single cottage near the lake, seemed so anxious to give us some trout and eggs that we ordered a little meal, and down ran the boys to catch the fish in the clear lake, and off went some wild-looking girls for the eggs. In less than a quarter of an hour a table was spread among the rocks, and our appetites were in excellent order to do justice to the old woman's good cheer.

We met several Spanish peasants, with fine banditti countenances and long red caps, some folded and placed flat on their heads, and others hanging down over their shoulders : some of their jackets were embroidered, and the red sash round the waist was of rich silk. They were driving richly-caparisoned mules down the dizzy height.

Though the scenery of the lake was very stern and sombre, yet I think it has a less gloomy aspect than the situation of Luchon. The high walls of rock which rise perpendicularly on each

330   THE CURÉ'S GARDEN.

side of this town give such a bird-in-a-cage sensation that I feel as if I could never get out.

Tuesday, 13.—We intended to have started this morning at six o'clock, if the weather had been fine, for the Porte de Venasque, to set our feet once more on Spanish ground. We looked out anxiously at five, but nothing but mists were visible, so I went to sleep again, as I was much tired from yesterday's long expedition. The weather cleared up a little at eleven, and we walked to a cascade above the opposite village of Montauban.

The curé has made a very pretty walk up to it, through his garden. After the rolling sharp stones which covered the corkscrew road we had yesterday to climb, it was a great relief to find a green path between hedges of lavender and verbina, winding gently upwards through fruit trees and large chesnuts, and sometimes along a straight terrace full of flower-beds, bordered with vines. During our ascent, we rested several times on rustic benches, and luxuriated in the fine view and delicious perfumes, and then suddenly emerged upon a scene of romantic grandeur, worthy of Scott's pen or Salvator Rosa's pencil. The cascade is in the deep recess of a narrow cleft in the rocks, and the large trees which overhang it, render the effect more dark and imposing.

I should think the sun can never shine on that body of falling water, or penetrate far into the recesses of the sort of open cave where it falls. The body of water is not great, but the sight is certainly very imposing and beautiful: the woman who shews the garden said that the waterfall is always frozen in winter, and the approach so covered with ice that they cannot go near it. The curé has planted, and, indeed, built the garden—for much of it is built up or raised on terraces—entirely at his own expense; and it cost eleven thousand francs. He now bestows upon the poor of the parish whatever gratuity visitors may give for their agreeable promenade.

Wednesday, 14.—This waiting, and hoping, and watching for a clear sky to go to Venasque, recals the disagreeable sensation I have generally experienced when waiting at a sea-port for a fair day to cross in the horrible steamer. Up half a dozen times in the night to see if the clouds were breaking—servants up at half-past five—breakfast ordered—and then comes rain !

I believe we are all more or less slaves to sight-
seeing. I long to leave the place, but we have
made it a point not to do so till we have seen
the lions. This is very foolish; and I am sure
a great deal of unnecessary fatigue and trouble
is taken in mountainous countries to go over
difficult passes &c., when, after all, the high
roads are often far more beautiful, and afford
the additional enjoyment of a comfortable carriage. From all I can judge, this is the case
with the carriage road from Bigorres here.

Evening.—In spite of clouds and showers, we
started at nine, on horseback, for the Valley du
Lys. We passed close to Castel Bielle, and
the road is the same as the one leading to
Venasque till the bridge of the Valley du Lys,
when we turned to the right, and entered the
lovely valley. It was beautiful even in mists
and rain, for the large forest trees grow in wild
fantastic forms on either side of the rushing
river Lys, and clothe the steep sides of the glen,
as far as the mists would allow us to see.

Sometimes the valley becomes wider, and the
great uneven plain is interspersed with cottages,
or rather stables, for there were no inhabitants :
they only serve as shelter in the winter for the

cattle. At that season, one man alone lives there for a fortnight at a time : how solitary, and dangerous, too; for we saw in many places the destruction that avalanches had caused—a line cut in the forest from the summit to the bottom— the gigantic beach and oaks actually mown down, and scarcely a trace of them left.

Yet, with all these marks of destruction and desolation, the Valley du Lys is a pleasant and peaceful-looking spot. The three cascades, which are precipitated down the sort of half cirque—a high wall of rocks—at the extremity, are very beautiful; the source of the Lys is in the centre, and this fall is called the Cascade de l'Enfer. At the base of the fall, there still re- mains an arch of snow, under which the foam- ing torrent passes, large trees spring from the clefts to ornament the scene; others overhang the high wall of rock down which the water rushes, and beyond are the snow mountains. Alas ! the mists veiled their forms, and deprived us of the most striking features of elevated scenery—fine trees, clothed in all their luxuri- ance of summer foliage, growing close to large fields of ice and snow ! We walked over the bridge of snow, though I felt rather nervous on it, from having heard that part of it had broken away a few days ago. The scenery at that spot is awfully grand, and well accords with its name, Cascade de l'Enfer.

Some boys picked me a bunch of lilies from the rocks, close to the single arch of snow we saw at the bottom of the waterfall : it is their abundance which gives the valley its picturesque name.

This valley belongs to the villages of Castillon, St. Aventin, and Cazon, which we passed through on our way to the Lac d'Oo, and was left to these villages ages ago by an ancient Count d'Arbon,— in the same way that in former times the celebrated St. Bertrand de Comminges granted valleys which belonged to him to various villages—that leading to the Port de Venasque, to Bagnères de Luchon, though in those times Luchon occupied a position on the mountain ; the valley where it now stands was a lake, which was afterwards drained by the English, who removed a rock which obstructed the passage of the river.

This M. de St. Bertrand seems quite to have been a kind of Pyrenean St. Patrick, as, beside all the miracles I have related, he had the power of destroying serpents with a wand ; and in proof

of this, one is shewn in the church at St. Bertrand—a huge one, which is said to have infested
the country in those days; but on our visit we
found it was the body of a crocodile, probably
brought by some crusader from the East.

We passed several detached "ecuries" (stables),
where the cattle, are kept during the winter:
higher up the valley, we saw two villages of
these establishments, now unoccupied. The
timber is very carefully attended to: no trees are
cut but under the direction of the proper officer;
a sale takes place, and the tenth of the produce
goes to the government, to keep up the roads
of the district; the rest goes to the benefit of the
commune. Timber is dear: we met a load carrying home for our guide, who had purchased
twenty-six trees, at thirteen francs each—he to
cut and carry home, and pay the government
tithe: they were fir-trees for planks, and would
stand him at twenty francs a-piece.

In this valley we saw a greater variety of timber, and of finer quality, than we had before met
with. The ash, and, I believe, the poplar and
sycamore, are valuable, as their leaves, particularly those of the ash, afford excellent spring
food for lambs. The young branches are taken

336   GOOD BREAKFASTS.

off while the leaves are on, and made into faggots for use, and are far more nutritious than hay.

There is a little wooden chalet at the end of the valley, where a family lives in summer, and provides refreshments for visiters; our *déjeûné* consisted of some very good curds and cream, besides an excellent omelette, which I saw the old woman make while I dried my dress at the kitchen fire.

On our return, the view of Castel Bielle,* on its high, rocky mound, the venerable guardian of three valleys, and the first glimpse down that of Luchon, was very fine. We had heavy rain all the way home, and arrived about three, very wet, and covered with mud.

Our guide's tradition agrees with the legend I related in the last chapter—that in ancient times a lake filled the valley of Luchon, whose waters were kept in by a rock, which was removed by the English; the waters were thus permitted to flow off, and the fine valley was created. We were shewn the spot, on the side of the mountain, to the left of the present town,

* A sketch of it, from the Promenade at Luchòn, is given at page 806.

where our guide said the old one formerly stood, overlooking the lake. If such was the case, this scenery just here must have been much more beautiful, for there is a flatness in the valley, which looks formal; the steep sides rise with a uniform abruptness, which would be beautiful if reflected in a clear lake, but, as I said before, there is now something almost awful in their gigantic height and even sides.

Thursday, 15*th.* — Sun-shine this morning, but the higher mountains are covered by clouds, so we wavered about going any expedition, after yesterday's wetting, till all the guides and horses were engaged; out of upwards of sixty guides not one to be found, even so early as seven o'clock. The clouds have descended lower, so we have had no loss, and gained a little time to finish sketches, &c.

Friday evening, 16*th.* — Another rainy day! We have had several days in the south of France such as I never saw even in that most traduced climate, Ireland; days in which the sun never shone.

Sunday, 18*th.*—Still prevented by rain from seeing anything; it poured all yesterday, but, contrary to our expectations, the mountains were

338   SPLENDID VIEW OF THE MOUNTAINS.

visible, in all their splendour, this morning—in increased splendour too, for a great deal of snow has fallen since they were last visible, five days ago, so that now they look like a new and finer range.

Our intention is, when the weather permits, to enter Spain by the Port de Venasque, to proceed to Viella in Catalonia, and from thence descend the Valley of Aran to St. Beat, there to meet our courier and the carriage.

339

CHAPTER XVIII.

Excursion into Spain—Splendid forest scenery—Hospice de Venasque — Spanish honesty, and veneration for the mountain pass — La Maledetta — Pierre Barran — Sad effects of parting in anger.

July 19*th.*—We were up at five o'clock, and had the happiness to see the mountains perfectly distinct, and a brilliant morning; departure for Spain, of course, resolved on. I in a chaise à porteur, carried by two men, with two to relieve, for which we are to pay forty francs : the rest of the party mounted, and our guide, Benoit, carries on his horse a portmanteau, and various other things—provisions for the men, and a leathern wine bottle, to be used à l'Espagnolle—that is, to be held a certain distance from the mouth, and the stream of wine directed into

z 2

340   THE CAGOT'S HUT.

the mouth, thus really " making the throat a thoroughfare for wine."

The ride up the valley was delightful; woods, and mountains, known before under the gloomy influence of mist and rain, now appeared in all their beauty. We passed the Tour de Castel Bielle, standing out in its fine position, and I found that the " porteurs" kept up to the usual mountain pace, for in less than an hour we reached the point where the road to the Vallée de Lys branches off, and we entered the Vallée of the Hospice — a valuable property of the Commune of Luchon.

We soon reached the Cagot's hut; the Cagots seem to have ceased to be considered as a separate race—the only present distinction being their own inclination to remain in the mountains. The family occupying this hut lost a remarkably fine young man, who was killed at Constantine, and their remaining son has now been drawn in the conscription; I saw the wife loading a horse with wood, to sell at Luchon.

We continued to ascend, enjoying a good view, of which the Pic de Pecade, not visible from Luchon, formed the great attraction : it is a complete sugar loaf of smooth shist, and looks

almost as if it had been chiseled. We now
reached the forest of Charagan, growing very
fine beech and fir, with other trees, and I saw a
large cherry lately cut, which is a wood much
esteemed for building.

Soon after leaving the forest, we reached
the Hospice, having, by degrees, neared the
great heights to which, for many days, we had
looked forward with so much anxiety; behind us
we saw the fine pasture height of Sobra-Bag-
nières, and could judge that the view from it
must be very good, commanding all the heights;
a visit to it might be combined with the expedition to the Valley du Lys. (Mem. for future
travellers.)

The Hospice is a large, substantial house, for
which a considerable rent is paid; the tenant is
obliged to keep the road to the Port from the
Hospice in order, as it is called; and in winter,
when he descends into the valley, must leave
bread, wine, and firing in the house for the relief of any traveller who may call.   It is a point
of conscience, which is almost invariably observed, to leave money equivalent to the quan-
tity of provisions consumed.

Another trait of honesty connected with this

342   CURIOUS CUSTOM.

passage is the sacredness of property left at the
Port de Venasque. By law, the carriers do not
cross the frontier; the bales of goods are depo-
sited at the Port, and there they often remain for
the day and night, before being removed by the
parties to whom they belong, and yet the plunder
of a bale is a thing never heard of. And whence
is this? Is it that scenes like these, that the
sight of nature in its sublimity, the awful ter-
rors of the avalanche and storm in these high
regions have the power of elevating the mind,
and rendering it incapable of base and sordid
actions?

A strong religious feeling, too, is connected
with the pass: it has all been consecrated, so
that the bodies of those lost in the passage may
lie in holy ground. I was pointed out a spot,
at the side of one of the small lakes, where
lie the bodies of five men, who were carried
away by an avalanche of snow, in attempting a
passage during the winter. It was two months
before they were discovered.

Our cortège stopped at the Hospice a few
minutes: we walked forwards, about to penetrate amongst the great heights around us, and
with a feeling of curiosity as to how we were to

get on—a feeling destined to be far more strongly
excited.   We had, from a height reached in a
few minutes, to halloo loudly before we could
move the main body, still lingering at the Hospice below us.

And now our hard work began.   We ascended
by the side of a torrent, the young Pique, I fancy,
forcing its passage through a bed of snow.   The
men took me in my chair over the snow-bridges,
being, I conclude, a more practicable mode than
passing through the torrent; but this proceeding much increased my alarm, for I could not
help thinking how easily the fragile bridge might
be carried into the valley below.   We knew that
part of the snow-bridge over the cascade in the
Valley du Lys had been carried away the very
night before we were there.   We thus cork-
screwed our way along, wondering by what
miracle we were to get out; for never did I see
a passage, where the effect of enclosure is so
complete; even to the last quarter of an hour,
the perpendicular wall of rock seems to bar all
further progress.

We continued our ascent, and reached a spot
which, to my surprise, was only half way: I did
not see how more than another hour could be

344   PIC DE SOBRAGARDE.

required to reach the summit which appeared to
be so close.

The Pic de Sobragarde, the highest point to
the right of the port, was now finely before us.
" It is not," said our guide, " very difficult of
access, and the view from it is very fine; the
top, when clear of snow, is covered with turf."
The Montaignette lies in front of the pass, and
amidst the snow which lay below the point
around us, are four or five small lakes, all now
unfrozen, except one. The water over the snow
at their edges, of a beautiful blue colour.

We now had a proof of the intelligence
of our horses in getting round a projection in
the path, a short, but nervous pass, covered
with snow. After fording a torrent with some
difficulty, we came to so narrow and steep a
passage in the snow, that it was thought better
to dismount: even on foot it was a formidable
business— a false step would have carried one
to a great depth, probably to the frozen lake,
far, far below.

Nothing could exceed the desolation of the
scene; all appearance of vegetation gone —
splintered rocks around us — and, below, the
dreary little lakes partly frozen, and fringed with

snow. We reached the rock called "l'Homme," which serves in winter to mark the direction of the Hospice. It appeared at an immense depth below us, yet, in winter, the guides glide from this to the bottom, over the snow, with great velocity, and in an incredibly short space of time; they direct and steady themselves with a pole, but it requires much skill to do so; for once started, there is no stopping, and any blundering would be fatal.

We toiled on, the chairmen and horses astonishing us by their power and steadiness. At last, when all further advance seemed impracticable, we rounded a projection, and, between its giant portals, saw the "Port" above us. The view here is too terrific to be picturesque; but it is truly sublime: we looked back upon the track we had passed, and could scarcely comprehend how the journey had been accomplished. At a quarter to eleven, we reached the Port de Venasque. Then, after all this upward toiling, we did not even attain a platform. No, the ridge passage through the narrow "Port" is not above a few feet level! And there we looked down—down both ways—there was no help for it—no end to the apparent danger. Nothing would have in-

346   THE MALEDETTA.

duced me to return the way we came, and yet,
on looking down the Spanish side, it appeared
quite as bad. I could see nothing to prevent
our slipping straight down into the deep ravine
which separates the Port de Venasque from the
most awful of savage mountains—the snow-
clad, accursed, unclimbed, almost unlooked-upon
Maledetta.

It is the highest of the Pyrenees—the highest
mountain in Spain or France; and yet it does
not shew its giant head in, I believe, any of the
distant views one gets of the Pyrenees. But
there it was. We entered the Port, and though
far distant, it suddenly appeared close before us.
" Port" is the term used for all the numerous
passes in the mountains between France and
Spain: they are, many of them, curious cuts
in the gigantic wall of rock which separates the
two countries, and at the Port de Venasque, so
narrow is the opening, that a good pair of gates
might serve as a barrier.

The Brêchede Roland is another of these; and
so exactly do they appear to have been cut, that
I do not wonder the imaginative peasantry of
these regions should have attributed that near
Gavarnie to the sword of their great hero Ro-

land. As we stood in the Port de Venasque, I thought with pleasure on Ariosto's beautiful descriptions of Roland and the Paladins of ancient days. Indeed, it would appear as if he had the very spot, and scenery through which we had passed, in his mind, when he relates the wanderings of Bradamante in search of the enchanter's castle:—

> " Prese la via per una stretta valle
>   Con Brunello ora innanzi, ora alle spalle.
>   Di monte in monte, e d'uno in altro bosco
>   Giunsero, ove l'altezza di Pirene
>   Pùo dimostrar, se non è l'aer fosco,
>   E Francia, e Spagna, e due diverse arene."

The passage is about ten or twelve feet wide, between two rocks, which rise apparently about forty or fifty feet above it; the level is only a few feet; we passed it, and were in Aragon. Here were lying some bales of wool, left by Spanish carriers, to be conveyed to Luchon. We arrived only just in time, for, fine as the day was on the French side, the Maledetta was collecting clouds around it; we were so high that this Queen of the Pyrenees did not look to the advantage which she ought; but still a fine object, and the view over her desolate territory is

very impressive. The Maledetta, owing to fis-
sures in the ice, is more dangerous of access,
than difficult. We saw, round the summit,
what appeared to be a road; it is a chasm in the
glacier; this chasm, according to Benoit, our
guide, is sixteen pans (10⅔ feet) wide, (a pan is
eight inches.)

" Poor Pierre Barran !" said our guide, as he
saw me looking at those fearful clefts in the
glaciers of the Maledetta; " I never see that
spot without thinking of our good Pierre, who
was the bravest and best guide in all the Hautes
Pyrénées. It is now full twenty years ago, yet
it seems only like yesterday. And his unfortunate
son ! I shall never forget the poor young man's
sorrow. God grant none of us may see the like
again !"

" What was it ? What happened to him ?"
we inquired.

" Ah, it's a sad story !" said our guide; " and
we had better get safe over all this snow, and
down yonder scala, and reach the other side of
the frozen lake, before we talk of anything so
dreadful; for I would not answer for my own
footsteps, much less for the ladies', if I was
thinking of Pierre Barran."

We went on; and the way, indeed, soon became so difficult as to require all our attention. After descending the scala, and over, or rather through, an awful waterfall, we sat down under shade of some fine chesnut trees. It was now so hot that our thoughts reverted with great pleasure to the frozen regions through which we had passed, and I reminded our guide of his promise.

" Pierre Barran," said he, " was the bravest and most honest man I ever knew; indeed, there was never one like him, except his son— his only son, Charles; and when any strangers wanted to go up to the Port in bad weather, or when there was great danger of avalanches, Pierre Barran was sure to be employed.

" The father and son loved each other more than any two mortals I ever saw; yet both were passionate, and I have seen them quarrel violently. Charles sometimes accused his father of being fool-hardy, and said he was sure that, sooner or later, he would come to some untimely end. Late in the autumn of 1812, two gentlemen, engineers, came to Luchon, and inquired for a guide to the Maledetta. All the passes were covered with deep snow, and every one of us laughed at the idea of any man thinking

350   THE GUIDE'S RESOLVE.

of going even over the Port de Venasque, much
less up the Maledetta, at such a time of the
year.

" However, Pierre Barran did not laugh ; but
when it was proposed to him, he gravely said
he would go.   Whereupon his son flew into a
great passion, and said he might as well commit
suicide at once ; and he swore a solemn oath,
that nothing should tempt him up—no, not even
as far as the Hospice.

" Barran was very unhappy at his son's
anger ; but still he had pledged his word to go
with the gentlemen, and would not retract.   It
was the custom of both father and son to go
and pray together every evening at the cross
near Montauban church, but on the night before
this dangerous expedition, neither of them were
seen there.   The next morning at five o'clock,
a neighbour who lived in the adjoining cottage
overheard Barran saying to his son—' Do not
let us part in anger, my dear boy, for perhaps
we may never meet again !'

" ' If you think so, then, father, why do you
go ?   For my part, it seems downright madness.'

" At that Pierre got angry again, and went
out without even wishing his son good-bye.

" The day had hardly dawned when Charles was seen walking up and down before the cottage, in great agitation. ' Oh, that I had not sworn that fearful oath !' he said. ' My poor father, I know he will perish, and I shall not be near to save him. Cursed be my folly !' He was aware of his wickedness in having been so violent, and yet went on swearing still, and saying, ' And to think that I had not even his blessing !'

" All day Charles Barran was like one wild ; and when night came on, the gentlemen returned, but poor Barran was not with them. Everything had gone on well till they came to the lowest glacier you saw in the Maledetta. Though he had succeeded in getting the travellers across, by some unaccountable accident his foot slipped and he fell in. The gentlemen could hear his groans for a long time, but they had no means of rendering him any assistance ; all they could do was to hasten back, and inform us of the sad event.

" The moment Charles heard of it, he threw himself on the ground in despair. The neighbours tried all they could to pacify him ; and one said, perhaps, after all, his father might not be dead, and offered to go with him as soon as morning dawned, and see if they could find him.

352   A SON'S DESPAIR.

" The moment Charles heard this, he started up, and exclaimed, ' I will give all I possess to any two who will go with me this very minute to the Maledetta !' But none were found to venture.

" The impetuous young man would not wait ; so he went alone, and none of us ever expected to see him again alive. However, next morning we went up to the Port, taking with us ropes, and irons, and everything necessary to restore animation, in case they had not perished. It was a rough morning—more snow had fallen— and none of us expected to return safe. However, the Barrans were both so much beloved that no one murmured, and we were all resigned to risk our lives for their sakes. It was past twelve when we reached the Port de Venasque, and we all looked with the greatest anxiety towards the Fente.

" Fortunately the weather became a little clearer, yet I could see nothing at that distance ; but Jean fancied something black moved near the crevice, so we hurried on. Two hours more passed before we could reach it, for the snow began to fall again right in our faces. Joseph fancied he heard a faint cry, as we approached the fatal spot.

" 'They are both dead!' exclaimed Joseph. 'But I am sure I heard a cry as if from the glacier.'

" We hallooed as loud as ever we could, and a faint voice, that sounded like a distant echo of our own, was heard; so, on approaching we saw Charles standing on a ledge of ice in the chasm below. We immediately let down to him some rope and a bottle of spirits.

" ' Let them down further,' said he; ' I will go down for my father's body, if it is at the very bottom of the mountain!'

" So Charles fastened the ropes round his body, and we let him down full twenty feet. He had tried to climb down, but could only get part of the way; and, as we had promised to come, he resolved to wait. And so he had passed all the night half-way down that terrible place, clinging to a projecting bit of ice, not to save his own life, but that he might be alive in the morning when we came, to fetch up his father's body.

" ' All night long,' he afterwards said, ' I prayed to God that he would enable me to live till I saw my dear father's body buried in our own church, and he has heard my prayer. Oh, if we had both not been blinded with anger on

354   BARRAN'S BODY DISCOVERED.

that fatal night till we forgot to pray! 'Twas
the only time in our lives we did not ask God's
blessing on our undertakings, and we have been
fearfully punished.'

" Well, we let down the ropes, but it was
long before Charles found the body, for poor
Pierre had fallen in some way further along the
cleft; and then Charles was so benumbed and
exhausted he could not lift it for some time.
Joseph offered to go down and help him, but
Charles begged him not, as he was determined
no one should risk the danger but himself.   At
last, he succeeded in fastening the rope round his
poor father, and we drew them both up.

" ' Thank God!' said he, as they reached the
light of day—' His name be praised! my dear,
dear father has a smile upon his countenance!'

" And so it was indeed, he had never looked
so peaceful before.   Poor Charles fell into a
faint, and it took some time to recover him ; but
at last we succeeded, and got as far as the
Hospice that night.

" The next morning Charles was hardly alive,
but implored us to hurry forwards.   ' If I can
only live to see him interred in our church I
shall die content!'

". God heard his prayer. We all reached Montauban by four o'clock that evening; and the good curé and the greater part of the villagers met us, and the mournful ceremony was performed.

" But Charles Barran never spoke again; as soon as the body was placed in the earth, he fell down senseless on the spot, and two days afterwards was buried in the same grave.

" And ever since, when any dear friends quarrel, or any of us are going to part in anger, we always remember poor Pierre Barran and his unfortunate son."

I will now return to our expedition by the Port de Venasque, from which I made this long digression, and thus anticipated our arrival in southern regions, after the toils of snow-paths, and all the difficulties of our route. As we looked from the "Port" towards the noble chain of mountains before us, Benoit told us that the highest point is the Maledetta; the next, the Pic de Natou, lying more to the south; on the right, the Pic de Perigeo; and at the extremity, the Pic de Paderme. On the left is the Forca-

356   FATIGUING EXPEDITION.

nada, and then the fine Pic de Pomero, little inferior to the Maledetta, and which afterwards,
as we descended the Vallée d'Artiga de Lin, was
so fine an object.

We descended on the Spanish side, which,
though steep, is much less formidable, and arrived at our resting-place, where the men and
horses were to feed, at three-quarters after eleven.
Here we thought our troubles ended; but we
were mistaken.   Below us lay a wild valley, on
the left of the Maledetta; but it was not our road
—it leads to the town of Venasque.   At twenty
minutes after twelve we again started, and, after
occasional ascents and descents, found ourselves
mounting to reach a bed of snow above us, over
which, some time before, we had seen some
Spanish mules toiling, though we little thought
then we should have to follow their example;
but so it was.   We had to pass the Pecade,
which separates Aragon from Catalonia.   At the
commencement of the valley below us we saw the
cascade, which loses itself in the Trou de Taureau,
or Toron, and which, after having passed under
a part of the range, re-appears, as it is said, in
the wood of the Pomero, at what is called the
source of the Garonne.   Our guide told us
the connexion has been verified by means of

saw-dust thrown in at the fall.* To descend to the cascade and return, would have occupied two additional hours ; with six hours still before us we were obliged to give it up.

We continued to ascend, and found ourselves at last higher than the Port de Venasque ; we passed, on our left, the path which leads to the Port de Pecade, and which would have been our way had we returned to Luchon ; the view of the Maledetta, which we had hitherto enjoyed, was now shut out by a projection of the ridge, and we saw her no more ; but a new view opened upon us—that of the summits of the eastern Pyrenees ; a vast number of pyramidal points, all partially streaked with snow, and one of much greater elevation than the rest; it is curious, from the number of heights, and the similarity of their shape.

We passed a circular pile of stones—the division between the two provinces of Aragon and Catalonia. We now entered Catalonia, and reached the ruins of some huts, where troops were stationed during the war.

---

* This is the spot into which the evil spirit is said to have thrown the Lady of Fronsac, as I related in the legend at page 312.

358

CHAPTER XIX.

Passage of the Gorge de Pomero—Desolate scenery—Beautiful flowers in the Spanish valley of Artiga de Lin—Tale of Catarina de Comminges and Alphonso, King of Aragon.

AND now we commenced a very steep descent over snow, through " La Gorge de Pomero ;" it looked an awful plunge. For a considerable distance we scrambled over the rocks at the side of the snow, but often they were so steep that we were obliged to walk through it, and in some places we sank in up to our knees ; yet this, though very disagreeable, was much safer than the harder snow-paths we had sometimes to pursue — those winding and steep scalas, only a few feet wide, with a deep abyss yawning below on one side, a wall of rock on the other.

The desolate grandeur of this scene was to me most depressing; no signs of vegetation could

DESOLATE GRANDEUR.   **359**

be anywhere perceived, and soon a dreary mist
came slowly winding upwards from the valley,
and veiled all distant objects from our eyes.   As
we toiled through the tedious beds of snow or
bare chaos of rocks, I experienced a sort of hopeless feeling, and despaired of ever again seeing
a blade of grass, or any sign of animated life,
and almost fancied that we had passed into another planet.

When at last we came to a few patches of
stunted vegetation, I hailed the sight with surprise
and with more delight than I ever felt at entering
the finest garden in the world.   So powerfully
does a very new and striking scene sometimes impress our minds that we seem absorbed by its present influence, and the past fades for the time from
our recollection ; we fancy everything else except
the striking scene before us was only a dream,
and cannot even imagine any other future—at
least, I find it so, though I do not indeed often
meet with any impression sufficiently powerful
to produce the feeling.   Our descent from the
Port de Pecade put me again in mind of Bradamante's search for the Enchanter's Castle,—

> " Quindi per aspro e faticoso calle
>   Si discendea nella profonda valle."

360   WILD FLOWERS.

There was, too, at the bottom of the upper
ravine, a rocky height so steep and isolated as
quite to agree with Ariosto's account of the
Enchanter's Palace :—

> " Vi sorge in mezzo un sasso, che la cima
>   D'un bel muro d'acciar tutta si fascia ;
>   E quella tanto verso il ciel sublima,
>   Che, quanto ha intorno, inferior si lascia.
>   Non faccia, chi non vola, andarvi stima ;
>   Che spesa indarno vi saria ogni ambascia.
>   Brunel disse : Ecco dove prigionieri
>   Il mago tien le donne e i cavalieri.
>   Da quattro canti era tagliato, e tale,
>   Che parea dritto al fil della sinopia ;
>   Da nessun lato nè sentier, ne scale
>   V'eran, che di salir facesser copia :
>   E bene appar, che d'animal ch' abbia ale,
>   Sia questa stanza, nido e tana propria."

                                        Canto iv., p. 20.

After a long and most fatiguing descent, but
very fine and wild, with the Pomero towering
above our heads, we left the snow, the mists
cleared away, and we rejoiced to find ourselves
amid the milder beauties of vegetation. A variety
of lovely wild flowers welcomed us back to the
world below, and we approached a wood of fine
beeches and chesnuts.

Before we entered its umbrageous depths,

however, we had to pass through a deep and
rapid torrent, just above a large waterfall, on
each side of which the scattered and riven trunks
of trees bore evidence of its fury.   I felt sure
that the horses and men would never be able to
stem this fearful torrent.   The guide went first,
on horseback, and reached the other side in
safety, and we all followed; but the men who
carried my chaise à porteur and me, were above
their knees in the rapid current, and declared that
it was indeed a " *mauvais pas.*"

After this (to me) terrific passage, we came
into a scene of exquisite sylvan loveliness : it
was a sudden and delicious transition from the
barren, piercing cold of polar regions, to all the
glowing and luxuriant vegetation of the south.
Wild flowers grew under the wide spreading
branches of gigantic oaks and chesnuts, in such
profusion and variety, that it seemed as if all the
conservatories of England had emptied their rich
stores in this chosen spot.

I do not know the names of many flowers, but
I never before saw any so beautiful, and their
vivid and rare hues were only equalled by the
gorgeous wings of innumerable butterflies which
sported among them.   Some of these lovely

creatures hovered close around us, and one,
whose wings must have been full six inches long,
rested for a moment on my dress. I hope it was
of that kind which, I hear, is called the Angel, for
it is supposed to be a good spirit, and that it
brings happiness to the fortunate mortal it
approaches.

For nearly half an hour we proceeded through
these woodland conservatories, where the flut-
tering "angels" made me almost imagine that
the spirit of harmony which seems to pervade
this happy valley had brought together the most
beautiful parts of the flowers to form a butterfly,
or rather, as if the half-breathing flowers had in
the very glee of their existence escaped from
their green stems, rejoiced themselves into life,
and risen up to pay a livelier adoration to the
sun's vivid rays.

Since I heard the wild Legend of Chambord
Forest,* in which spirits once innocent and lovely
are said to be imprisoned in flowers, I have
looked on my favourite plants with more interest
than ever. I am, too, more delighted with their
perfume, because that strange Spirit of the Violet
said the only intellectual pleasure they felt was

---

* This tale I did not insert, for want of room.

when mortals were enjoying their perfume. I delight, too, in thinking that we are surrounded by spirits, and there is nothing the coldest reason can urge against the pleasant idea that flowers and trees, and all the lovely works of creation, which minister so much to our daily happiness, may be the dwelling-places of good spirits. The thought makes everything more companionable—to imagine those beings look upon us with kindness, and breathe peace and delight into our hearts with every gentle air that wafts their perfume towards us! How well Mrs. Norton expresses this idea in the following beautiful lines :—

> " Go! let the scoffer call it
> A shadow and a dream;
> Those meek subservient spirits
> Are nearer than we deem:
> Think not they visit only
> The bright enraptured eye
> Of some pure, sainted martyr
> Prepared and glad to die;
> Or that the poet's fancy,
> Or painter's colour'd skill,
> Creates a dream of beauty,
> And moulds a world at will:
> They live! they wander round us,
> Soft resting on the cloud;
> Although to human vision
> The sight be disallow'd;

64   FOREST SCENES.

> They are to the Almighty
> What the rays are to the sun—
> An emanating essence
> From the great supernal One :
> They bend for prayer to listen,
> They weep to witness crimes ;
> They watch for holy moments—
> Good thoughts—repentant times :
> They cheer the meek and humble,
> They heal the broken heart;
> They teach the wavering spirit
> From earthly ties to part;
> Unseen they dwell among us,
> As when they watch'd below,
> In spiritual anguish,
> The sepulchre of Woe :
> And when we pray, though feeble
> Our orisons may be,
> *They* then are our companions
> Who pray eternally."

We were now continually in a forest. By a rough and very steep road we again reached the stream, which we passed on some trees thrown across it.

Here Benoit and W—— left the party, to see what is called, (but why, I know not,) "La source de la Garonne." The spring which gives rise to the river (the Garonne), which flows by Viella, is surely more deserving of the name. W—— said he passed a torrent, which he would have

had great difficulty in accomplishing by himself,
and had a scramble of about ten minutes through
the forest to reach the spot where the stream, of
considerable volume, issues from among the
rocks, and is certainly worthy of being a great
river's source. Unfortunately, the rocks are so
numerous immediately at the issue, that they
divide the water, and injure the effect. On the
return, Benoit made the capture of an enormous
frog, which he rejoiced in, as being very fat, and
excellent eating.

Again we started, and kept descending through
the forest—a source of great wealth; the road
now improved, and we at length emerged from
the wood, and, after a rapid march of three
hours, reached the hermitage of Artiga de Lin,
the first habitation we had seen. Here refreshments may be had. There is a small chapel near
it, where a priest attends on festivals. Our
bargain with the porters extended no further;
but as we had three more hours to travel, and
some rough ground still before us, I dreaded the
fatigue of riding; so we made a further agree-
ment to pay twenty francs for the chair to Viella.

At the Hospice a number of Spanish peasants,
genuine Catalonians, came out to see us, and

accompanied us into the dark and solemn chapel. The contrast between the French and Spaniards is more decided than that of any two other nations I ever saw, and is much more striking here than it was in our journey from Bayonne to St. Sebastian, for all the inhabitants of the Basque provinces, on whichever side of the frontier, are the same people, and quite unlike the French.

Here, in Catalonia, the Spanish women have a most sedate, and quite a regal air. You may fancy them born to be arch-duchesses. Their countenances are expressive of sound judgment and good sense, and totally devoid of that frivolity which may be often seen in the French peasantry. They appear, too, far less amiable and desirous of pleasing, but to possess more solid goodness. They are very handsome, and have peculiarly fine lips and eyes, with clear and rather fair complexions, and the most beautiful colour in their cheeks, exactly where it ought to be.

After the horses had fed, we again, about four o'clock, got under weigh. At first, the road was delightful, passing through meadows, surrounded by wooded heights, which were now, however, beginning to be clothed in mist. We descended rapidly, and reached some stables, the winter refuge of the cattle, but now deserted.   We again crossed the branch of the Garonne, but now in a gentlemanlike way, by a bridge, and again ascended for some time in the forest of Balican, occasionally having the river some hundreds of feet immediately below us, until we reached a projecting eminence, from which we had a charming view of the Valley of Aran.

The first Spanish town we saw was Villa Hermosa, so called·from the beauty of its situation, as well as the splendid buildings it once contained.   And, indeed, though the ancient palaces have long since fallen to decay, it still deserves the name of Hermosa, from the extreme beauty of its position, being built on one of the loftiest of those rocky heights which characterize the Valley of Aran, and seemed formed expressly as resting-places, from which to admire the lovely scenes below.

Villa Hermosa, now Villamos, is the most elevated town in the Vale of Aran, and being situated just where the valley makes a curve, it commands two different views.* As I was borne

---

* I afterwards made a sketch of Villamos, and the village under it, called Bebos, with the town of Castel Leon, on the opposite side of the valley.   It forms the frontispiece to the second volume of this work.

luxuriously along the woody slope, and gazed on these romantic scenes, I thought of the beautiful Catarina, heiress of the Comte of Comminges, by whose marriage with the King of Aragon this valley became a portion of Spain.

In the year 1198, Comte Bernard of Comminges, accompanied by his only daughter, passed through this valley, and was nobly entertained by the principal inhabitants of Villa Hermosa.

The young heiress was betrothed to Alphonso, King of Aragon, who was one of the most accomplished and handsome princes of the age — at least, rumour described him as such; but the beautiful Catarina had never seen him, and therefore, as she journeyed towards his court, a thousand fears and apprehensions caused her to tremble, and she gladly seized an opportunity to delay the journey. Her father was obliged to use the utmost persuasion to urge her forward; yet he was by no means a harsh parent, and, unlike most fathers of those times, he had himself superintended her education, and always treated her as a friend and companion; and now he endeavoured, by every tender endearment, to cheer and support her drooping spirits.

" My darling, noble child," said he, as they

stood on the balcony of the castle at Villa Hermosa, while a bright moon illumined the scene below—" You have, I well know, sacrificed the dearest wishes of your heart for the good of your country; it has been, certainly, a great trial, but God will reward your unselfish conduct."

" I want no other reward than your approbation," replied his daughter; " that look of deep affection quite compensates for what I have suffered.   After all, too, what a foolish fancy mine was !" she continued, blushing deeply; " but indeed I knew not that stranger-minstrel had made such a deep impression on my heart till you announced the King of Aragon's proposals; then, indeed, I felt——but I will never think of him more," she added, with a sigh.

" Dearest child, I well knew your feelings : I was aware that such noble sentiments as breathed in the poetry sung by that Spanish minstrel were well calculated to fascinate the pure taste of my darling girl, and had I been blessed with a son, or were France more kindly affected towards my people, I would never have demanded the sacrifice of your affections, but allowed you to dream in peace of the gentle poet, even though my fears had been confirmed, that his rank in life was far too humble ever to aspire to my child."

" Nor would he ever, I am certain," said she; " for, if you recollect his song, it only spoke of hopeless love, of the ennobling effect of deep affection whenthere was no prospect of its ever being returned."

" I well remember it, my child, but indeed we must both try to forget the handsome minstrel. You have declared that the consciousness of acting for the good of our dear vassals has been sufficient reward, and this conviction must support you, even should the King, your husband, not prove so worthy or agreeable as fame declares him to be. And now go to rest, darling, for we have promised to honour the good Abbot of Mitz-Aran by breakfasting in his old monastery, and after that, our journey is long."

" And at the end of the day we shall then reach St. Liestra, the place where the King has appointed to meet us," thought Caterina, as she retired to rest.

Poor Caterina tried hard to occupy her thoughts with her royal bridegroom, yet tradition says, that in her dreams that night she saw the nameless minstrel who had appeared, a year before, at her father's court at Comminges ; and the next morning it was with a heavy heart that she pursued her way.

That night they reached St. Liestra, but the King was not there : he sent, indeed, a numerous retinue and a splendid litter to convey her to Saragossa. It was a great relief to Caterina ; and as she retired to her room, she rejoiced to think that sleep might once more give her the bliss of such dreams as had visited her pillow the night before, without a crime.

Perhaps it was this thought that inspired them, but certainly on that night the unknown minstrel appeared to her again, and his songs were more beautiful, and his appearance more fascinating, than ever.

The next morning, the Count begged her to hasten as much as possible, as they were expected at Saragossa at noon.

Caterina obeyed with a heavy heart, and, attired in her most costly robes, entered the royal litter ; but it was near evening when they reached the splendid palace of Aragon, and Caterina became so agitated, she could scarcely see anything.

But what is this ?—a well-known voice greets

her ear.   Can it be that of the minstrel?   Yes ;
he stands by her side, attired in his simple blue
velvet mantle.

"A thousand welcomes, fairest Princess," he
says—" in the King's name, I bid thee welcome,
and have his orders to conduct thee to his presence."

Caterina trembled more than ever ; for it was
very strange the king should have chosen a person of his low rank to greet her, and it seemed
cruel in the minstrel thus to intrude.   And now
he takes her hand, and presses it to his lips.   She
was almost disposed to be angry, and she scarcely
dared to look at him ; and yet she could not help
wishing that fate had given her such a husband.

" Come, fairest of mortals, the banquet waits,
and the nobles are impatient to do homage to
their beautiful Queen."

They enter the gorgeous chamber, and the
minstrel conducts her to a splendid throne.
There he casts off his simple attire, and stands
before the astonished Caterina arrayed in royal
splendour.   Shouts of " Long live our gracious King Alphonso, and his lovely Queen !"
echo through the lofty halls.   It was the King

himself, who, disguised as a simple minstrel, had won the heart of his bride.

"Pardon me!" he exclaimed, "adored Princess, for deceiving you."

"Nay, it was my doing," interrupted the Count of Comminges : "I wished to try if my daughter was worthy of the devoted affection of such a prince, and whether she would sacrifice her own inclinations to the good of her people. I am now satisfied. The dearest wish of my heart is accomplished ; and may God shower down his choicest blessings on your heads."

The marriage ceremony was performed, and Alphonso and Caterina reigned long and happily over the united states of Aragon and Comminges.

374

CHAPTER XX.

Entrance into the Valley of Aran—Numerous villages—
Aubert—Moncorban—Catalonian peasants—Arrival at
Viella—Miserable quarters.

As we proceeded further, the density of the population in this beautiful valley of Aran was very
striking.   From the point where we rested for a
few minutes, six well-built villages, with their
churches, were in sight.   Castel Leon in the
bottom of the valley; Aros immediately before
us; Villa Hermosa higher up the mountain;
Aubert· on the right.   We had now a very
agreeable ride towards Viella, looking over the
rich valley, with the Garonne rushing on below
us. We laughed at the rough descent to the river,
though, without the experience of the morning,
it might have alarmed us, for the path was none
of the widest, with a very respectable precipice

on the left, and the river far below. We thus reached the high road of the valley, and cantered triumphantly into Aubert.

One of our horses had lost a shoe en route, and had long shewn evident symptoms of his loss. It was here replaced by a smith, a fine specimen of a Catalonian peasant—tall, slight, but muscular, long limbed, and as erect as an arrow; he wore a brown jacket, with culottes of the same colour, open at the knees; his well-shaped leg was covered with a blue stocking, kept up by a coloured garter, and the espartillos, the mountain slipper of cord, the ancient cothurnus, was bound with a lace round the ancle; on his head was the red cloth cap, with the long pendant end,—sometimes this end is folded on the top of the head, with good effect, like the capulets of the Basque women.

Our appearance brought out the population, and among the spectators, I saw many faces, shewing that this place deserves the reputation which the valley has for beauty. At Aubert, we crossed the Garonne, and saw about its rocks, and along its banks, numerous "rouleaux" of timber, left by the last flood, to be forwarded by the next.

The timber of this valley is much esteemed, and gives rise to a considerable trade. The river is the mode of conveyance : each log, with its peculiar mark, is thrown into the stream, and finds itself, at last, at St. Beat. It is a high misdemeanour to take a log, and is punished with " dix ans de galère ;" so that property to a great amount is thus scattered along the river in perfect safety. Every step we took disclosed some new beauty, and I longed to stop and sketch, every minute ; but it was getting late, and the men shook their heads ominously whenever I asked to stop. Fortunately, however, just before we came to the beautiful village of Moncorban, my porteurs waited for a minute or two to take breath, and I then hastily made this sketch, and afterwards put in our own party as they were grouped at the moment.

Before reaching Viella, we passed what had been a convent of considerable size, called Mitzaran, from its position half-way up the valley. It shews traces of high antiquity, and of Moorish architecture ; the church still remains, but many of the buildings have been pulled down, and what is standing has been converted into a farmhouse.

Sketched by Lady Chatterton and drawn on stone by Bichebois.   Printed by Lemercier Benard und Cᵉ

THE VILLAGE OF MONTCORBAN

in the valley of aran. Spain.

It was nearly dark before we reached Viella, and the shades of evening gave a still more desolate appearance to the blackened ruins of houses which had been burnt in the late war. Every object assumed a gloomy appearance, and I could not help thinking of the horrors which had so recently occurred in this spot.

There is something peculiarly dreadful in the idea of a civil war—of brothers fighting against each other, and sons entering into conflict with their once-loved parents. In England, the recollections of internal wars are in some measure hallowed by time, and we look with interest on the old castles, though their blackened ruins still shew that they owe their destruction to civil conflict; but here, where fires of civil discord and hatred seem still to smoulder—where we see no town or village that does not bear traces of recent war, I could not help shuddering as we entered the blackened gateway of Viella, and saw a multitude of ferocious and banditti-looking figures crowd around us; nor could I repress a fear that hands which had been so lately died in the blood of their own kindred, might be lifted against us for the sake of gain.

These disagreeable fears were not diminished

378   THE ALCALDE'S HOUSE.

by the spectral look of burnt houses and the
ruined bridge over which we crossed, or the aspect
of the Alcalde's dwelling, where we were destined
to pass the night, or the clamour and sensation
caused by our arrival there.

Viella is the chief place of the valley; and
some way up the mountain is a kind of fort,
where the Governor resides. We caused quite a
sensation, and made our entrée amidst the bark-
ing of dogs, and the anxious faces of young and
old, who turned out to see us: Benoit led the
way, followed by those on horseback, and I, the
great object of wonderment, borne in my chair
and surrounded by a crowd of children, closed the
procession; such an apparition having, perhaps,
never shewn itself before.

We went to the Alcalde's. The exterior of
the house did not promise much, so, when we
got inside, we could not say we were disappointed; nothing could well be more wretched
and dirty. However, there was no remedy, so
we had to make the best of it: indeed, the
streets through which we passed looked as if
the plague was in them, and the Alcalde's
house as if many a foul murder had been committed within its walls. The old and half-

ruined staircase groaned under our weary footsteps; and the large, lofty room, with its
dark rafters and walls, to my apprehensive
sight, seemed stained with blood. The five
doors, opening from it on mysterious galleries and rooms of all sizes, and none of
which would fasten, or scarcely shut; the large
dark bed within a deep recess, and, above all,
the ominously serious look with which the Alcalde pointed to it, and hoped we should sleep
well in his state bed; the solemn countenances,
too, of the Spanish women, who stood in silent
stillness around, their dark faces shaded by the
white mantilla, and their majestic figures attired
in black; all this had such a new, and, to my
tired imagination, fearful air, that it put me
most disagreeably in mind of a tragedy I saw
when a child, representing murder committed
in a forest inn. Some delay occurred before
we could procure a fire in this gloomy apartment, every one appearing to be absorbed in the
surprise of our arrival and the earnest contemplation of our interesting selves. At last, after
many intreaties, a royal-looking donna slowly
approached the gigantic hearth with some sticks
and a candle, and we had the pleasure of seeing

380   BAD PROVISIONS.

them soon in a blaze, and of drying our feet and
clothes, which were still very wet from our knee-
deep wading through the snow.

We imagined ourselves extremely hungry;
but when, after the lapse of two weary hours,
some black-looking dishes were brought, we
could not find anything eatable. The bread was
mouldy; the soup—I know not of what compound
of horrors it was made—but, after the first mouth-
ful, we hastily abandoned it. We asked for milk
—there was none; for eggs—"no hay," (not
any.) I then turned all my attention to the prospect of repose; but in this we seemed destined
to be disappointed, for we were surrounded by a
large concourse of people, who paid very little
regard to our repeated wishes to be left alone.

In vain I urged extreme fatigue—having
arisen at four o'clock in the morning, and had a
most tiring expedition over the mountains. They
pointed to the bed, and advised me by all means
to go to sleep, but did not appear at all to understand why their presence should prevent my
doing so.

Some, indeed, went away—but others entered, and it was past eleven o'clock before we
could clear the room and go to bed; but, in

spite of extreme fatigue, it was long before I could sleep. The doors creaked every minute on their rusty hinges; and I fancied, by the fitful glare of the expiring fire, that dark heads and gleaming eyes were looking in upon us. The solemn tones of the old church bell, too, which began to toll, increased the ominous gloom, and I almost regretted we had sent away those nun-like women with the white mantillas, whose presence might perhaps have protected us from their more ferocious companions.

At last I slept; and, on awaking, a bright sun was streaming through the lofty windows, and the Alcalde's pretty daughter was smiling near me. Hers was the first countenance on which I had seen a smile, for a wonderful gloom seemed to pervade the whole establishment. "My mother is not so ill to-day," she whispered, in a gentle voice, "and I hope we shall be able to give you something better for your breakfast, than you had last night." We found that the Alcalde's wife had been dangerously ill, but he did not like to tell us of it, lest we should have scrupled to enter his dwelling.

The pretty girl then withdrew, and I began to rise; but before I had time to get out of bed

382   THE ALCALDE'S APOLOGY.

she returned again, followed by several women, to whom she had given the apparently joyful tidings of my having awoke. Soon the room was half full of people; and, as the different doors opened, I saw with great dismay that several men were about to enter.

I entreated the pretty daughter to prevent their entrance, and to withdraw the whole party. She could not understand my objection to have a regular levée at my toilette, but with great good humour she and her sedate companions slowly departed. I felt very stiff and uncomfortable, and as if I could never undertake the long ride of twelve hours which must be performed before we could reach the French frontier.

As soon as I was dressed, the Alcalde came in, and expressed his regret—as well as his broken French would permit—that the severe illness of his wife prevented things from being as well as he could wish.

On going down stairs, I saw through an open door the poor mistress of the house in bed, surrounded by at least a dozen nun-like figures. Three or four were kneeling on each side of her, and the others were standing in a row behind them. A profound stillness reigned in the

room, and the pale countenance of the poor suf-
ferer, and the sedate looks and praying attitudes
of her attendants, put me in mind of the sculptured forms on some of the old monuments in
our English churches.

Certainly, the Spaniards must have the organ
of order strongly developed, or a great taste for
symmetry. In each church I have entered there
were always figures kneeling and standing in
regular rows, with candles placed on the ground
before them at equal distances ; and thus whole
groups, forming as it were patterns, were scattered over and adorned the building.

END OF VOL. I.

T. C. Savill, Printer, St. Martin's Lane.

EDITORIAL NOTES

p. 17, l. 10: *Louis XI*: Louis XI (1423–83), King of France from 1461 to 1483. His love of scheming and intrigue made him many enemies, including his father. Shrewd and often vicious, he plotted and spun webs of conspiracy which earned him the nicknames 'the Cunning' and 'the Universal Spider'.

p. 17, l. 25: *William the Norman*: Also called William the Conqueror (*c.* 1028–87), he was the first Norman King of England, reigning from 1066 until his death in 1087. After a long struggle to establish power, by 1060 his hold on Normandy was secure and he launched the Norman conquest of England in 1066.

p. 18, l. 6: *Bayeux tapestry*: An embroidered cloth nearly 230 feet long depicting the events leading up to the Norman conquest of England concerning William, Duke of Normandy and Harold, Earl of Wessex, later King of England, culminating in the Battle of Hastings.

p. 20, ll. 18–21: *There are many ... Times*: Lady Chatterton's narrative on Abbeville and on the Battle of Crecy is based on F. C. Louandre, a French historian who wrote an interesting and well-documented *Biographie d'Abeeville et Environs*. The Battle of Crecy (1346) is also depicted in A. Ayton, P. Preston and F. Autrand, *The Battle of Crecy* (2007), p. 112, in J. Bradbury, *The Medieval Archer*, p. 187, Rev. Anglo-Fr., iii. 1835, pp. 245–70 and Rt Hon D. H. Madden, *A Chapter of Medieval History* (London 1924).

p. 21, l. 2: *Louandre*: I cannot discern whether the *History* Lady Chatterton refers to was written by François César Louandre (1787–1862) who was born in Abbeville, or if it was written by his son, Charles Léopold Louandre (1812–82), also born at Abbeville and also a historian. I am inclined to believe that it could have been the work of François César Louandre, as the first important work by his son Charles is dated 1842.

p. 21, ll. 3–9: *Et reçu de ce prince l'odieux misión de plonger ... vers 1095*: 'And he received from this prince the horrible task of locking up in a dungeon Princess Bertrade. She was shut again at Montreuil-sur-mer in a tower that bears her name and that still exists in the citadel, the unlucky Queen that died of sadness and misery around 1095' (French).

p. 21, ll. 23–4: *l' affront fait à son sang*: 'the affront to his blood' (French).

p. 23, ll. 9–10: *Je suis ici... defendre*: 'I am here in my lands and I want to defend them' (French).

p. 23, l. 19: *Froissart*: Jean Froissart (*c.* 1337–*c.* 1405), often referred to in English as John Froissart, was a medieval French chronicle writer. For centuries *Froissart's Chronicles* have been recognized as the chief expression of the chivalric revival of the fourteenth-century kingdom of England and France.

p. 24, ll. 23–4: *Tuez-moi cette... là!*: 'Kill all this mob!' (French).

p. 25, l. 25: *Ich dien*: 'I serve' (German). The correct form is 'Ich diene'.

p. 26, ll. 3–6: *L'an mil quarente ... Behaigne*: 'The year one thousand three hundred forty-six, as the chronicle says, was brought and placed here, Jean Luxemburg, King of Behaigue' (French). Epitaph of D'Alençon.

p. 26, ll. 23–8: *Puis a Crécy.... de guerre*: 'Then at Crecy I lost my gendarmes / thirty five thousand notwithstanding their great weapons / despite their armours and chaperons and other clothes / that floated everywhere in the earth, and that were not good for good people to fight' (French). For more information on the battle of Crecy see G. F. Beltz, *IX. An Inquiry into the existing Narratives of the Battle of Cressy, with some Account of its Localities, Traditions, and Remains. By George Frederick Beltz, Esq. K.H., F.S.A., Lancaster Herald, in a Letter to Sir Henry Ellis, K.H., F.R.S., Secretary* (1839). This text was chosen by Lady Chatterton to depict the Battle of Crecy in *Archaeologia: or miscellaneous tracts relating to antiquity. Published by the Society of Antiquaries of London* (London: Nichols and Son, 1840) vol. 28, p. 191.

p. 27, l. 19: *jeux floraux*: 'floral games' (French).

p. 28, l. 7: *moult triomphalement*: 'very triumphantly' (French).

p. 28, l. 14: *Sa coiffure*: 'her hair' (French).

p. 28, ll. 15–17: *à la façon de son pays ... de ses templettes*: 'following his country's way, it was enriched with precious stones around its temples' (French).

p. 28, l. 17: *beaux mystères et honnestes*: 'beautiful mysteries and honest' (French).

p. 29, l. 6: *Alle cloque, je n'en veux mie, attaqu'me*: 'Come on, listen, I do not want more of it, attack me' (French).

p. 40, l. 25–p. 41, l. 1: *moulded by ... fame*: Mary of Orleans (1813–39), a French princess who became Duchess of Wüttemberg (1837) through marriage. With a solid education she took up sculpture and drawing, becoming a talented artist in these two disciplines.

p. 41, ll. 2–3: *Mrs. Hermans ... loveliness*: 'Joan of Arc, In Rheims' by Felicia Hemans (1793–1835). See F. Hemans, *Records of Woman: With Other Poems*, 2nd edn (Edinburgh: William Blackwood and London: T. Cadell, 1828), pp. 109–15. To some readers Hemans offered a woman's voice confiding a woman's trials; to others a lyricism apparently consonant with Victorian chauvinism and sentimentality. Among the works she valued most were the unfinished 'Superstition and Revelation' and the pamphlet 'The Sceptic', which sought an Anglicanism more attuned to world religions and women's experiences. In her most successful book, *Records of Woman* (1828), she chronicles the lives of women, both famous and anonymous.

p. 41, ll. 17–18: *So ist des Geistes Ruf an mich ergangen, / Mich treibt nicht eitlesn irdische Verlangen*: 'The spirit's call was to me. / No earthly vain desire forces me' (German).

p. 43, ll. 10–12: *splendid collection of Spanish ... fine*: Francisco de Zurbaran (1598–1664) was a Spanish painter. He was primarily known for his religious paintings depicting monks, nuns and martyrs, and also for his still lifes.

p. 54, l. 15: *La Tour de Malbrouk*: This refers to John Churchill, first Duke of Malborough (1650–1722).

p. 54, l. 23: *Malbrouk est allé à la guerre*: The air 'Malbrough s'en va-t-en-guerre' ('Marlbrough Has Left for the War') was a burlesque lament on the Duke of Malborough's death.

p. 60, l. 21: *gaiété*: 'gaiety' (French).

p. 60, l. 22: *plein de l'enfance*: 'full of childhood' (French).

p. 66, l. 22–p. 67, l. 8: *L'ANTI-MARSEILLAISE...coeurs*: 'The anti-marseillaise. / Sacred love of the Motherland, / Motherland! is the universe. / Let us dream this loved law /, This is the law of the various peoples /, This is the law of Providence /, Who created us for the happiness / of the great and holy alliance / of peoples to their Saviour / More weapons and do not talk any more / Our destructive swords / breaking our swords / Let's swear, let's swear / that a holy love that will unite all our hearts' (French).

p. 67, ll. 10–11: *Benit soit celui... comprises*: 'Blessed the one who wrote these lines / may they be understood' (French).

p. 72, l. 24: *De nos delicieux deserts de Fontainebleau*: 'From our delicious desserts of Fontainebleau' (French).

p. 73, ll. 6–8: *In the apartment of ... signed*: The Marquise of Maintenon (1635–1719) was the second wife of King Louis XIV of France, whose marriage to him in a private ceremony was never officially announced or admitted. Owing to the disparity of their social status she could not marry the king openly and become queen, and their marriage was morganatic. No written proof of the marriage exists although it is widely accepted by historians. She was known during her first marriage as Madame Scarron and after her marriage to the king as Mme Maintenon.

p. 77, ll. 14–20: *The group which Inglis describes ... the present statue*: For further reading see H. D. Inglis [Derwent Conway], *Switzerland, the South of France, and the Pyrenees in 1830 by Derwent Conway in Two Volumes* (Edinburgh: Constable & Co. and London: Hurst, Chance & Co., 1831), p. 305.

p. 80, ll. 21–22: chere petite maitresse: 'dear little Lady' (French).

p. 87, l. 9: *Catherine de Medicis*: Catherine de' Medici (1519–89). Queen consort of France as wife of King Henry II of France from 1547 to 1559. Throughout his reign, Henry excluded Catherine from participating in state affairs and instead showered favours on his chief mistress, Diane de Poitiers, who wielded much influence over him. Henry's death thrust Catherine into the political arena as mother of the frail fifteen-year-old King Francis.

p. 88, ll. 21–3: *The people expected ... Nostradamus*: To read more, see *The Prophecies of Nostradamus*. 3/51–1588, p. 27. The term regularly used to describe Nostradamus was 'a Medieval mystic'. Born in 1503 at St. Rémy in Provence, he was a child of the Renaissance. He had the benefit of a traditional classical education together with Jewish teachings in the natural sciences still forbidden to Christians.

p. 89, ll. 1–2: *Paris conjure un grand meurdre commettre ... plain effet*: 'The committing of murder plotted in Paris, / will be carried out openly at Blois' (French).

p. 89, ll. 8–11: *En l'an qu'un oeil en France regnera ... en mal et doute double*: 'In the year in which an eye will reign in France, / that court will be in very unpleasant trouble, / the great of Blois will kill his friend; / the realm placed in harm and double doubt' (French).

p. 89, ll. 19–20: *Quand* bonnet rouge *passera par la fenêtre ... et* tout *perira*: 'When the *red cap* goes through the window, for *forty ounces* they will cut off your head and *everything* will perish' (French). Lady Chatterton mistakes Cardinal Richelieu for Cardinal Mazarin as stated in A. V. de Vigny, *Cinq-Mars: or, The conspiracy*, tr. W. Bellingham (London: George Routledge & Co., 1850), p. 244.

p. 90, l. 15: *Eveché*: 'bishopric' (French).

p. 91, ll. 20–3: *in a manner ... testimony*: Chatterton is referring to Enguerrand de Monstrelet (*c.* 1400–53), a French chronicle writer and author of the *Chronicle de Enguerrand de Monstrelet*. To read more see H. Wijsman, *History in Transition. Enguerrand de Monstrelet's Chronicle in Manuscript and Print (c. 1450–c. 1600)* and H. Chrisholm (ed.), *Encyclopaedia Britannica*, 11th edn (Cambridge: Cambridge University Press, 1911).

p. 92, ll. 22–3: Rien ne m'est plus, plus ne m'est rien: 'Nothing is more to me, more is nothing to me' (French).

p. 93, l. 13: *J'ai fait l'obseque de madame*: 'I made the exequies of Madame' (French).

p. 93, ll. 14–16: *I will quote ... this Queen's life*: Mrs Agnes Strickland (1796–1874) was a British historian. She grew up as one of nine children; five of them, besides Agnes, were distinguished by their literary talent. The pecuniary situation of the family made it desirable that the sisters, who had already commenced to write, should regard their literary talents as a part of their means of livelihood. Agnes's first publication was 'Monody upon the Death of the Princess Charlotte of Wales', which appeared anonymously in the *Norwich Mercury* in 1817. In 1827 she published by subscription *Worcester Field, or the Cavalier*, a metrical romance written long before. *The Seven Ages of Woman, and other Poems*, followed in the same year (another edition appeared in 1847). In about 1827, she made her first visit to London and stayed with a cousin, in whose house she met Campbell and Sir Walter Scott. At this time, her sister Elizabeth was editing the *Court Magazine*, and had written some biographies for it about female sovereigns. It occurred to Agnes that historical biographies of the queens of England might prove useful. The two sisters planned a book together, under the title of *Memoirs of the Queens of England from the Norman Conquest*, and obtained permission from the young queen, who had just ascended to the throne, to dedicate it to her. But before the first volume was published the title was appropriated by another author, Miss Hannah Lawrance (1795–1895), whose *Historical Memoirs of the Queens of England* appeared in 1839. The Stricklands then changed their title to *Lives of the Queens of England*, and the first and second volumes appeared in 1840.

p. 93, l. 17: *J'ai fait l'obseque de madame*: see note to p. 93, l. 13 above.

p. 94, ll. 25–7: *Some of his ... the Tower of London*: Charles, Duke of Orleans (1391–1465). After the death of his beloved wife, he was taken prisoner and carried to England, which became his residence for a full quarter of a century. Above all, he had leisure to devote himself to literary work. Charles's work consists of hundreds of short poems, a few in various metres, but the majority either ballads or rondels. The chronology of these poems is not always clear, still less the identity of the persons to whom they are addressed. Some, perhaps the greater part of them, belong to the later years of the poet's life. But many are expressly stated in the manuscripts to have been 'composed in prison'. He has the urbanity of the eighteenth century without its vicious and prosaic frivolity, the poetry of the Middle Ages without its tendency to tediousness. His best-known rondels – those on Spring, on the Harbingers of Summer, and others – rank second to none of their kind. His son, afterwards Louis XII, was not born until 1462, three years before Charles's own death. Many of his later poems are small occasional pieces addressed to his courtiers and companions, and in not a few cases answers by those to whom they were addressed exist. The best edition of Charles d'Orleans's poems, with a brief but sufficient account of his life, is that of C. d'Hericault in the *Nouvelle Collection* Paris, Jannet (1874).

p. 94, ll. 28–9: *says Saussaye*: Louis de la Saussaye, member of the Institut de France and rector of the académies of Lyon and of Poitiers was the historian of the Loire Châteaux de Troussay, one of the smallest châteaux of the Loire Valley. Lady Chatterton says that they had purchased 'a very interesting account of Blois, written by M. Saussaie' (see note to p. 109, l. 17–p. 110, l. 10, below).

p. 95, ll. 8–21: *Le temps a laissié son manteaux ... et de pluye*: 'The season has laid its mantle by / Of wind and cold and rain / And donned embroidered garments / Of radiant sunshine, clear and fair. / There is no beast nor bird / That in its own tongue does not sing or cry: / The season has laid its mantle by / Of wind and cold and rain. / River, fountain and brook / Wear, as pretty livery, Drops of silver jewellery. Each thing clad itself anew' (French).

p. 97, ll. 10–14: *L'air de Blois me donna un rhume épouvantable ... les gens que je voyois*: 'The air of Blois gave me a terrible cold that lasted three weeks, I didn't go out, I did not sleep, and I could not eat either; I enjoy playing, because it bothered me less than entertaining the people I saw' (French).

p. 97, l. 18–p. 98, l. 5: *On alla diner à Blois ... toujours la petite reine*: 'We went to dinner at Blois, where my father offered a banquet to the king in the castle. My sisters came to the bottom of the steps (the grand staircase) to welcome his Majesty. Unfortunately, some flies known as cousins, had bitten my sister; as she is of a more beautiful complexion, they were so bad and her throat so thin, as was usual with girls of fourteen, it was a pity to see her. Add to this grief, she was believed to have married the king. He had always held this speech, and always called her the little queen' (French).

p. 98, ll. 19–20: *L'on ajusta fort ma soeur*: 'We tried to convince my sister' (French).

p. 98, ll. 22–3: *parceque l'on là vouloit marier à quelque prix que ce fût*: 'because they wished to marry her at any price whatsoever' (French).

p. 99, ll. 4–5: *Allison says ... Europe*: Lady Chatterton included the whole text from A. Alison, *History of Europe from the Commencement of the French Revolution in 1789 to the Restoration of the Bourbons in 1815*. Chatterton's text was extracted from the British version by William Blackwood and Sons (Edinburgh and London, 1842, vol. 10, p. 494). Alison's *History of Europe* was also published in New York (Harper & Brothers Publishers, 1855) and the extract can be found in vol. 4, ch. 75, p. 404.

p. 102, ll. 14–15: *the great staircase du Lys*: See note to p. 106, ll. 10–21, below.

p. 104, l. 24: *Souvent femme varie,/ Mal habile qui s'y fie*: 'Often women change their minds, / badly skilled the one that relies on them' (French).

p. 106, l. 8: *Madlle. De Montpensier*: For more information see M. M. Michaud, *Nouvelle Collection des Mémoires pour servir a L'Histoire de France. Depuis le XIII Siècle jusqu'a la fin du XVIII; Précédés de Notices pour Caractériser quelque auteur des Mémoires et son Époque*. Troisiéme Série. IV. *Mémoires de Mademoiselle de Montpensier Fille de Gaston D'Orleans, Frére de Louis XIII*. Première Partie 1637 (Paris: Chez l'Éditeur du Commentaire Analytique du Code Civil, 1838), p. 5.

p. 106, ll. 10–21: *Une des plus curieuses et plus remarquables ... quand je l'eus joint*: 'One of the most curious and remarkable things of the house is the staircase, done in a way that a person can go up and another go down without meeting, although they can see each other, which the Lord (her father) took pleasure in playing on with me. He was at the top of the stairs when I arrived; he went down when I went up and he laughed out loud at seeing me running around thinking I had to catch him: I was glad that he took pleasure in this, and I was even more glad when I had joined in' (French).

p. 109, ll. 4–6: *Un abrégé de ce que peut effectuer l'industrie humaine*: 'A summary of what human industry can make' (French).

p. 109, ll. 7–10: *Il a passa quelques jours ... età très grand foison*: 'He had spent a few days delighted in hunting the deer who were there in one of the most beautiful parks in France, and with great abundance' (French).

p. 109, l. 17–p. 110, l. 10: *When," she says an old ... visible*: Although Lady Chatterton usually includes the origin of texts she copies in her historical narratives, with Theobald of Champagne, she only refers to an old chronicle without adding any other reference about its author. For more information on Theobald, Count of Champagne and Blois, see *L'Art de Vérifier les Dates, ii.*, part 2, p. 618. Also in the Life of St Bernard and in the Letters of that Saint (Opp., i., col. 380) in the Publications of the Surtees Society Established in the Year, 1834 and J. Raine, *The Priory of Hexham, its Chroniclers, Endowments and Annals*, (Durham: Andrews and Co., London: Whittaker and Co., and Edinburgh: Blackwood and Sons, 1864), vol. 1, p. 165.

p. 109, l. 19: *herbe qui égure*: 'On the grass that loses us' (French).

p. 111, ll. 5–7: *and we begin to see … scenery*: Chatterton's description could also refer to that of *Six Weeks on the Loire* written by 'a lady of quick observation, much reading, and possessing a sound and wholesome philosophy. The Language is pure and elegant and proves the fair author to have a mind not only alive to the varied charms of nature, but overflowing with charity'. In *Fraser's Magazine for Town and Country* (London: James Fraser, 1833), vol. 7, p. 716.

p. 112, l. 5: *Honoré de Balsac*: Honoré de Balzac (1799–1850), French novelist and playwright. Due to his keen observation of detail and unfiltered representation of society, Balzac is regarded as one of the founders of realism in European Literature. His main work was a sequence of short stories collectively entitled *La Comédi Humaine* which presents a panorama of French life in the years after the 1815 fall of Napoleon.

p. 112, ll. 5–6: *"qui," as Balsac says, "repose l'ame"*: 'which', as Balsac says, 'soothes the soul' (French).

p. 112, l. 13: *Diane de Poitiers*: Diane de Poitiers (1499–1566) was a French noblewoman and a prominent courtier at the courts of King Francis I and his son, Henry II of France. She became notorious as the latter's favourite. It was in this capacity that she wielded much influence and power at the French court, which continued until Henry was mortally wounded in a tournament accident. At this tournament Henry's lance wore her favour (ribbon) rather than his wife's favour.

p. 112, l. 13: *Henry II*: Henry II (1519–59), King of France from 1547 to 1559. Henry II's reign was dominated by war against the House of Habsburg, chiefly in Italy. He suffered an untimely death in a jousting tournament held to celebrate the Peace of Cateau-Cambrésis at the conclusion of the conflict. During Henry's reign, Protestantism became an important minority religion in France, in spite of his efforts to suppress it. His death led to a weakening of French royal authority that helped spur decades of religious violence between Protestants and Catholics.

p. 115, l. 24: *Charles VIII*: Also called 'the Affable' (1470–98), he was King of France from 1483 to his death in 1498. Charles VIII was a member of the House of Valois. His intervention in Italy initiated the long series of Italian Wars which characterized the first half of the sixteenth century.

p. 117, ll. 10–11: *Le temple Saint Gatien sentit aussi le feu … que bien peu*: 'Saint Gatien's temple also felt the fire, / but being rescued it was but very little burnt' (French).

p. 119, ll. 9–11: *description given by … Chambord*: in *Mémoires de l'Acadèmie – des sciences de l'Institut de France* (Paris: De L'Imprimerie Royale, 1724), p. 130.

p. 120, ll. 21–3: *"Le service" says the chronicler … à moitié nues"*: 'The service', says the chronicler, 'was performed by the half-naked, most honest and beautiful ladies of the court' (French).

p. 125, ll. 8–11: *Qu'à m'égarer dans ces bocages … j'aime ces flots argentés*: 'That I lost my heart in these groves of pleasure! / What I like in these shades! / I love the silvery waves' (French).

p.128, ll. 24–5: *Zieren würde sie … sie verschmäht ihn*: 'She would decorate / the first throne of the world, but she spurned it' (German).

p. 129, ll. 12–3: *La "Gentille Agnes"*: 'the charming Agnes' (French).

p. 129, ll. 14–7: *Plus de louange et d'honneur tu merites … ou bien devot hermite*: 'More praise and honor you deserve, / The cause of France is recovered, / What can you craft in a cloister, / a closed Nonain, or a devout hermit' (French).

p. 134, l. 16: *La Pucelle Inconnue*: 'the unknown maiden' (French).

p. 136, l. 25: *son ami*: 'his friend' (French).

p. 141, l. 12: *Mary Queen of Scotts*: Mary, Queen of Scots (1542–87), also known as Mary I of Scotland or Mary Stuart, was Queen Regent of Scotland from 14 December 1542 to 24 July 1567, and Queen Consort of France from 10 July 1559 to 5 December 1560.

p. 145, ll. 10–16: *Pensò al fin ... fiero*: For further reading see A. Panizzi, *Orlando Furioso di Ariosto with Memoirs and Notes* (London: William Pickering, 1834), p. 132 [s 36–9].

p. 145, ll. 10–11: *Pensó al fin di tornare alla ... di Merlin profeta*: 'At last he thought to go back to den, / where there were the bones of the prophet Merlin' (Italian).

p. 145, ll. 13–16: *Con questo intenzione prese il cammino ... in loco alpestro e fiero*: 'With this intention I took the road / towards the woods next to Pontiero, / where the tomb of Merlin was concealed and proud' (Italian).

p. 147, l. 26–p. 148, l. 4: *A Claude Venerille ... monument à ses frais*: 'A Venerille Claude, daughter of Claudius Consul Verenus. The City of Pictons voted the Funeral, a place of Sepulture, a statue, a public monument. Marcus Censor Pavious, Lieutenant of the Emperor, Governor of the Province of Aquitaine, inscribed Consul, her husband, touched of so much honour, has ordered to raise the monument at his expense' (French).

p. 148, l. 5: *touché de tant d'honneur*: 'affected of much honour' (French).

p. 148, l. 7: *honore contentus*: 'satisfied in his honour' (French).

p. 148, l. 18: *beau pays*: 'beautiful country' (French).

p. 148, l. 19: *Pierre levée*: 'Standing Stone' (French).

p. 150, ll. 3–4: *our Richard Coeur de Lion*: Richard I (1157–99), also known as Richard the Lionheart even before his accession, was King of England from 1189 until his death. At sixteen he commanded his own army, putting down rebellions in Poitou against his father King Henry II.

p. 150, l. 5: *Queen Berangaria*: Queen Berangaria of Navarre (*c.* 1165–70) was Queen of England as the wife of King Richard I. She was the eldest daughter of King Sancho VI of Navarre and Sancha of Castile.

p. 166, ll. 8–9: *The Castle of Blanquefort ... description*: See *Dublin University Magazine: A Literary and Political Journal*, No. 127 (July 1843), vol. 22, p. 155.

p. 175, l. 18: *Rue d'Enfer*: 'the Street of Hell' (French).

p. 178, l. 6: *La Belle*: 'the Beautiful' (French).

p. 180, ll. 4–30: *The following epitaph ... die!*: For further reading see A. Strickland, *Lives of The Bachelor Kings of England by Agnes Strickland*, Author of *"Lives of the Queens of England"* and *"Lives of the Queens of Scotland"* (London: Simpkin, Marshall, and Co; 1851).

p. 200, ll. 9–12: *an Etudiant de Médécine, qui ... le triomphe de la liberté*: 'A medical student, that "died gloriously in Paris, July 29, 1830, for the defense of our rights, and the triumph of freedom"' (French).

p.200, ll. 14–16: *Les revolutions justes/ Sont le chatiment/ Des mauvais rois*: 'The just revolutions / Are the punishment / Of the bad kings' (French).

p. 202, ll. 8–10: *Richard and fair ... it*: A. Strickland's *Lives of the Queens of England, from the Norman Conquest with Anecdotes of Their Courts* (Philadelphia, PA: Lea and Blanchard. 1841), vol. 2, p. 13; for further reading: M. E. Hewitt (ed.), *Heroines of History* (New York: Cornish, Lamport & Co. Publishers, 1852), p. 54. The chronicle that Chatterton alludes to is that of Bernard le Tresorier in Ginzo's edition. When describing the first time Richard Coeur de Lion saw the beautiful Berangaria, Lady Chatterton copies the exact words that we can read in the above-mentioned book, also taken from the *Biography of Eleanora of Aquitaine*, vol. 1.

p. 207, l. 16: conducteur: 'driver' (French).

p. 209, l. 13: *faubourg*: 'neighbourhood' (French).

p. 210, l. 1: *(Ventres-blancs)... (Ventres-rouges)*: '(white bellies) ... (red bellies)' (French).

p. 210, l. 14: *Charles V*: Charles V (1500–58) was ruler of the Holy Roman Empire from 1519. As Charles I he was ruler of the Spanish Empire from 1516 until his voluntary retirement and abdication in 1556 in favour of his younger brother Ferdinand I and his son Philip II.

p. 210, ll. 17–18: *ont péri*: 'have died' (French).

p. 210, l. 19: *l'une par l'autre*: 'one by the other' (French).

p. 210, l. 26: *Isle des Faisans*: 'Isle of Pheasants' (French).

p. 212, l. 17 : *moza*: 'waitress' (French).

p. 212, l. 22: *Plaza*: 'square' (Spanish), in some cases it can mean 'arena' when used for bull-fights.

p. 213, l. 12: *mantillas*: 'embroidered lace' (Spanish).

p. 214, l. 7: *Carlists*: Traditionalist and legitimist political movement in Spain seeking the establishment of a separate line of the Bourbon family on the Spanish throne. This line descended from the Infante Carlos, Count of Molina (1788–1855) and was founded due to a dispute over the succession and widespread dissatisfaction with the Alfonsine line of the House of Bourbon. The movement was at its strongest in the 1830s, but had a revival following Spain's defeat in the Spanish-American war in 1898, when Spain lost its last remaining significant colonies: Cuba, Puerto Rico and the Philippines. The first Carlist War was a Civil War in Spain from 1833 to 1839 fought between factions over the succession to the throne and the nature of the Spanish state.

p. 214, ll. 13–14: *Lord C—'s interesting work*: It is difficult to ascertain what work Lady Chatterton is referring to as it could have been a published or unpublished work. I am inclined to think that it could refer to H. Southern and G. W. F. Willers Claredon, *The Policy of England towards Spain: Considered chiefly with reference to 'A review of the Social and political state of the Basque Provinces, and a few remarks on recent events in Spain, &c. By an English Nobleman'* (London: James Ridgway and Sons, 1837).

p. 221, l. 11: *The Queenites*: The Queenites were the supporters of the Regent Queen Consort Maria Cristina, acting for the Princess Isabella II.

p. 221, l. 18: *the war*: In the Siege of San Sebastián (from 7 July to 8 September 1813) Allied forces under the command of General Arthur Wellesley, First Duke of Wellington, captured the city of San Sebastián in northern Spain from its French garrison under Brigadier-General Louis Rey. The attack resulted in the ransacking and devastation of the town by fire.

p. 224, ll. 1–2 : *diner à l'Anglaise*: 'English dinner' (French).

p. 225, l. 5 : *La Fête Dieu*: Corpus Christi.

p. 230, l. 3 : *Fueros*: 'privileges' (Spanish).

p. 232, l. 6: *mantillas*: see note to p. 213, l. 12, above.

p. 237, ll. 1–2: *Beltran de Cueva*: The first Duke of Albuquerque (*c.* 1443–92) was a Spanish nobleman and the presumed lover of Queen Joan of Portugal.

p. 237, ll. 6–8: *the Castle of Urtubi ... Montreal*: For further reading on this historic place see *Victoria Magazine*, 7 (May 1866), p. 195. This magazine was edited from 1797 to 1869.

p.286, ll. 17–18: *Dix mille grenouilles ne valent pas la tête d'un saumon*: 'Ten thousand frogs are not worth the head of a salmon' (French).

p. 287, l. 6: *Charles II*: Charles II (1661–1700), Spanish king. Was the last Hapsburg who reigned in Spain (Castile and Aragon). He also ruled the Spanish Netherlands and

Spain's overseas empire, stretching from the Americas to the Spanish East Indies. He was noted for his extensive physical, intellectual and emotional disabilities – along with his consequent ineffectual rule – as well as his role in the developments preceding the War of Spanish Succession.

p. 287, ll. 17–24 : *Dans les époques de lutte ... quelque sorte fataliste dans ce but ?*: 'In times of struggle and social work, wealth and power belong to those who have chosen a goal, *who in conscience,* have dedicated to this purpose their intelligence and energy. See Rome, Mohammed, Charlemagne, Napoleon, did not they all have a purpose and a belief somewhat fatalistic for this purpose?' (French)

p. 288, ll. 19–21: *Soutez-moi, mon frère, j'en ai besoin ... je suis fort*: 'Hold me my brother, I need it.' *Napoleon answered, with a smile,* 'Lean on me and do not be afraid, I am strong.' (French).

p. 289, ll. 7–9: *D'ailleurs ces arrengements ... je donne Naples à Lucien*: 'Of course, these arrangements end our arguments, I gave Naples to Lucien' (French).

p. 290, l. 26–p. 291, l. 3: *In the mountains beyond ... Rolan*: Also called the Roncevaux Pass, it is a high mountain pass (1057 m) in the Pyrenees near the border between France and Spain. The pass itself is in Spain. According to tradition, it is the place where Roland died during the Battle of Roncevaux in AD 778, a landmark in the history of the Basque provinces. There is a tombstone near the pass commemorating the area where it is traditionally believed that Roland died.

p. 291, ll. 12–13: *various songs and legends ... battle*: The poem included by Lady Chatterton was taken from *Bentley's Miscellany,* an English literary magazine founded by Richard Bentley. All its volumes were published between 1836 and 1868.

p. 299, l. 4: *Froissart*: Jean Froissart (*c.* 1337–*c.* 1405). See note to p. 23, l. 19, above.

p. 300, ll. 8–10: *En beau Pré sert et plaisant ... Entre Pau et Ortais seant*: 'In a pleasant meadow / Over the River Gave / Here between Pau and Ortais' (French).

p. 302, l. 18: malaise: 'discomfort' (French).

p. 303, l. 3: *the brave Palafox*: José Rebolledo de Palafox, first Duke of Saragossa (1780–1847). Aragonese general who fought in the Penninsular War.

p. 307, ll. 10–17: *Go, travel ... Nature*: Elizabeth Barrett Browning (1806–61) was a woman's rights activist and a crusader in the anti-slavery and labour reform movements. The extract is taken from her poem 'A Sea-side Walk'. According to Beverly Taylor, 'Other poems in the collection attest to Barrett's kinship to the Promethean quality of the major Romantic poets. "The Tempest" and "A Sea-Side Meditation," for example, evoke the sublime through imagery of thunder, lightning, and raging winds and seas and describe the interchanges between nature and the human mind, which perceives in nature's threatening grandeur glimpses of immortality'. See B. Taylor, 'A Brief Biography of Elizabeth Barrett Browing', in W. B. Thesing (ed.), *Dictionary of Literary Biography, Volume 199: Victorian Women Poets* (The Gale Group, 1999), p. 4.

p. 311, ll. 4–6: *une petite Athenes ... tout pleine de jolies maisons*: 'a small Athens, such a cute town, full of beautiful houses' (French).

p. 312, l. 24: *treaty of Bretigny*: This treaty was signed on 9 May 1360, between King Edward III of England and King John II of France. In retrospect it is seen as having marked the end of the first phase of the Hundred Years War (1337–1453) as well as the height of English hegemony on the Continent. Signed at Brétigny, near Chartres, it was ratified as the Treaty of Calais on 24 October 1360.

p. 313, ll. 15–16 : *Oh, Monsieur, vous ne faites pas gentillesse*: 'Oh, sir, you are not being kind to me' (French).

p. 313, l. 26 : *La vue des precipices me fait mal*: 'the view of precipices hurts me' (French).

p. 324, l. 5: *tricoterie*: 'knitwear' (French).

p. 348, l. 25: maigre: 'thin' (French).

p. 360, l. 4: *Cascade de l'Enfer*: 'Cascade of Hell' (French).

p. 362, l. 6: déjeûné: 'lunch' (French).

p. 365, ll. 8–9: *chaise à porteur*: 'an English litter or sedan chair' (French).

p. 366, l. 8: *porteurs*: 'carriers' (French).

p. 366, l. 14: *the Cagots*: The Cagots were a persecuted and despised minority found in the west of France and northern Spain in the Navarrese Pyrenees, Basque provinces, Béarn, Aragón, Gascony and Brittany. Evidence of the group exists as far back as AD 1000.

p. 373, ll. 2–3: *Ariosto's beautiful descriptions*: Ludovico Ariosto (1474–1533), Italian poet. He is best known as the author of the romance *Orlando Furioso* (1516). The poem describes the adventures of Charlemagne, Orlando and the Franks as they battle against the Saracens.

p. 373, ll. 9–14: *Presse la via per una stretta valle ... e due diverse arene*: 'He took the way running along a narrow valley / Brunello now forwards now in his shoulders. / From mountain to mountain, from wood to wood. / They reached Pirene. / One can see, if the sky is not dull / either France and Spain, two different arenas' (Italian).

p. 385, ll. 25–6: *Quindi per aspro e faticoso calle / Si discendea nella profonda valle*: 'Therefore, the hills fell steeply away through a rough track' (Italian).

p. 386, ll. 5–18: *Vi sorge in mezzo un sasso ... Sia questa stanza, nido e tana propria*: This is from Tasso's Orlando Furioso, Canto 4. To read more see *Quattro Poeti Italiani, Dante, Petrarca, Ariosto, Tasso* Edizione Fatta su Quella di A. Buttura (Parigi : Baudry, Libreria Europea, 1845), p. 263.

p. 402, ll. 6–7: *dix ans de galère*: 'ten years of misery' (French).

For Product Safety Concerns and Information please contact our EU
representative GPSR@taylorandfrancis.com Taylor & Francis Verlag GmbH,
Kaufingerstraße 24, 80331 München, Germany

Batch number: 08158359

Printed by Printforce, the Netherlands